Feeding the Brain

How Foods Affect Children

Feeding the Brain

How Foods Affect Children

C. Keith Conners, Ph.D.

PERSEUS PUBLISHING
Cambridge, Massachusetts

Library of Congress Cataloging in Publication Data

Conners, C. Keith.
  Feeding the brain: how foods affect children / C. Keith Conners.
    p.   cm.
  Includes bibliographical references and index.
  ISBN 0-7382-0620-2
  1. Food allergy in children—Psychological aspects. 2. Behavior disorders in children—Nutritional aspects. I. Title.
RJ386.5.C66   1989   89-16071
613.2′083—dc20   CIP

Perseus Publishing books are available at special discounts for bulk purchases in the U.S. by corporations, institutions, and other organizations. For more information, please contact the Special Markets Department at the Perseus Books Group, 11 Cambridge Center, Cambridge, MA 02142, or call (800) 255-1514 or (617)252-5298, or e-mail j.mccrary@perseusbooks.com

10 9 8 7 6 5 4 3

Preface

The premise of this book is that what children eat can profoundly shape the course of the brain's growth, its functions, and its capabilities. Children's brains are actively changing, dynamic structures, strongly influenced by what, how much, and when they eat. Food nurtures the brain, providing key nutrients and energy for growth. Food protects the brain, shutting out harmful threats from a toxic and polluted environment. Food alerts as well as calms brain activity. Food changes the moods of the brain, both through the pleasure it affords and by its chemistry.

Foods, like drugs, are ultimately chemicals. But they are more than that. Foods are symbols, a part of rituals, pathways to body images, and vehicles through which love is expressed. Food is part of human culture, habits, and lifestyles. Language, culture, and social environment are intertwined with food, and they powerfully affect brain growth in their own right. They interact with food, determining the course of the brain through its perilous journey from conception to adulthood.

Important new understanding now exists about the ways that food changes behavior, mood, and mental proficiency in children; and how human behavior in turn affects nutrition. But little of this information is available to parents, educators, and others who must decide how and what children should eat.

This book tries to help parents and educators to become

good consumers, not just of food, but of information. We argue that much useful information is prematurely dismissed by some scientists with biased agendas. But there is also a good deal of misinformation, too readily swallowed as if it were fact.

This is not a diet book, nor a self-help book. But we do attempt to show how one may learn for oneself, through experiments at home, whether some of the ideas in the scientific literature apply to one's own child. Science is nothing more than a set of rules, devised to prevent one from kidding oneself and others, about some idea of how nature works. Much of this book presents the back-and-forth dialogue among scientists about food and behavior. To the lay reader, who wants to know what to do now, these debates may seem at times to lead to a mystifying impasse. But we argue that the debates show us what to look for in our own, personal experiments, and how to use food as a tool in optimizing mental and behavioral function in children.

I am grateful to Richard Wurtman, John Fernstrom, Bonnie Spring, and Ernesto Pollitt for inspiration and helpful discussions about many of the issues in this book. Dan Raiten provided me with many helpful suggestions and the benefit of a professional nutritionist's perspective.

Grants from the National Institutes of Mental Health, Kellogg's Foundation, General Foods, and the Sugar Association were all helpful in my own research on sugar, breakfast, and brain function in children. Without the unstinting support of James Egan, M.D., I would not have had the freedom or resources to pursue my interest in this subject.

I am very grateful for the patience and encouragement of my editors, Linda Regan and Victoria Cherney, who ruthlessly pointed out the passive voice, dangling participles, and other bad habits from a lifetime of academic writing.

Finally, I am especially grateful to my wife, Karen Wells, for insisting that I eat the way I preach to others; and to my daughter Katie, for showing me just how marvelous a growing brain can be.

C. Keith Conners

Contents

CHAPTER ONE

Food, Mind, and Behavior

BELIEFS AND EMOTIONS ABOUT FOOD

This book is about food and its relationship to behavior and mental processes in children. Everyone knows and accepts that foods are important to the functioning of the body. Not everyone believes that foods affect the mind, however. Many people feel that as long as children are well-nourished, what they eat has little relevance to the way they learn, think, feel, and act.

It may be easy to accept that foods cause certain *transient* changes of mental state, such as when discomfort or drowsiness follows overeating, when sedation ensues from imbibing alcoholic beverages, or when our morning coffee makes us more alert. Most people can easily recognize these minor effects from their own experience. It may also seem reasonable to believe that some very *extreme* nutritional conditions, such as severe protein malnutrition, lead to failure of brain growth, much as poor nutrition stunts the growth of the body. But there is more to the food–mind connection than transient subtle changes or the extreme effects of major nutritional deficiency.

Food has profound effects on higher mental functions, even in well-nourished children eating ordinary foods in ordinary amounts. Foods can enhance problem-solving ability, optimize alertness, and improve mood and behavior in normal children. Contrarily, foods can also impair children whose behavior and learning are already in trouble from other causes, hampering their efforts to concentrate and maintain self-control. Over an extended period, food affects basic intelligence through effects on brain growth and by altering the way the environment changes the developing brain.

But some scientists see the idea of food changing behavior as just another popular fad. Our culture glorifies nostrums and special diets, promising to improve everything from longevity to beauty and sexual potency. Tabloids routinely announce "secret diets" or miracle foods that restore lost powers, increase IQ, or even enhance spiritual communications. There is something inherently appealing, almost mystical, in the idea that "You are what you eat." Such beliefs seem to fulfill a deep need to have some control over one's own mental functions, other than the more commonly accepted—and arduous—methods of education or psychotherapy. Yet, more often than not, people adopting these ideas become disillusioned, until the next fad appears. The cycle of failed promises from bogus remedies eventually leads to skepticism.

Scientific scrutiny of these claims about the mental and behavioral effects of foods is not always dispassionate and objective. There is something about the subject that seems to provoke inflamed debate. Sometimes scientists learn to be so skeptical about fads that they overreact and dismiss *all* ideas about food and behavior out of hand.

The response of the American Academy of Pediatrics to a study of megavitamins and mental retardation illustrates the emotions surrounding this issue.[1] In a 1981 article which appeared in the *Proceedings of the National Academy of Sciences*, Dr. Ruth Harrell and coworkers purported to show that a group of 16 retarded children had a 5- to 10-point rise in IQ after a short period of nutritional supplementation with trace minerals and megadoses of vitamins (issues we will take up in detail later).[2] This study was roundly criticized and dismissed by a committee from the American Academy of Pediatrics (AAP). But Dr. Bernard Rimland, a well-known researcher on autism and mental retardation, pointed out a half-dozen errors of reporting and interpretation contained in the AAP's statement. He had this to say:

> What we have here—clearly—is a temper tantrum by a group of pediatricians who find themselves unable to tolerate the frustration resulting from the destruction of several of their most cherished beliefs by well-designed and well-conducted research. What a shock it must be to learn they have been wrong all these years: first, mentally retarded children *can* be helped; high potency nutritional supplements *can* be beneficial. . . . The lack of professional integrity and of concern for the welfare of retarded children and their families by the AAP is shameful. Come on fellows, grow up! If you are skeptical, try the supplements on some of your own patients.[3]

There are some flaws in Dr. Harrell's experiment, but Dr. Rimland has caught several errors and misinterpretations by the AAP committee itself. In turn, he responds with vehemence to what he sees as professional imperialism and entrenched conservatism. The argument has shifted from questions of fact to questions of motives and professional bias. We will see other examples of the deep distrust between practitioners who believe in the power of diet and scientists who regard it as fraud but who then go on to display bias in their own handling of the issues.

It is understandably difficult to remain cool and objective when certain members of the professional community commercially exploit complex and unsubstantiated dietary routines for curing serious mental illnesses, with little or no evidence to support their schemes. For example, some practitioners charge large fees for developing elaborate profiles of nutrients based upon samples of human hair, claiming that the right balance of minerals will cure serious emotional problems. Perhaps such a profile of minerals for a particular individual *is* related to his or her mental health; the idea itself is not unreasonable. But the experiments needed to prove the truth of that idea have not been done by the people who proposed it. Until others do that work for them, it seems reasonable that the practitioners should desist in their claims. Meanwhile, their operations only serve to increase scientific skepticism.

A medical colleague of mine recently told me a story about a patient of his who perfectly illustrates the way fringe practitioners prey upon patients. The patient, a young woman, had a problem with tension and fatigue unexplained by her doctors. She heard of a doctor who used diet to cure "the tension–fatigue syndrome." The doctor took a blood sample and had it analyzed by a company in the Midwest, at a cost of several hundred dollars. The report prescribed a complex series of dietary changes, supplements, mineral, and vitamin combinations which would take several months to complete—presumably at a very high cost.

What made the report interesting in the eyes of my colleague, however, was the disclaimer it contained at the end: "Although the recommendations of this report are backed by scientific research, they still must be established by clinical correlations." In other words, "We have to proceed by trial and error at your expense, and don't blame me if it doesn't work."

Some practitioners rely upon unproven methods of detecting food allergy, such as placing foods under the tongue and watching for a behavioral reaction. Now, *allergy* is a much misused term, and though it is a complex subject covering a wide array of bodily reactions that are often hard to pin down, it does have specific scientific meaning. As we will see in a later chapter, specific tests that provoke the immune system can verify the presence of true allergy. But the advocates of dietary schemes for treating allergy, who use unproven diagnostic methods, seldom feel the need for proven laboratory findings or critical thinking to support their theories, relying instead upon colorful anecdotes to bolster their claims. Scientists learn to regard such frivolous claims with caution because there are clear monetary motives behind those making them. Skepticism is usually increased by the unwillingness of those making the claims to carry out the supporting research necessary to document them.

The individuality of human responses to foods is also a cause of skepticism that food alters mental functioning. Not everyone reacts to foods in the same way. It may therefore seem as though the effects of foods are random or inconsistent. If certain foods always changed a certain behavior or learning ability, then there would be no dispute. That there are important individual differences in the way children react to food, however, should be no more surprising than differences in response to drugs.

Certain psychoactive drugs (drugs that affect mental processes and behavior, such as antidepressants and antipsychotic drugs) have quite different, even opposite effects, depending upon the genetic makeup of the person taking the drug. Drugs often have quite different effects on normal people and those with some biological dysfunction. For instance, some antidepressants improve mood only in people with a certain type of depressive illness, but they have no effects or even unpleasant effects in normal people. Foods, too, act differently on children, depending upon their unique biochemical makeup.

We will see that the druglike specificity of some foods on the minds of children is not just an analogy to psychoactive chemicals. Foods are made up of chemicals and, like drugs, can produce psychoactive effects which depend upon the chemistry of the recipient and on the particular circumstances in which the food is eaten. But fringe practitioners exploit this idea, precisely because it makes it hard to pin down clear-cut reactions to particular foods.

FOOD AND THE BRAIN

There are certain nutrients designated as "essential." This word has a specific meaning in nutrition: we must replenish these chemicals by eating them, since the brain and body do not manufacture them. For example, many of the brain's neuro-transmitters—chemical messengers—are either essential amino acids found in proteins or derived from essential amino acids. The functions of the brain therefore depend very much on eating protein foods with the right amount of amino acids in them and ensuring their availability at the right time.

Although not essential in this same sense, almost all the fuel for the brain's work comes from a sugar known as glucose, which the brain cannot manufacture. Glucose must be made from carbohydrates. (There is also a process called *gluconeogenesis*, which makes glucose from some proteins when carbohydrates are unavailable.)

Perhaps as much as 30 to 50% of the calories consumed by children go to meet glucose energy requirements of the brain. The body maintains a supply of glucose and other energy sources (such as glycogen) which is usually adequate to meet the constant demands of the brain. If this surplus pool of sugar becomes depleted (as happens, for example, when there is too much insulin), then even a few minutes of insufficient glucose will lead to faintness, unconsciousness, coma, and ultimately, death. Many foods we eat are quickly converted to blood glucose, raising the blood sugar level. The brain must receive a constant, accurate, steady flow of this fuel in order to survive. Sugar, therefore, has often figured in speculations about mental illness and brain disorders. We will review evidence later showing that sugar can act much like drugs on the brain and that sugar interacts with drugs commonly used to treat children's hyperactivity.

But if foods like sugar and proteins do influence the brain's basic energy supply and chemical messages (and therefore mental functioning and behavior), what prevents each meal from radically upsetting our mood or altering our behavior in unpredictable, unpleasant, or even dangerous ways? And wouldn't each meal be like blindly swallowing a bunch of psychoactive pills? Finally, would the human species evolve in a way that allows foods to have a major impact upon mental functioning?

Although the brain and body have evolved a highly elaborate system for protecting the brain, there are special circumstances which allow the chemicals in foods to penetrate through the protective barriers of the brain, where they then interact with the brain's own chemicals. Recent discoveries in nutritional research have clarified some of these circumstances, which we will discuss in detail later. Yes, foods are psychoactive, but only under particular circumstances, and it is these circumstances which we must understand if we want to take advantage of the possibilities for enhanced mental function and avoid the harmful consequences of eating the wrong food at the wrong time.

FOOD AND THE WORLD AROUND US

Not only are there special circumstances which permit a connection between food and mental functioning, there are also subtle interactions between food and the environment, often disguising the connection of food with behavior. Eating is not an isolated behavior that one engages in just to obtain sustenance. Rather, it is highly integrated with every aspect of our physical, cultural, and social environment, and the effects of food depend to some extent on the environment.

Consider, for example, the question of the mental effects of severe protein malnutrition. Scientists have established that during certain periods of early development, brain damage results from inadequate protein intake. But long-term effects of such deprivation are quite different from one child to another. Some children have much better functioning after early malnutrition than others starved to the same degree. They register higher IQs, and their behavioral deficits are fewer than other children with similar early nutritional disadvantages. What accounts for such inconsistency?

Careful study of children in the early stages of malnutrition reveals that some mothers stop responding to their infants because the infants have stopped sending out the signals mothers usually depend upon. Mothering becomes impaired when a baby becomes listless and apathetic, no longer cries, and ceases responding to the mother by looking and smiling at her, which would encourage continued interaction. The lack of mothering—rocking, soothing, talking, stimulating—in turn causes more impairment of brain growth in the child. The reasons are not well understood; but the brain needs social stimulation in order to grow, just as it needs food. Without this "social nutrition," brain growth slows down even if adequate calories are available.

Similarly, the fussy and irritable child, whose "colic" is the result of intolerance to cow's milk, can turn a mother against the child and lead to a prolonged, hostile battle over feeding. This back-and-forth chain of events is an example of what psychologists call *transactionalism* in child development—the intertwining of child and parent responses, so that both are causes and both are effects. The child's behavior causes the mother to react in a certain way; this effect—the mother's reaction—then causes a further reaction in the child; and so on. When such systems develop, they are often hard to disentangle. The child's behavior and emotional functioning may appear to be the result of parenting behaviors alone, whereas the child's behavior is part of a whole cycle of influences, including reactions to foods.

Family and cultural belief systems affect what, when, and how often certain foods are eaten. Certain convictions, like the belief that "natural foods" promote health, lead to selective diets which can have unexpected consequences for mental functioning in children, as we shall see when we look at the relationship between intelligence and diet. These beliefs are part of our culture and family life, so their profound effects may go unnoticed and taken for granted. Like the air we breathe, food is such a familiar part of our environment that we may fail to take notice of it until it becomes scarce or produces some toxic effect.

The amount of money people earn, where they live, and what they eat are often tied together. If you are wealthy you are less likely to live in polluted environments. Then, even if your diet is suboptimal, it might be of little consequence. On the other hand, because some foods have a protective effect against pollutants, that same suboptimal diet might be hazardous to your IQ if you are poor and live in an area exposing you to toxic chemicals. Here it is not just the lack of a particular nutrient or foodstuff that is the problem, but a lack which occurs in the presence of an environmental hazard. Thus, we may overlook nutritional effects on brain function because the effects occur only in a particular environmental context. We will discuss such problems when we look at the effects of heavy metals, such as lead, and their relation to diet and IQ.

PROBLEMS IN STUDYING FOOD AND BEHAVIOR

Most people may not spot the flaws in studies purporting to prove something about food and behavior, or the logical flaws in the counterarguments used for the other side. If even reasonable scientists get caught up in biased and heated debates, how can the ordinary citizen expect to sift the evidence?

In this book I try to speak to that citizen, not to scientists locked in unresolved controversies. Laypersons often misunderstand the goals of science, which concerns itself with general laws applying to large populations. Behavioral science, in particular, deals with statistics and averages, not with individual cases.* Experiments on food and behavior with large groups of children are especially difficult; manipulating and controlling diets is hard, and there are ethical limits to what can be done in most experiments. As a result, many experiments remain flawed, inconclusive, and difficult to interpret or replicate.

Even successful experiments resulting in support for a hypothesis may not tell us what we need to know. Parents and teachers usually want to know what to do about a *particular* child, and an experiment seldom reveals which children are exceptions to the general findings. Rather than waiting for resolution of all the scientific squabbles, parents and teachers need to know what can be done now. Unlike scientists, parents don't require certainty about general laws, but guidance about individual decisions.

To some extent then, parents and teachers must become experimenters themselves, because they cannot wait for resolution of all conflicting evidence. There are many important ideas about food and behavior testable at home by careful observation. Scientists may conduct experiments or carry out studies on groups of people, only to find that the results are inconsistent, perhaps because there are too many variables out of their control. But many important *ideas* tested by scientists are worth exploring with individual children in the home. The results of home experiments may not satisfy scientists who are looking for generalizations that apply to large groups of children. But they may unlock secrets of value for the one child we most care about—our own.

Before one begins experimenting with foods as a cause or

---

*Behavioral psychologists often study individual animals, finding very precise laws governing their behavior without resorting to statistics and averages. But these animals are usually genetically pure, and they live in controlled environments impossible to achieve with humans.

cure for misbehavior and mental dysfunction, it is important to become alert to some of the pitfalls of such experiments, whether by scientists or ourselves as self-experimenting food consumers. A personal experience of mine illustrates some of these pitfalls.

Several years ago I was trying to find the truth of a theory that artificial colors and flavors cause children to be hyperactive. The theory was first put forth in 1974 by Dr. Benjamin Feingold, a respected pediatric allergist, who claimed that the behavior of many hyperactive and learning-disabled children improved with the introduction of a diet free of artificial colors (such as the red and yellow food dyes). He suspected that these chemicals had something in common that affected the brain. He observed that children sometimes improved in learning, sometimes in behavior, and sometimes in both, when on a diet free of food additives.

The apparent epidemic rise of hyperactivity in the past few decades appeared to Feingold to coincide with increased use of artificial flavors, colors, and preservatives in our food supply. It was the artificial colors which he most suspected, because they have a certain chemical similarity to substances known to produce allergic responses. Having seen many children in his practice who showed "dramatic" improvement when placed on an additive-free diet, Feingold assumed that the additives were causing the condition. But he had never done a controlled study of the problem.

To test Feingold's contention experimentally, my colleagues and I selected children whose behavior markedly improved when we put them on his diet. We randomly divided them into two groups. While keeping strictly to the diet, one group received daily challenges of chocolate cookies laced with artificial colors, while the other received a placebo—regular chocolate cookies with no artificial colors.

This is a type of study known as "double-blind," meaning

that both the patient and the doctor are "blind" to which treatment is being given. Although both types of cookies contained chocolate, sugar, and other ingredients, only one contained the suspected offending agents, the artificial colors. Since the two kinds of cookies looked and tasted alike, it was impossible for the subjects or the observers evaluating the response to have a bias about the outcome. Parents who might believe that food additives caused the behavior were unaware of which type of cookie their child received. Typical biases avoided by this method were the wish of the doctor to see a significant effect and the wish of the subject to accommodate the doctor.

A 7-year-old severely hyperactive boy (whom we later came to call the "cookie monster") improved remarkably while on the Feingold diet. He was the first subject we entered into the study. I became both concerned and excited when the patient's mother called up the day after the child received his first cookie and shouted at me, "I don't know what you put in that cookie, but I am taking my son out of the study! He has gone berserk and become a monster. He got a knife, sliced up our couch, took a hammer to a neighbor's motorcycle, and has been running around like a wild man." All after one cookie!

I was "blind" to which type of cookie the child received, but because the response was so much like the dramatic cases reported by Feingold, I assumed at once that the boy had eaten the cookie with the artificial colors. As sorry as I felt for this frightened mother, I couldn't help feeling the excitement that comes with a new discovery. What if Feingold was on the track of something important, and what if he had found a simple explanation for why there are so many hyperactive, impulsive, aggressive, inattentive youngsters? Here was a boy with a severe disorder showing marked improvement while on the diet and marked deterioration during his first double-blind challenge.

Of course I knew that such responses needed verifying by

many other cases, but when the first subject reacted so dramatically and so much like Feingold's description of many similar cases, my original skepticism gave way to hopes that a discovery of great consequence had been made. Not only would we be solving a problem defying many scientists over many years, but the discovery would provide a simple cure: simply omit things in food which weren't necessary in the first place.

Here was a child who *precisely* fit the picture described by Feingold in his reports to Congress and medical societies and decidedly met objective criteria for a diagnosis of the hyperactivity syndrome. These were not mere "brat" behaviors but dramatic symptoms undeniably in the severely abnormal range. The cause of hyperactivity in children has been a mystery long awaiting a solution. Perhaps the answers to why some children are hyperactive had been under our noses all along, hiding in various things we eat.

As it turned out, we dropped this particular boy from the study because we genuinely feared that the artificial colors might be hazardous to his mental health (to say nothing of his family's and neighbors' safety). The scientists conducting the study therefore opened the sealed envelope containing the code of active and placebo cookies with considerable excitement. But alas, the "cookie monster" *had received the placebo cookie!*

This is not an isolated instance. During controlled studies I have experienced many such cases. Scientists are quite familiar with similar episodes proving the power of the placebo, of human wishful thinking, or of just plain chance events which happen to coincide with the treatment.

But why had this boy shown such a remarkable improvement while on the diet? Were the apparent changes just a product of wishful thinking on his mother's part? Or did he pull himself together in order to please all the adults hoping for some miraculous cure? Was it a real behavior change or only the *report* of a change by parents eager to believe in Feingold's theory?

More than likely, there is some truth to each of these speculations. It is easy to see how hopeful parents might magnify a
small, temporary change in the behavior of a child and how
their behavior to the child might further encourage the child to
change.

Some scientists wondered whether all the extra personal
attention received by children on Feingold's diet might have
caused real improvement in behaviors originating in the need
for attention. Children whose bad behavior is just an attention-
seeking mechanism are well known. The children on the diet
became quite involved in selecting and preparing the foods,
gaining a lot of attention from everyone at home and at school.
Everyone was optimistic about this treatment because of publicity about the diet. Hope and optimism for change are powerful ingredients in most successful psychiatric treatments.

We cannot be sure about any of these speculations, but I am
sure that the cookie monster's behavior was *not* caused by the
artificial colors. Episodes like these contribute to one's skepticism whenever a parent alleges that their child's behavior is a
dietary, not a psychological, problem.

Even though the evidence to the naked eye seems unequivocal—a clear association between a dietary and a behavioral
event—without the placebo control and the double-blind experiment, dramatic cases like the cookie monster's fool even the
most experienced observers. I am a scientist, but like many parents, I *wanted* to believe in the effect of food additives on behavior, and I was only too ready to believe it based on a single
case. But fortunately, scientists have learned to protect themselves from wishful thinking by designing safeguards, such as
techniques like the double-blind control.

Even professional mental health workers and doctors, like
Feingold, are easily misled into believing in a food and behavior
connection when there is none. One can easily understand
Feingold's conviction and fervor about this theory, for he had

experienced many cases similar to the cookie monster's in his practice. But the authority of being a doctor, even a very good one, is insufficient as a basis for accepting a scientific conclusion. Keeping a balance between healthy skepticism and open-mindedness is therefore essential, both for the scientist and for those people who suspect foods might account for the aberrant behavior of their children or themselves.

There are other reasons to be cautious about the causal connection between diet and behavior. People often undertake a treatment just when the symptoms reach their peak and are about to subside. Parents in desperation, after many other failures, may enroll themselves or their child in a dietary program, just as their own efforts result in change for the better. Initiating a special diet and then seeing these symptoms disappear could make one a believer in the diet, when the changes simply reflect motivating oneself to do something about the problem.

Bloodletting was a treatment for sickness for hundreds of years because the patients often got better anyway—*in spite of* the treatment, not because of it. Of course, the surgeon was always eager to take the credit when health improved and willing to forget the case when the patient died. A simple controlled trial would have laid the issue to rest immediately. Folk wisdom, such as hanging garlic around one's neck to relieve a cold, survives precisely because the symptoms usually go away in a few days anyway. Many children have transient behavioral disturbances (stuttering, nail biting, nightmares, extreme shyness) which go away most of the time of their own accord.

There *are* important effects of foods on the way children behave, learn, and feel, but it is important to resist the temptation to jump to conclusions without careful safeguards. In the coming chapters we will see examples of both real and artifactual relationships between food and behavior, and we will see that such relationships are often a two-way street, in which eating alters behavior, and behavior of parent, child, and social community shapes eating. We will see examples of how food enters into transactions between parents and children which have important consequences. We will see that food and the environment around us become linked in important ways worth understanding if we are to optimize children's mental and emotional potential and prevent tragedies that are avoidable by common sense.

BEHAVIOR PATTERNS IN CHILDREN

If we are to understand the ways in which foods affect mental processes and the behavior of children, we need to know something about the major behavior patterns of children, for these patterns themselves reflect important aspects of the composition and chemistry of the brain upon which foods act.

While behavior patterns in children are the product of many interacting forces, including social learning, these patterns are strongly influenced by certain aspects of brain function. Therefore, these patterns can become an important clue to brain neurotransmitter systems. Neurotransmitters in turn are crucial in understanding how foods affect mental and behavioral processes.

Externalizing Children

One broad group of children includes those whose problems are visible to the naked eye and mostly bother people external to the child (thus the label "externalizing"). These children are abnormally intrusive and are easily noticed because they elicit strong reactions from others, such as annoyance, frustration, anger, or punishment. They are overactive, impulsive, and inattentive. They violate rules and are sometimes destructive of property or harmful to people. Such children are often happy-go-lucky types who are blissfully unaware of their problems. They seem to be lacking in internal distress and are always focused outwardly (until they get older and their self-esteem has become damaged by constant conflict with others).

Of course, all children are externalizers at some times and not others, and in certain circumstances. Whether externalizing behavior is normal or abnormal depends both upon the age and the setting in which the behavior occurs. For example, it is normal for a 3- or 4-year-old to run around between mouthfuls at the dinner table or to stay seated only for a short time during play. This same behavior is deviant when it persists in a 10-year-old. The same rowdiness or aggressive play considered acceptable on the playground may be abnormal when it occurs in the classroom.

The *level*, or *degree*, of the behavior is also crucial in defining what is normal for a particular age and setting. A 10-year-old who occasionally fidgets during the reading lesson is normal, but constant wriggling and fiddling with everything in sight could be a sign of an abnormal motor control system. We understand that impulsively running into the path of oncoming cars is expectable in young children, and so we take precautions to avoid it. But the same behavior in a hyperactive 7-year-old is usually abnormal and evidence of poor impulse control.

There are two major types of externalizing behavior patterns, though the two types are often seen together in varying degrees in many children.

Hyperactive Children

One of the most common subtypes of externalizing behavior disorders in children is hyperactivity also known as "hyperkinetic syndrome," "minimal brain dysfunction" (MBD), "attention deficit disorder" (ADD), and by many other labels. The many labels are a reflection of the confusion and changing views of the true nature of this problem. There are probably many causes for this behavior pattern, and it is one most often suspected as caused by foods, food additives, toxic chemicals, or by lack of certain micronutrients (minerals and vitamins that occur in tiny amounts).

Perhaps as many as 3 to 5% of all children are sufficiently hyperactive that they require some form of treatment. These children comprise most of the cases seen in mental health clinics. The successful drug treatment of hyperactive children (with stimulants like Dexedrine and Ritalin, for example) has served to strengthen the belief that they suffer from some dysfunction of brain processes, involving the neurotransmitters affected by the stimulants.

For convenience we will refer to this class of children as "hyperactive," in recognition of the prominence of excessive activity in the earlier stages of the disorder. But the term hyperactivity is somewhat misleading in that the *symptom* of excessive activity level is only part of a more complex picture, which also includes impulsive and heedless behavior, poor concentration or attention, and trouble relating well to other children. An additional complication in about half of these children is learning disabilities such as poor reading, spelling, and arithmetic. Sometimes these learning problems get better with drug therapy, suggesting that they are secondary effects of the behavior problems of paying attention and sitting still. Other times the learning disabilities persist, and appear to reflect intrinsic dysfunctions in the brain's learning centers.

It is not clear whether hyperactivity is a true disease, a syndrome (collection of symptoms), or several different disorders with different causes. But because the true condition can have severe long-term consequences for both the child and his or her family, it is important to distinguish it from mere unruly behavior stemming from lax parenting or overindulgence. There are children who superficially resemble truly hyperactive children but who probably deserve the label of ordinary "brats." But unlike such children, hyperactive children have a more pervasive inability to sit still, to conform, and to attend; and their basic behavior pattern does not change even after correcting the poor parenting. Parenting skills may improve when the hyperactive child responds well to treatment, showing that poor parenting is sometimes the result, not the cause of misbehavior. Therefore, while poor parenting can make hyperactive children worse, it can also be the result of a child who does not respond to the ordinary rules, rewards, and punishments of social and family life. Some have even suggested that the inability to profit from rewards in learning is at the heart of the disorder, prompting them to link the problem to the neurotransmitters involved in the brain's reward centers.

Conduct Disorders

Some externalizing children are not hyperactive but are aggressive, antisocial, bullying, destructive, or in other ways likely to violate ordinary social proprieties and rules. When the normal negativism and self-centeredness of the 2-year-old persists in the 5-year-old, it may be a sign of an *oppositional disorder*. It is as though defiance of authority becomes its own goal. Truanting, stealing, fighting, and lying may become evident in such children as they grow older.

Conduct disorders refers to a pattern of early aggressive behavior persisting into young adulthood, along with a pattern of violation of social authority. Like hyperactivity, there are probably several forms of conduct disorders, and also like hyperactivity the contributions of genetic temperament, environment, and traumatic insults to the brain may all have a role in creating the pattern. Again, because certain neurotransmitters linked with aggressive behavior are also affected by diet, speculation about dietary therapy for conduct and aggressive disorders has been rife.

While hyperactivity, conduct, and learning disorders may all occur quite separately in some children, it is not uncommon for them to overlap with each other within a single child. Often one disorder *causes* another, as when continual lack of control over behavior in the classroom eventually leads to learning failure, or when learning failure eventually results in rebelliousness, defiance, and oppositional behavior. Although these behavior patterns may blend together into a variety of combinations, they are sufficiently distinct in their natural history, outcome, and response to treatments that most professionals regard them as different disorders, requiring different causal explanations.

Internalizing Disorders

Another broad class of problems are those in which it is the children who suffer more than those around them. Children who are excessively anxious or frightened for no apparent reason and who cry easily and are very afraid of separating from their parents are exhibiting an *internalizing disorder*. So are depressed children who are melancholy and hopeless about the future, as well as children who are not notably anxious or depressed but who withdraw from all social contact and who are exceedingly shy and socially awkward, sometimes even with no apparent desire to be sociable.

Many people readily accept that externalizing disorders in children might have a basis in brain dysfunctions. After all, it was the very similarity of hyperactive children to brain-damaged children that initiated such terms as "minimal brain damage syndrome" for such children. But they may draw the line at the idea that anxiety, depression, and other internalizing conditions result from chemical abnormalities in the brain. Recent advances in human psychopharmacology and genetics nonetheless show that even these apparently pure psychological conditions have an important connection with brain chemistry.

One of the conditions most psychiatrists held as purely psychological for a long time was the anxious, ritualistic behavior of the hand-washing, frightened obsessive–compulsive. These people have ideas they can't get out of their mind (obsessions) or rituals they must carry out over and over (compulsions). But recent experiments with a new drug (clomipramine) have produced remarkable improvements in such patients, even after a lifetime of suffering. Brain imaging is a new technique in which X rays or radiation-labeled chemicals produce computer images of the brain's deep structures. Brain images of these patients reveal abnormal brain structures and patterns. Similarly, infusions of a chemical called lactate have produced classic "panic reactions" in certain vulnerable people, exactly reproducing symptoms of anxiety and panic long believed to be purely socially acquired. These developments do not imply that brain dysfunction or disease causes all these internalizing states. But they remind us that almost all behavior has important foundations in biological functions of the brain. They encourage us to consider all types of behavior, not just those most clearly attributable to brain damage, as possibly influenced by the foods we eat.

These broad classes of disorders—externalizing and internalizing—probably reflect very basic aspects of brain organization. Just as work with drugs has revealed that drugs work differently depending upon the type of individual receiving them, so the effects of foods may depend upon specific brain behavior patterns. Much research work on both animals and humans now suggests that these behavior patterns are strongly influenced by genetic factors and by the brain's chemical messengers, the neurotransmitters. It is for this reason that it makes sense to ask how different behavior patterns relate to the chemical effects of foods we eat.

In Chapter 2 we will look at a new class of foods, artificial sweeteners, and their possible role in hyperactivity. We will see that young children in particular may experience dramatic behavioral and personality changes from these new sweeteners, though the evidence remains tentative and scanty.

In Chapter 3 we will see how breakfast is a meal that can have either very beneficial or very harmful effects, on both normal children and hyperactives.

Chapter 4 looks at the role of sugar in hyperactive children. We will see that common myths about sugar are partly true and partly false, with sugar being either helpful or harmful depending upon the type of child, the contents of meals, and the timing of the sugar dose.

In Chapter 5 we will see whether sugar leads to aggression and violence and whether special diets can affect criminality. We will turn a critical eye toward recent attempts to alter the diet of criminals in hopes of reducing their violent tendencies and discuss the role of sugar in aggressive behavior of hyperactives.

Chapter 6 deals with the effect of foods on the growth of the brain and intellectual function. We will discuss recent experiments showing that vitamin supplements increase IQ in school-children, and we will see that diet in pregnant mothers can affect the IQ and cognitive skills of their newborns.

Chapter 7 discusses the Feingold diet and food allergies as causes of behavior problems in children. Again, we will see that the theory that food additives cause hyperactivity is partly true, but not entirely so. We will examine recent evidence that some diets help improve the behavior of children with allergies.

Chapter 8 examines the controversies and dangers surrounding the use of huge doses of vitamins—megavitamin therapy—and critically discusses the evidence both pro and con for its use.

Chapter 9 looks at the possible role of diet in the way children react to stress, how certain foods may inoculate against stress, and how stress can lead to life-threatening eating disorders. Finally, in Chapter 10 we will present some simple methods for carrying out experiments in the home and tracking children's suspected reactions to foods.

Scientists are innately conservative, and in each chapter we will see that much controversy exists. But parents, teachers, and mental health professionals must make daily decisions about food with children, and they need not wait for resolution of all controversies in order to make educated decisions and be knowledgeable consumers of available remedies. Though our knowledge is tentative and subject to revision as new data emerge, prudent action regarding food management for children can often be taken in ways that at least will do no harm and at best may optimize the child's behavior and mental function.

Thus, we believe that foods do affect the minds of children in many subtle and important ways. The foolish claims of popular culture and pseudo-science should not discourage us from acknowledging the real connections between the chemicals in foods and the chemicals in the brains of children.

CHAPTER TWO

Hyperactivity and Artificial Sweeteners

A CASE OF SEVERE REACTION TO ASPARTAME

I was skeptical when Jamie's mother called me and said that her 4-year-old son was totally out of control after drinking some cherry Kool-Aid. Phone calls like this one occur often, and usually the problem turns out to be much more commonplace than a reaction to food or drink. Instead, the issues most often involve more familiar problems in relationships between parents and child, such as lack of balance between authority and nurturance, poor parenting skills and lax discipline, or inappropriate models of behavior in the home. But people will often look for easy answers first.

However, Jamie's mother did not appear to be someone avoiding hard choices; she had already investigated the problem like a scientist. She observed her son carefully and carried out some experiments. She told me that during the summer Jamie drank Kool-Aid for about 3 weeks, usually about three glasses a day (20 ounces or so). Over this period of time she noticed that he became increasingly erratic, with gradually escalating levels of frustration, anger, and emotionality. He easily burst into tears, was very irritable, and had violent, unprovoked, angry outbursts. Eventually he had an episode when he became so hyperactive that he had to be sent to his room, whereupon he proceeded to throw himself against a wall, knocking himself to the floor, repeating this behavior until restrained. He was totally out of control in a way she had not seen before.

Jamie's mother called her pediatrician, who questioned her carefully about anything the child might have swallowed, thinking that he may have ingested some poison. After eliminating several possibilities, his mother mentioned that the Kool-Aid was new to Jamie's diet. A pitcher was kept in the refrigerator and Jamie had free access to it. The pediatrician suggested removing it, and after doing so Jamie's behavior seemed to return to normal over a 10-day period. The mother, thinking logically, decided to reintroduce the drink, doubting that this seemingly benign product could be the cause of her son's trouble.

However, the second time Jamie drank the Kool-Aid, within about 30 minutes he became even more violent than before and complained of severe headache. Although the episode subsided within the day, both mother and child felt frightened, and the mother called me asking for help.

She described him as usually a normal boy, "a great baby, a good sleeper, and a good eater." The Kool-Aid episodes were aberrant and superimposed upon an otherwise normal pattern. Jamie was a cute, well-nourished 4-year-old who was friendly, affectionate, and playful, with an endearing twinkle in his eye. Nevertheless, there were some subtle signs of potential problems in several areas.

Though Jamie was large at birth, weighing over 10½ pounds, he was now a thin and wiry youngster, at only the 30th percentile for weight (that is, 70% of children his age weigh more). His mother had gained a whopping 55 pounds during pregnancy, which is twice the recommended amount. Though by no means an inevitable cause of hyperactivity, large weight gain and problems during pregnancy are sometimes part of a picture contributing to a suspicion of some birth damage.

When I first asked about Jamie's behavior, his mother replied that on the whole Jamie was a happy, bright, and precocious boy. But as we talked, it became apparent that Jamie's behavior was not perfect. Far from it; he was a very active boy, "going all the time." One of the best tip-offs that his activity pattern was excessive came when his mother said, "he acts like he is driven by a motor." After periods of intense activity, Jamie appeared to suddenly wind down; however, he would have an afternoon nap every day, somewhat unusual for a 4-year-old.

Though 4 years old, Jamie still showed the 2-year-old's characteristic pattern of saying "no" to everything. He could also be quite aggressive, and according to his mother, on occasion would "beat his brother to a pulp." (This must have been quite an accomplishment since his brother was 3 years older.)

There were also some indications of problems with parenting skills. Jamie's mother was tender and solicitous with him while they were in the waiting room, but she admitted that she often became exasperated with him and mostly tried to manage him by yelling and screaming, a strategy that is easy for parents to fall into, but one that is usually totally ineffective. I made a note to myself that I would have to recommend some training in parenting skills.

At first I thought that Jamie's picture was that of a classical hyperkinetic syndrome. Jamie's mother had filled out a 93-item checklist of Jamie's behavior, and all the major categories were within the normal range except for a group of items dealing with restless and impulsive behavior, such as blurting into conversations and not waiting his turn; on these, Jamie was worse than 90% of children his age. Jamie's mother had checked off on the symptom list Jamie's explosive behavior and temper outbursts and his habit of throwing himself around and breaking things.

Similarly, he engaged in repetitive activities, had sudden

mood shifts, and acted as if "driven by a motor." But when I interviewed the mother and went over each item she had checked, she said the various symptoms were severe *only when Jamie drank Kool-Aid*. Thus, the drink seemed to exacerbate patterns of response that were already there.

Moreover, Jamie's "motor-driven" behavior, sudden mood changes, and destructive outbursts only became a real problem after exposure to Kool-Aid *sweetened with aspartame*. This now familiar artificial sweetener had only recently become available, and because aspartame had a delicious sweetness without an aftertaste, it would soon begin to replace less palatable sweeteners like saccharin.

There were hints of other problems with food, though nothing conclusive. From the beginning there were some feeding problems, and though such problems are not uncommon, they seemed to reflect a pattern of food intolerance. He had constant rhinitis (stuffy nose) and diarrhea following formula feedings, and he was eventually switched to a cow's milk formula with alleviation of the symptoms. His mother had a suspicion, though not documented by an allergist, that Jamie was allergic to both milk and molds. She herself could not eat apples, pears, peaches, or plums because of allergy to pectin, and said that she was also allergic to jellied candies, pollen, penicillin, and some other medicines.

THE NUTRASWEET (ASPARTAME) STORY

Like many scientific discoveries, aspartame was the unintended product of luck. A chemist working on an ulcer medicine in the 1960s inadvertently licked the powder on his fingers and found it pleasantly sweet, and unlike saccharin, it had no aftertaste. When Jamie was just 2 years old, Searle Pharmaceuticals introduced this revolutionary new artificial sweetener to the market as a table-top sweetener, and then during the same year I first saw Jamie, in 1983, the Food and Drug Administration (FDA) permitted its use as a sweetener for drinks. I was curious why it took 20 years for the manufacturer of aspartame to receive approval to market it. Aspartame (trade names "Equal" and "NutraSweet") was originally approved in 1974 by the FDA.

But animal studies by a neuropathologist, Dr. John Olney, suggested that aspartame might lead to brain damage. This finding caused suspension of aspartame's approval by the FDA, which was sensitive to this issue, knowing that other sweeteners, such as sodium cyclamate and saccharin, are carcinogenic (cancer causing) in animals.

There was also a question of how adequate the execution of the animal studies was. Searle's performance with several laboratory studies on aspartame and other drugs had led the FDA commissioner, Dr. Alexander M. Schmidt, to testify earlier that "recent investigations by the agency have raised questions about Searle Laboratory's conduct of animal experiments and their reporting of data."[1] The FDA therefore appointed a six-man team of scientists to evaluate Searle's animal data regarding aspartame and other drugs.

Two years later, in 1976, the report of the scientists was damning: "Searle made a number of deliberate decisions which seemingly were calculated to minimize the chances of discovering toxicity and, or, to allay FDA concern." The commissioner of the FDA had no choice but to tell Congress that Searle had engaged in "a pattern of conduct which compromises the scientific integrity of the studies," and he even requested the U.S. Justice Department to investigate whether Searle had concealed data or made false statements in support of aspartame.

The legal suit was eventually dropped, but meanwhile, over 80 studies questioning aspartame's safety, most having to do with its cancer-causing potential, had accumulated. By now the task of independently reviewing this mass of data was so large that Schmidt and the FDA decided not to waste more public funds on the issue, and the FDA and Searle agreed to hire an independent research group to evaluate the findings. However, this group could review only 15 of the 80 studies, and a public board of inquiry later appointed to do a more extensive review also found the 140 volumes of documentation overwhelming and ended up focusing on the same set of 15 studies examined by the scientific panel. Although this review panel found no evidence that the sweetener was likely to cause brain damage, they did find that they could not rule out the possibility that aspartame caused cancer, and they recommended that the FDA withhold approval.

Despite this resounding defeat for aspartame's endorsement, Searle persisted, and the day after the Republican administration took office on January 21, 1981, they petitioned for approval from the newly appointed FDA commissioner, Arthur Hull Hayes. Hayes approved, and shortly thereafter resigned. Perhaps unfairly (considering his distinguished record of public service), newspapers such as the *Washington Post* noted that a month after granting approval Hayes resigned, and that "he became senior scientific consultant to the public relations agency that has Searle's account for aspartame, Burson-Marsteller."

It is easy to see why one might construe this sequence of events as evidence of a sinister government–industrial plot to promote a monumentally successful commercial venture. The facts do not warrant such a conclusion. The FDA has to make a reasonable judgment that protects the public interest from harm, but it also has to consider the benefits of a new product and not obstruct its availability. Further research has continued to suggest that aspartame is not carcinogenic. But what is striking about this whole episode is the narrow focus on *physical* risks, with no attention paid to possible *behavioral* risks. Behavioral toxicology hardly came into the discussion at all.

Much of the earlier concern about brain damage in newborns and children arose because aspartame consists of two amino acids (aspartic acid and phenylalanine) used in the brain's neurotransmitter systems. Phenylalanine, like many other amino acids, is "essential," because it must be eaten in order to provide the brain with sufficient amounts to manufacture its basic chemical messengers, the neurotransmitters. In this case, phenylalanine is a "precursor" used in the synthesis of the neurotransmitters dopamine and norepinephrine—two chemicals that we will hear much about in connection with foods children and adults eat.

In the condition called phenylketonuria (PKU), one of the enzymes required to break down phenylalanine is missing at birth, and as a result, excessive amounts of phenylalanine accumulate in the brain, eventually causing brain damage and varying degrees of mental retardation.

One of the treatments for this inborn metabolic error is a diet low in phenylalanine. Some scientists therefore immediately raised the question whether aspartame might pose a threat to those suffering from PKU or those who have some of the genes necessary for the disease but who do not have the disease itself. Fortunately, most of the animal and human studies appeared to reassure scientists that aspartame in moderate doses posed no hazard for these populations (though some worry on this point persists).

But apart from brain damage and cancer, a sudden influx of phenylalanine might affect *behavioral* functions of the brain. To understand why, some technical background is necessary. Phenylalanine is one member of a class of amino acids (large neutral amino acids, or LNAA) that gain access to the brain only in competition with one another. Since they all have to compete for a place on the carrier molecules that transport them across the barrier from the peripheral blood supply into the brain itself, when many amino acids are eaten together (as usually happens in a protein meal), they cancel out so that none gains precedence in the competition to enter the brain. Thus, when eating a hamburger, phenylalanine is taken in along with other LNAA such as leucine, isoleucine, valine, tyrosine, and tryptophan. The competition from these other amino acids limits the access of phenylalanine to the brain.

We seldom eat a *single* amino acid protein, though we commonly assume that "protein" refers to a single type of food. When drinking an aspartame-sweetened drink, however, the phenylalanine is heavily concentrated, and hence the *ratio* to other amino acids increases markedly. It is this ratio which finally determines which of the many substances get to the brain and to what extent. A high ratio of any one amino acid to the others gives it a competitive advantage for getting to the brain.

The brain is normally protected from a sudden infusion of just one amino acid by this competitive relationship among them. Most foods contain many different amino acids, so that when digesting food there is a balanced entry of the amino acids into the brain. Only under unusual circumstances is it likely that a single type of amino acid gains sufficient precedence that it can overcome the competition for transport into the brain. One might consider the system similar to a lot of people trying to find seats on a bus. Ordinarily people of all kinds will line up for seats. But if the local football or hockey team happened to arrive, they would be overrepresented on the bus and get to their destination at the expense of the ordinary citizens.

Among the arguments often used for the safety of aspartame, is that the increase in the amount of phenylalanine in the blood following a diet drink, or even several diet drinks, is equal to or less than the phenylalanine increase after eating a hamburger or other protein-based meals. But there is a fundamental fallacy in this argument, for as we have already noted, it is not the total amount in the bloodstream but the concentration compared with other amino acids that finally determines how much gets into the brain.

Considerable controversy centers on how much aspartame is sufficient to cause important changes in the brain. Most of the research on this question has involved laboratory rats. But rats metabolize phenylalanine quite differently than humans. Whereas rats convert phenylalanine in the liver to the amino acid tyrosine, this does not happen with humans to anywhere near the same extent. Fundamental differences between these laboratory animals and humans are so great that they call into question many of the conclusions regarding the effects of aspartame on humans, especially regarding how much increase there is in brain neurotransmitters from eating aspartame.

Another important point ignored in the rat studies is that the amounts of aspartame getting to the brain can be markedly altered by certain dietary conditions. Dr. Richard Wurtman, a leading researcher on these questions at MIT, has pointed out that eating sugar or other carbohydrates at the same time as the aspartame (for example, eating cookies along with the soft drink) compounds the problem. One of the immediate effects of eating sugar or other carbohydrates is a rapid insulin response. Insulin is the main counter-regulatory hormone which acts to keep blood sugar within bounds. One of its effects is to purge the bloodstream of most of the circulating amino acids. So, the insulin effect would tend to reduce most of the amino acids at precisely the time when the liquid intake of aspartame in a diet drink is increasing the available phenylalanine, thus giving it an even greater competitive advantage over other amino acids in the fight to enter the brain.

Another concern about aspartame has been its possible effects in producing convulsions or seizures. Scientists know that brain neurotransmitters which are dependent upon phenylalanine (such as the neurotransmitters dopamine and norepinephrine) are important in the regulation of seizures. It has been shown that animal brains treated with large doses of phenylalanine develop a lower threshold for seizures provoked by certain seizure-causing substances. Since it is not possible to investigate this type of problem experimentally in humans, little direct evidence is available regarding the effects of aspartame on seizures in children or adults.

But scientists working on aspartame, and the Center for Disease Control (a public health agency in Atlanta), received many reports of incidents involving headache and first-time seizures when aspartame was first introduced. We have to recognize that *any* newly approved food item will cause many such anecdotes to occur, but some are compelling enough that they at least raise our concerns and suggest needed areas for further research.

For example, one letter received by Dr. Wurtman was from a 26-year-old registered nurse who gave a very detailed clinical description of her experience after she began using aspartame. She was using 6 to 10 packets a day of Equal (a powder version of aspartame) and occasional drinks with NutraSweet for about a week when she began experiencing a "left-temporal headache" (just above the left ear). That night she had a major seizure. The seizure began in her right hand and "marched" in a typical fashion through other parts of her body. After hospitalization, she had many tests, all normal. No cause was found for the seizure.

Meanwhile, unawares, she continued using Equal. One day she consumed more than her usual amount and developed the left-temporal headache again. That night at a party she had a drink of rum (probably not a good idea for someone prone to seizures) and while dancing she experienced another major seizure, which was witnessed by several doctors who were present. She continued having two to three headaches a week, and about a month later she had a 1-ounce drink of rum with guests at dinner and again had a seizure.

Several interpretations of these incidents are possible,

which is typical of many such anecdotes. Was it just the rum in a seizure-prone individual that triggered the attack, or was it the combination of excessive aspartame intake and the rum, or just the aspartame alone? We noted earlier that anecdotes are only suggestive, never proof, and the present case is no exception. What sets this account apart from most, however, is the careful description of details, made by a professional observer, and the repeated close correlation of symptoms with excessive intake of Nutrasweet.

Although such anecdotes by themselves prove nothing about the headache and seizure-causing role of aspartame, laboratory studies with animals show that such an effect is *possible*. One method of testing for a drug effect on seizure threshold is to give a substance to an animal which is known to lower the threshold for seizures in that animal (that is, making seizures more readily triggered) and then examine the effect of the drug on that threshold. One such agent is metrazol, which in rats will lower their seizure threshold. Aspartame has been shown to lower the level at which metrazol-induced seizures occur. Because the levels of aspartame had to be very high to produce the effect, most scientists concluded that it was unlikely to be a predisposing factor in seizures for humans.

But experimental animals differ in so many ways from humans that one cannot be sure that the same levels of the amino acid cause similar effects in humans. What is a high level for animals may be very different from the level required to produce a problem in humans. One prominent scientist estimates that as little as 15–20 mg per kg of body weight could lower the seizure threshold. For a 30-kg child this means that three or four cans of soda containing about 100 mg of aspartame would reach this level of risk. Even that might seem to be an unlikely amount for very many people to consume.

But another letter is worth quoting in some detail, because

it highlights how easy it is for some youngsters, because of their lifestyle, to use diet drinks to excess, thus exposing themselves to enormous doses of aspartame:

> I suppose the best way to sum up the past three years of my life would be to call them a living hell. I was trapped in a deep, dark and seemingly endless state of depression that neither my doctors nor I could find reason for. The only way to explain the magnitude of my turmoil would be to start from the beginning and therefore give you a clear impression of my life before and after aspartame entered it.
>
> Before aspartame was introduced to the public my life had been full and very rewarding. I was a top student and very active in all sports and social activities. The highlight of those years being when I competed in [World Championship games in Europe]. It was just months after this event . . . that aspartame was introduced . . . into my daily life. This low calorie sugar substitute instantly became a success and the "savior" of teenage girls like myself who were diet and health conscious. With this product in the new diet sodas we could drink as much as we wanted and not have to worry about our waistlines or possible health hazards that saccharin was reported to have.
>
> I would drink a diet soda to quench my thirst after a workout and it soon became a regular routine for me to opt for a diet drink over all other drinks whenever possible. It soon became a well-known fact amongst my friends that I was a total addict of the drinks. A fact we all laughed at because what could be the harm in such an addiction? It got to the point where I would always have a huge bottle of the stuff in my locker so that I could take a swig in between classes. The teachers even kidded me that they should have the stuff analyzed to see if it was spiked. They even documented the fact by mentioning my "addiction to Tab, Fresca and Coke" (all diet drinks containing aspartame) in [class pictures].
>
> The last two years of school . . . were radically different from the previous years. I became gradually more and more depressed. Many times unable to leave the house for classes or to see my friends. I began to lose interest in all extra-curricular activities and rarely could bring myself to do those things that I used to thrive on such as jogging, biking, dancing or just horsing around. Nothing was FUN anymore.
>
> It's only now, four years later that I have learned about the side effects of aspartame that I have realized the correlation between the introduction of aspartame into my life and my gradual

growing depression. But back in high school I had no idea why I was feeling the way I was. It honestly seemed at the time that the only enjoyment I was getting out of life was a cold can or bottle of diet soda. I had somewhere along the line lost the ability to enjoy anything else.

It got to the point where my daily routine consisted of watching TV, eating, and the consumption of at least 10 to 15 cans of diet sodas. But to add to the problem I began to gain weight because of my inactivity and poor eating habits brought on by my depression. In those few years I had gone from a vibrant outgoing person to a lump of flesh on the family-room couch.

I tried many times to overcome my depression but with no avail. I just continued to drain can after can after bottle after bottle of the stuff hoping that I would somehow just snap out of it. [She then goes on to describe her unhelpful experiences with a series of doctors. After seeing a news report about aspartame she stopped drinking it. She continues:]

In conclusion I'd like to say that since I've stopped using aspartame I have noticed an improvement in my attitude. When I first tried to stop use I experienced shaking, nausea and a tremendous urge to have a diet drink. I wasn't able to stop immediately so I gradually cut down the number of cans each day until I had quit altogether. . . . I have experienced other discomforts which I'm not sure were caused by aspartame but . . . I will list them for you: a) acidic feeling in chest and throat; chest pains; b) blurred vision; c) skin rash; d) headaches in temple area.

Again, we cannot know whether this is a response caused by aspartame or merely coincident with its use; the "experiment" does not rule out many alternative explanations. The picture is a typical one for adolescent depression: inability to experience pleasure anymore, inactivity, hopelessness, and dejected and sad mood. But this same story of excessive use with similar symptoms is one I have heard from other teenagers and children.

It is also striking how many of the unsolicited letters contain references to the last three symptoms this girl mentioned: blurred vision, skin rash, and temporal headaches. These could be coincidence or influence of public media (one news report or letter can spawn dozens of identical symptoms). Nevertheless,

the addictive quality of the experience stands out, suggesting
the possibility that gradually over time some important chemical
adjustments took place in the brain, much as happens with true
addictive substances.

A CONTROLLED CASE STUDY WITH ASPARTAME

Now that we have learned something of the background of
aspartame, it is time to return to Jamie's story. Though reluctant
to further expose him to aspartame, I had little trouble persuad-
ing Jamie's mother to carry out a double-blind trial in order to
more rigorously document her son's aberrant response to aspartame. Her major concern was that continued exposure to the
chemical might have disastrous consequences, and in this she
proved to be partially correct, as we shall see.

We saw earlier how double-blind trials are usually carried
out on *groups* of subjects, one group receiving the active ingredient, one the placebo. In the double-blind study of a single
person, the trial involves observations taken with the same person receiving the drug and the placebo at different times, usually some days apart. The drug and the placebo days are then
compared to control days when neither agent is given. If a reaction occurs on the days when the active ingredient is present,
and not on the placebo or control days, it tends to confirm that
the reaction is due to the active ingredient and not to random
effects or placebo effects. Jamie's mother had already carried out
a similar experiment, using regular Kool-Aid. But, of course, she
was not blind to the changes, and she could have been influenced by knowing which drink contained aspartame.

For Jamie we had a ready-made drug and placebo: regular
Kool-Aid sweetened with sugar, and Kool-Aid with aspartame
(NutraSweet). The two drinks were indistinguishable in taste
and color. Jamie's mother had said that his symptoms usually

showed up about a half hour after exposure, so we started observing him over a period of about 1 hour immediately after he drank a 6-ounce glass of the cherry-flavored Kool-Aid, with continuing observations by his mother over the course of the day after they left the laboratory.

We studied Jamie on four separate occasions about a week apart. For 10 days his mother recorded his symptomatic behavior using a behavior checklist, as she had done when she first brought Jamie to the laboratory. (In Chapter 10 we will show how parents and teachers can use this checklist to track the effects of foods in their own children.) On 2 later days he received the aspartame-flavored drink, and on 2 days the sugar-flavored drink. About 1 week separated each of the four visits, and in between, his mother continued recording his daily behavior. Our dietitian prepared the drinks and the order of administration without informing either the child, parent, or observers.

We set up two methods to observe Jamie. First, two psychologists videotaped and observed him by counting the number of times he engaged in aggressive, angry, or defiant behavior. We instructed Jamie to play with toys in the room any way he wished, while his mother sat over to the side quietly watching. After a half hour or so we instructed Jamie's mother to give various "commands" to put the toys away, clean up, and so forth. Second, Jamie's mother filled out the daily checklist of hyperactive behaviors at the end of each day. We could compare these checklist responses to thousands of parents of normal children of Jamie's age.

In one sense, nothing dramatic happened in the two sessions in which Jamie received the artificially flavored drink. We saw no wild, out-of-control displays or destructive behavior. But something was *beginning* to occur. During the aspartame days, Jamie's level of defiant and noncompliant behavior in the laboratory increased from the normal level on regular Kool-Aid and baseline days so that they were occurring over 70% of the time, a much higher level than on the placebo days. On both of the aspartame days, Jamie's mother marked many more hyperactive symptoms occurring later that day. The levels reached the abnormal range, whereas on control days and placebo days they were entirely normal.

More interesting still are the informal comments that Jamie's mother wrote at the bottom of the rating sheets on the two aspartame days. On the first of these she wrote:

> After we left Children's Hospital Jamie was very quiet (did not speak) all the way home and all through lunch. His grandmother noticed he seemed to be day-dreaming. He ate a good lunch, but seemed not to be with it (pre-occupied). He started complaining of a headache (approx 2:30 p.m.) and was somewhat cranky and nasty. He slept for 3 hours for his afternoon nap. When he awoke, he was not in the same disposition he was earlier in the day. He woke up crying and screaming. Proceeded to find fault with everything. Refused to eat dinner. Cried all through the meal. After dinner he played in the basement but instead of playing he stood in the middle of the floor and screamed for ½ hour at the top of his lungs. I put him to bed early (he was restless). Next morning he was all smiles.

There was nothing else going on that might account for these unusual behaviors. Jamie appeared to show signs of exhaustion and irritability, much as a child does when overtired. Instead of his outgoing personality he became more withdrawn. His headache was a tell-tale sign that something had happened to his central nervous system. Finally, when he woke up, and should have felt refreshed, he was instead completely lacking in controls, as though some basic capacity for restraint or inhibition in the brain had been lost.

In the intervening days his mother made comments like "very happy and sweet all day." On Jamie's second aspartame day (still double-blind), she said:

> When we left the hospital Jamie said he was very tired and had to go to the bathroom. We stopped at the restrooms as we were

leaving. We arrived at my parents around 11:40 a.m. and Jamie ate everything in sight, but looked as though he were falling asleep. His hands kept holding up his head. After lunch he had to go to the bathroom again. We left my parents to go home around 1:20 p.m. and Jamie went to the bathroom again. He fell asleep in the car 5 minutes before we arrived home.

When we arrived home he went to the bathroom again and said he couldn't wait to take his nap, he was so tired. I put him to bed around 2:15 p.m. (I was surprised his bladder appeared to be working overtime, as I'm lucky if he goes 2–3 times a day, maximum). I put him to bed with the feeling that he would sleep all afternoon since he appeared so tired. To my surprise, he never slept. I heard noises in his room at 2:45 [p.m.] and when I checked on him he was *running* back and forth from his room to his brother's and back again, running in circles over and over again.

As the afternoon wore on, he kept running and circling and seemed to be everywhere—he talked so much and *very fast*, I could hardly understand him. At dinner time Jamie ate nothing and couldn't sit still to eat. He kept getting up and running full speed through the house and talking fast and loud.

I had a baby sitter come at 6:30 p.m. so I could go to a class with my husband. The sitter's first reaction to Jamie was: "Who wound him up?" We were home by 10:30 p.m. and the sitter stated that Jamie was very argumentative with his brother and was like a rubber band wound up too tight. When she put him to bed at 9:00 p.m. she said he almost collapsed into bed and fell asleep right away.

Other signs of central nervous system disruption appear in these notes: a disturbance of appetite, sleep, and bladder control. These are what psychiatrists call "vegetative signs," very basic aspects of bodily function which are often impaired in people with serious mental illness such as major depression. Such signs are thought to reflect very primitive biological functions regulated by structures deep in the brain.

As telling as these vignettes may be, they are not conclusive. One still might have some doubts about the role of aspartame in Jamie's hyperactive behavior. Could it be possible, for example, that these 2 "hyper" days just happened to coincide with 2 bad days in the up-and-down life of a hyperactive youngster? Or could Jamie's mother have unconsciously guessed at the schedule, reporting biased observations because of her belief in the aspartame connection? The 10-day period which she recorded before the double-blind challenges was, of course, not blind. So perhaps she painted a rosy picture during those times and simply guessed when Jamie received the aspartame. These are all possibilities, but considering the entire story, they seem implausible.

We continued to follow Jamie over succeeding months, and intermittently his mother called with new episodes, each more worrisome than the last. For instance, on Halloween (about 2 weeks after our challenges), Jamie went to a school party where he accidentally drank some Swiss Miss hot chocolate (which the teacher thought was aspartame-free but later turned out not to be). Jamie was sent home for screaming, kicking, crying hysterically, being out of control, and threatening other kids. The same pattern reoccurred: hyperactivity, aggressiveness, intermittent somnolence, increased urine output, and slurred speech.

On another occasion, Jamie and his mother had lunch at a local family-style restaurant and drank root beer, which they knew to be naturally sweetened (one of the reasons they ate there). Later in the day the typical reaction occurred, with incessant talking, uncontrolled body movements, severe headache, and inability to stay asleep more than an hour at a time. This reaction continued through the following day, with almost no sleep over the 24-hour period. When Jamie's mother checked back at the restaurant, the manager was very sheepish and concerned, because they had run out of the regular supply of root beer and had taken the expedient of temporarily using diet root beer purchased nearby, without notifying the customers of the change. In some respects, these serendipitous double-blind experiments are more convincing than the carefully managed ones conducted in the laboratory.

The most important aspect of Jamie's story is the progressive change in his personality, which seemed to occur after each of these intermittent and terrifying episodes. He began to show signs of extreme nervousness; he had nightmares and fears of falling asleep because the "NutraSweet monster" was going to get him. At one point he drew a frightening picture of the monster about to devour him.

Television ads for NutraSweet now caused Jamie to fear going to sleep and to be withdrawn for the rest of the evening. One may wonder about the role of adults in sensitizing Jamie to these fears, but it seems unusual that a nonanxious and mildly hyperactive boy should shift from an externalizing orientation to an internalizing one. Jamie began to appear less like a hyperactive boy and more like a neurotic one.

Eventually I referred Jamie to a child psychiatrist who worked with him over the next several months. Despite this therapy, Jamie's depression and anxiety became progressively worse, and his ability to learn in school became impaired. Jamie's teacher reported that he was not the same happy, confident youngster who started the year and that he was more and more tearful, withdrawn, and afraid of being touched. In many respects this course of events is so similar to the adolescent girl who overindulged in diet drinks that we may well wonder whether a similar process is occurring in both cases. But unlike the adolescent girl, Jamie did not have to take in large amounts of aspartame to trigger a reaction.

We cannot be sure that aspartame began this disturbing cycle, nor can we even be certain that the dramatic bouts of hyperactivity, sleeplessness, and excitability were directly linked to NutraSweet. One could postulate that Jamie has an early variant of manic–depressive disorder, though such cases are very rare in children Jamie's age. Possibly Jamie's mother simply "pinned" the rap on the drinks, forgetting or minimizing those hyperactive episodes that occurred when there was no artificial sweetener in the vicinity.

As a scientist, I have to agree that these are *possible* interpretations, but ones I find to be much more farfetched than the obvious one—that Jamie has a severe reactivity to aspartame-containing substances.

This case raises many questions. Are the episodes those of someone especially vulnerable or sensitive (as in an allergic reaction)? Do they have something to do with Jamie's preexisting mild hyperactivity? Is there any connection with PKU? How many other children have such reactions? Are the reactions age-specific, possibly having something to do with age-related changes in brain neurotransmitter functions? Scientific data cannot yet answer most of these questions.

As for the relationship to hyperactivity, aspartame does have a theoretical connection. One theory of hyperactivity is that certain brain neurotransmitters work together in regulating functions like motor activity, alertness, and emotional responses. Scientists have theorized that these two transmitters, dopamine and norepinephrine, normally work to modulate each other in a coordinated way, but that in hyperactive children they are "uncoupled." There is some evidence that treating hyperactives with stimulant drugs restores the normal relationship between the two neurotransmitters. The dopamine system is especially important in brain structures involving restraint and motor control. The lack of coordination between the two neurotransmitters may also explain why hyperactive children are easily disinhibited but tend to show a lack of inner anxiety and emotionality. Control over emotional responses depends upon the norepinephrine system. The relative balance between the two neurotransmitters could account for the externalizing and internalizing patterns so often found in children's behavior.

These two neurotransmitters also develop in the brain over a period of time during early childhood, and some theories view hyperactivity as a disorder of development of these basic regulatory systems. One experiment with animals provides a revealing model of hyperactivity. Destroying the dopamine system of young rats causes the animals to become hyperactive and learning disabled. Treating them with stimulant drugs used to treat hyperactive children (like amphetamine) makes them normal, much like their human counterparts. As they grow older their hyperactivity diminishes, much in the same way that it tends to disappear with age in children. Presumably the gradual waning of hyperactivity with age in hyperactive rats and children reflects the growth of dopamine-containing neurons in their brains. Hyperactive dogs with dopamine deficiencies calm down when treated with amphetamine. Normally active dogs, on the other hand, simply get more excited.

As we have pointed out, aspartame contains phenylalanine, required by the brain for making dopamine and norepinephrine. It does not seem too farfetched to consider that an unexpected large influx of phenylalanine to the brain somehow disrupts the balance in the dopamine–norepinephrine system, especially in young children whose system is in the process of developing or in hyperactive children who already have a tenuous balance among their neurotransmitters. It is interesting that the second child I saw with a confirmed laboratory response to aspartame was also a mildly hyperactive 4-year-old boy.

We do not know if there is a genetic loading for PKU in Jamie, because his mother was not willing to subject him to the test for this (which involves taking a large dose of phenylalanine). One laboratory finding is consistent with this possibility. Jamie had an abnormally low blood tyrosine level. Tyrosine is another essential amino acid required for production of norepinephrine in the brain. High levels of phenylalanine tend to lower the available levels of tyrosine available to the brain. Lower tyrosine levels in the brain could upset the production of norepinephrine, which, as noted earlier, is an important neurotransmitter in many brain functions, including the "fight–flight" reaction, emotionality, and mood.

Lacking large-scale studies, it is difficult to know whether

Jamie's type of reaction is an isolated case. But unsolicited letters from parents raise the possibility that the reaction is more common than first suspected. For instance, one mother concerned about her 3-year-old son described a scenario remarkably similar to that of Jamie's:

> Last summer I purchased Kool-Aid drink mix with NutraSweet and made it for my children. The following day, my son, then two years and ten months, was absolutely unbearable, crying for no apparent reason, and not wanting to be a part of anything almost all day long. His behavior was so bizarre, that by the afternoon, I was going over the events of the past few days to try to determine if any single event could have upset his personality so drastically. When I could not pinpoint any emotional trauma, I began to recall his diet . . . and remembered he had consumed . . . about 16 ounces [of Kool-Aid] for the two days.

Just as with Jamie, this same little boy was subsequently exposed to Swiss Miss chocolate. After drinking about 8 ounces at supper, the mother reported that,

> . . . next morning he was grumpy and cranky and when I picked him up in the evening from his daycare, his teacher told me that he had been very "weepy" all day. After about an hour of non-stop crying and whining, [he] began to laugh hysterically and run around the house, the mood shift was so extreme that it triggered the memory of the summer behavior, and I then made the connection with the NutraSweet.

Another mother, who normally never allowed artificially sweetened drinks in the house, described what happened when some friends visited for Thanksgiving and left two large bottles of NutraSweet-flavored soft drinks:

> Johnny has always been exceptionally active, although we were always assured that he is not hyperactive as his concentration is quite good. Right after Thanksgiving, however, his activity level went from high to crazed. He became angry and violent, ripping apart the furniture in his room, breaking toys, having constant tantrums and being unable to exhibit any self-control. Before this he had had the most cheerful disposition imaginable. Then, as suddenly as it had begun, the behavior stopped. . . . Perhaps I

should add that Johnny had many food allergies as a baby, all of
which he has apparently outgrown.

The similarity in these stories is impressive, including the
ages of the children, the types of symptoms, the products involved, and even the mention of allergies. None of these parents knew each other and so were not influenced by the others'
stories. Each made discoveries of a connection between an artificial sweetener and hyperactivity that was at first never suspected until repeated exposures raised the issue. We might well
wonder how many other children have had similar episodes
where the connection went unnoticed.

It is particularly easy for such connections to escape notice
when the child has been hyperactive for some time, or when the
explosive outbursts or crying seem only like slightly exaggerated
variations of the normal ups and downs so characteristic of hyperactive youngsters. It takes a keen observer to notice the correlation between these fluctuations and what the child is drinking or eating.

Scientists and laymen alike might ignore such cases, especially if they are rare, claiming that the numbers are insufficient
to matter. After all, the argument goes, some people react badly
to aspirin, but few argue that such rare reactions should be the
cause of removing it from the market. The problem is that we
have no good estimates of the number of such cases, and artificial sweeteners are now so ubiquitous that we might fail to see
connections that were more obvious the first time they were
used. Only the most curious and careful observers, tracking the
behavior over time, with and without the sweetener, would be
likely to see the connection.

DIETING AND ASPARTAME

There are many apparent benefits of a nonnutritive sweetener for obese dieters, diabetics, and people worried about den-

tal decay or the cardiovascular effects of sugar. If real, we may choose to have these benefits despite the occasional rare reaction such as Jamie's. But what about these alternative advantages? How real are they? We have already recounted one case when aspartame not only failed to help dieting but eventually impaired the process entirely. Is there any more general basis for this occurrence?

The regulation of appetite is complex and still not completely understood. But we do know that both the taste of the food and its nutrient value (including the type of food and the amount of calories) are important in telling the brain when we should stop eating. Most food, of course, has both taste and nutrient values associated with it, and part of the regulation of eating depends upon how pleasant the food tastes. Once the food ceases to taste good, we tend to stop eating. Fasting or avoiding a particular food, on the other hand, will tend to make food tastier. (My wife, for example, is one of those disciplined people who loves chocolate but will deliberately forsake it in order to heighten the pleasure when it *is* eaten.)

But what happens to appetite when the taste of food gets uncoupled from its calorie content? A recent experiment by two British researchers suggests that aspartame acts paradoxically, compared with calorie-containing sugar such as glucose. When subjects were given large doses of glucose, their desire to eat lessened and their sense of fullness increased. In contrast, appetite suppression did not occur after drinking aspartame; instead, it *increased* significantly!

Apparently, the "residual hunger" created by aspartame leads to increased eating. It is as though the brain's food centers feel cheated, signaling that food is coming, but not receiving the promised calories. The investigators warn that

> This confusion of psychobiological information may lead to a loss of control over appetite, particularly in vulnerable individuals of normal weight who are dieting and who may be consuming large

amounts of dietary aids for weight control. In turn, this may contribute to disordered patterns of eating prevalent among certain groups of normal weight individuals.[2]

We learn from this observation what many people in a weight-conscious society already know: it is not only fat people who diet or watch their weight. People of average weight trying to maintain a steady weight level are probably much more numerous than fat people on diets. But they also stand to lose the most if their appetites become unregulated.

When we experiment with nature, we risk the possibility of producing unanticipated effects that may not be worth the apparent advantages. One only has to imagine what it would be like if no foods had any taste at all or if all foods had the same taste. There are psychiatric and neurologic conditions where exactly this occurs. The usual effect is that eating stops entirely or becomes very erratic.

Taste cues are closely integrated with the hunger and satiety system and undoubtedly evolved over many millennia in order to provide a type of automatic control system over when to eat and when to stop eating. We may wonder at the long-term consequences of providing an attractive taste, but no calories or nutrition to back it up as the brain has come to expect.

OTHER CONTROLLED TRIALS OF ASPARTAME
IN CHILDREN

In one of our studies, we wanted to see how sugars affected children's behavior in the classroom and on the hospital ward. In this study we used aspartame as the placebo drink, assuming it would not have any psychological or behavioral effects of its own. The children we studied were inpatients with quite severe conduct problems or hyperactivity.

Nurses observed 37 children who were eating their normal

diets (baseline) over a 1-week period and then for several weeks during which the children drank an orange drink at breakfast, containing either sugar or aspartame at a low dose. The nurses observed the children with a 60-item behavior checklist.

There was one set of items that the nurses rated significantly higher on days the children received the aspartame than either the baseline or sugar days. These items included headaches, fatigue, lethargy, diarrhea, aches and pains, and food refusal. Though no one of these complaints was significantly associated by itself with aspartame, as a group they were evident more often on the aspartame days. Not all children experienced these problems, but a majority did. We concluded that in this group of children, chronic exposure to a low dose of aspartame was creating an increase in bodily complaints.

In another experiment carried out in our laboratory, Dr. Mark Reader studied 30 normal preschoolers (3 to 5 years of age), on 3 different days: once after receiving sucrose (refined sugar), once after aspartame, and once after saccharin. These challenges were given after an overnight fast. The drinks were about the same in taste and color, with the experimenters blind to the assignments. We could observe the children through a one-way mirror while they played with their mothers. They also wore little instruments on their wrist and ankles called "actometers." These devices look like wrist watches but record the amount of bodily movement rather than the time.

On most of the measures there was no observable difference among the treatments. But 21 of the 30 children had higher scores on the actometers when they received aspartame than when they received the other treatments. However, a similar study conducted by Dr. Marcus Kreusi at the National Institutes of Mental Health found no differences between sugar, saccharin, and aspartame on actometer scores in 32 preschool children.[3]

Such differences in the outcome of scientific experiments

often occur. When findings are inconsistent there can be many reasons, such as different methods of selecting the children, different methods of observation, or different methods of treatment. On the whole, despite differences between studies, both of these controlled trials with normal preschool children are somewhat reassuring. If there are any aspartame effects, they are minimal and quite subtle. But such studies do not say anything about the effects of *repeated exposures* nor whether some predisposition to a reaction is important.

These studies also raise the question of just what constitutes a safe dose. Studies with humans base their estimates of an unsafe amount largely on the idea that normal consumption involves drinking one or two 6-ounce drinks per day. A 6-ounce diet drink contains about 100 mg of aspartame. Most drug studies adjust the dosage based on body weight, because drug effects depend upon the amount of body tissue in which the drug acts. If an average 4-year-old weighs about 20 kg, then two diet sodas a day would only expose the child to about 10 mg for each kilogram of body weight.

The manufacturers of aspartame estimated that about 34 mg of aspartame per kilogram would be a higher dose than 99% of the population would be likely to consume; that is, only about 1% of people would consume aspartame levels of more than 34 mg per kg of their body weight. Thus, according to these figures, young children would have to drink more than six cans of soda a day in order to consume as much as the upper 1% of consumers. But some scientists argue that this estimate may turn out to be very low.

Americans consumed over 3,500 tons of aspartame in 1984. One scientist estimated that 7- to 12-year-old children would consume over twice the recommended amount.[4] More important, based on studies in which loads of aspartame were given over a 12-week period to normal adults, the rise in the blood levels of phenylalanine could be 10 times the normal level.

Given the blood levels considered safe, 14% of the normal population would be at risk for unsafe pregnancies, and 35% of those who are genetically loaded for PKU would be at risk. Almost 5% of the normal population would be at risk for unsafe blood levels. Experiments have already shown that high levels of blood phenylalanine impair neuropsychological functioning. Obviously, these differences in estimation of safe levels among scientists argue for caution in using any amount with children.

Besides the risk of elevated blood levels of phenylalanine, it is worth stressing that little is known about the long-term impact of high levels of exposure to aspartame. This is of most concern with children expected to have many years of continued exposure, usually at escalating amounts as they become adolescents.

SUMMARY

Extraordinarily convincing anecdotes place us in an intellectual dilemma. On the one hand, our scientific caution reminds us how often and how easily we believe something is true when it is merely an artifact, or is simply gullibility, or the naive wish to believe in something clear, simple, and easily understood. On the other hand, when anecdotes provided by careful observers with no vested interests take on a pattern and display a close similarity of details, we feel compelled to pay attention to them. This is especially true when there is a good theoretical reason for expecting a connection between a food product and the brain's neurotransmitters.

Aspartame provides a powerful example of how a new food product raises serious issues about the *mental and behavioral* aspects of food safety. Devoting as much care to these aspects of toxicity as required with cancer-causing aspects of new foods and drugs only seems like common sense. I am fully satisfied that we have one unequivocal and well-documented case of a profound behavioral reaction to aspartame in a 4-year-old boy, and several other cases spontaneously described by parents. Perhaps there are many other such cases, or perhaps these are rare, isolated reactions applying to a very small segment of the population. The food industry seems unlikely to diligently pursue these questions.

If parents insist on using artificial sweeteners with young children, rather than simply avoiding them, I strongly recommend that they observe their children closely for acute reactions (using methods like those recommended in Chapter 10). Unfortunately, what the long-term consequences might be over the life of a child is anyone's guess. For my part, I think it is simply easier to avoid all such products as far as possible and instill in children early a concern for how such foods might affect their own mental health, much as we try to do with physical health.

Research on seizures and headache reactions to aspartame has not reached any definite conclusions. Nevertheless, I strongly advise any parents whose children have these problems to avoid artificial sweeteners altogether. The possibilities of harm are simply too great to take a risk for something that is easily avoided and of no nutritional value.

CHAPTER THREE

The First Meal of the Day

DOES EATING BREAKFAST MATTER?

Surveys of American schoolchildren consistently estimate that nearly 25% of children do not eat breakfast on a regular basis. Many busy parents who routinely drink only a cup of coffee in the morning function more or less well without breakfast. They therefore assume that missing breakfast probably doesn't matter for children. It is true that as long as the quantity and quality of calories for the day as a whole are adequate, both children and adults will grow normally and maintain adequate nutrition. But this is not necessarily the case for behavior.

There are many parallels between food and drugs: their effects depend upon timing, amount, and content. Any drug taken in the wrong amount can be harmful, even deadly. Some ingredients by themselves are harmless until mixed. Drugs have a time course whose effects on the body or the brain will vary widely from one time to another.

Similarly, studies show that when, how much, and what adults eat at meals changes the way they function. (For example, studies of industrial accidents show that adults are more likely to have an accident after a large carbohydrate meal than after a low-carbohydrate meal or a small meal.)

But there is reason to believe that the effects may be more important for children than adults. Just as a more capable, experienced driver may resist the disruptive impact of alcohol much longer than a poor driver, so adults may resist the negative effects of foods on performance more easily than children. Adult brains are more redundant—have more reserves of capacity and experience—than children's, whose brains are easily tipped into a dysfunctional state by rather subtle influences.

But foods don't just impair performance, they also enhance it. In the right amounts, under certain conditions, and with the right timing, children think, attend, and behave better than they might otherwise. These effects on behavior and mental function may not be obvious. They are subtle enough that scientists have disagreed about their existence and significance for children.

When a child's mood shows drastic changes, everyone notices. But a gradual shift from a normally cheerful youngster to a grouchy and irritable one may escape one's attention or make it difficult to relate the changes to some specific cause. When a busy, alert student begins to slide into a tired, apathetic state, the changes are readily attributed to other things happening at the same time or simply ignored as one of those mysterious quirks of child personality.

If a child is usually impulsive, hyperactive, and inattentive, a drop in his or her performance might not stand out, or it might perhaps appear as part of a chronic condition. One of the most familiar puzzles to parents is how their child can do so well at some times yet so poorly at others. Clinicians usually have no explanation for these fluctuations, and they seldom consider how diet may be affecting the child's ability to maintain a steady but flexible level of performance.

In some families there is chaos at mealtime, with children left to fend for themselves as they wish. No one even notices whether the child ate or not. Poor and illiterate families may not have the resources or knowledge to provide adequate breakfasts. On the other hand, there are many affluent parents who scrupulously insist that their children eat breakfast but pay little attention to what is in the breakfast itself, incorrectly assuming that one breakfast is as good as the next.

We will see that there are many reasons for believing that the first meal of the day is especially important for children; that learning, brain function, and behavior can all be significantly altered by breakfast. While we have to be mindful of the scientific controversies surrounding this subject, they should not deter us from the possible advantages of a good breakfast or from recognizing some of the dangers inherent in a bad one. Here we will see just what constitutes a "good" breakfast, as it relates to behavior and learning, and how some breakfasts can be harmful to a child's mood and ability to function optimally in the classroom.

SUPPLEMENTING BREAKFAST

Milk and Calcium

William, a 9-year-old boy, was having a very difficult time in school. He seemed to lack interest in school work, seldom volunteered in class, and was often disruptive to other children as well. At times he showed signs of being a lethargic and apathetic child, while at others he was noisy, intrusive, and difficult to manage. William was one of several children who often ate "only a hasty morsel or two" before school and was thought to be excessively "nervous."

As part of a study, and without his teacher's knowledge, William received milk supplemented with vitamin D, calcium, and phosphorus every morning for a 4-week period. Vitamin D plays an important role as a supplement, mobilizing changes in the gut which allow calcium and phosphorus absorption by the body. Without vitamin D, much of the calcium would pass through the body. To be useful, calcium and phosphorus must occur in a roughly equal ratio (1 : 1). (Whole milk usually comes in about this ratio now, but did not at the time of this study— 1931.)

The fortified milk supplement was given to William at 9:30 a.m., just before his homeroom class. His teacher was to keep careful notes about his behavior and that of other children in the study. At the end of the 4-week period, William's teacher reported as follows:

> There has been a marked improvement in this child during the past four or five weeks. He has appeared more interested in classroom happenings, which previously had no effect on him. [He] has even at times volunteered information without being asked, which was an unheard of occurrence. Lessons, too, have been grasped more quickly and given back in a more intelligent manner. Since this child was a real problem, and home conditions are far from what they should be, his expansion has been really wonderful.[1]

The last observation of the teacher hints that some of William's difficulties stem from problems at home, yet she still notices an improvement after the supplement. The supplement has not altered the basic causes of William's misbehavior arising from problems in his home environment (whatever they might have been). But he seemed better able to *cope* with those problems, or at least to leave them behind while he was in school. The food appears to have optimized his reserve capabilities to deal with both school and home demands.

By itself, such an anecdote would not mean much. But William's case was part of an experiment by Dr. Donald Laird and colleagues on diet and "nervousness," the results of which appeared in 1931. This was one of the earliest studies on the classroom effects of a breakfast supplement in school children, and it showed that William's case was not an isolated one. Considering the early date of this study, it was surprisingly well controlled and convincing. For example, the three breakfast conditions (no supplement, milk supplement, and milk supplement with calcium and other nutrients) were given to the children out of sight of the teachers, who were therefore "blind" to which treatment was given.

The authors focused on the effects of the breakfast supplement on what they called "nervous" behaviors. Many of these behaviors were much like the ones we now consider as conduct problems or hyperactive behaviors rather than anxiety or emotional problems. For example, some of the items rated were "sustaining attention," "impulsiveness," "acting on the spur of the moment," "blows up," "aggravating," "unmannerly or saucy," "difficult to keep on a task," and so forth.

The experiment showed that children receiving milk alone made an 8% improvement in the average number of "nervous" symptoms, compared with 2% in an untreated control group. But there was an average of 25% *or more improvement* in symptoms of communicativeness, fatiguability, and even-temperedness. A majority of the children became less irritable and more energetic. Children receiving the additional calcium supplement showed a 25% or more improvement in 15 of the 32 symptoms, compared with changes this large in only 3 symptoms in the milk group. While the milk by itself seemed to improve behavior to a mild extent, the supplement caused a dramatic improvement.

There are several possible explanations for these beneficial effects upon behavior. This study did not record how many of the children were simply undernourished. More recent studies in the New York public school system showed that hyperactive, noisy classrooms were considerably calmed when children not eating any breakfast were given morning milk. These changes could well be due to a reduction in hunger pangs in mildly undernourished and hungry youngsters. But in the 1931 experiment, there was a noticeable advantage for the group that got a calcium supplement, and hunger pangs cannot explain this effect.

In one of our own recent studies of apparently well-nourished 6- to 12-year-old hyperactive children, there are hints that calcium may be important in its own right. We found that the more hyperactive children had significantly lower calcium intake in their diets than less hyperactive children. Again, it is worth cautioning that these correlations cannot establish causation. Perhaps they reflect some differences in vitamin D intake or metabolism (though we couldn't find any). Perhaps the lower calcium is the *effect* of being a more active youngster. Scientists must still unravel the mechanisms that could account for the correlation between calcium and behavior.

Two years after this early 1931 study by Laird, a project involving over 4,000 school children found that 59% of normal children receiving a morning supplement of whole milk showed improved scholastic progress compared with 24% of children who did not receive the supplement.[2] Unfortunately, in this large study it was not possible to be sure that the milk alone was responsible for the greater numbers showing academic improvement. For one thing, the milk-supplemented group made more *physical* progress, suggesting that they were undernourished to begin with. It was not possible to be sure that social and economic status did not account for the different rates of progress. These studies took place in the days of a nationwide economic depression, when many children not only did not have regular breakfasts but also had poor general nutrition. If the children receiving the milk also came from the poorest home conditions, their greater academic progress may have reflected the benefits to their physical health rather than some special benefit to mental functioning alone.

But these studies ought to prompt parents to be mindful regarding the possible importance to mental functioning of calcium intake in young children. Normally we think of calcium as important for strong bones and teeth, but calcium is one of the most important nutrients in the proper functioning of nerve cells. It has been known for many years that chronic low levels of calcium can lead to irritability, social withdrawal, fatigue, depression, or even psychosis. Even neurotic symptoms, such as phobias, obsessions, and compulsions, may result from these deficiencies. Sometimes calcium deficiencies result from vitamin D deficiencies and, on occasion, from some abnormality in the parathyroid gland or the kidneys. This is why it is important that children with mental symptoms have a thorough physical examination to rule out basic physical problems that could be causing calcium deficiencies, which in turn might produce the mental symptoms.

Fruit Juice

Nursery school teachers are well aware that even normal children can have "good days" and "bad days." At times a child may appear nervous, fidgety, aggressive, irritable, whiny, or scattered. At other times the same child may be sweet, alert, compliant, and easy to manage. These behaviors may not reach the level requiring psychiatric intervention, but they interfere with learning and with social interaction, and over time they can have a cumulative effect on normal children.

In 1950, scientists conducted a well-controlled study in a university laboratory school over the course of a year.[3] In this study, 133 normal nursery-school children were given either a morning drink of pineapple juice or water on two different occasions. Trained observers blind to the treatment conditions watched the children on the playground, recording 30-second samples of various behaviors, such as hyperactivity, aggressive interactions, and nervous habits. Many such samples were taken and averaged to provide scores on behavior. The results showed that most of the undesirable behaviors (except withdrawal) declined when the children received the juice compared with the water.

As an aside, throughout this book the reader will note that most of the examples are about boys. This is not accidental nor unintentionally chauvinistic. It happens that many more boys than girls are hyperactive, perhaps by as much as a 5 to 1 ratio. The fruit juice effect on the normal children of this nursery school study was much more apparent in boys than girls. Perhaps this was because boys exhibit many more of the negative behaviors in the first place. The increased activity level and aggression in boys compared with girls at an early age is well known.

These differences have received a variety of explanations, but the reasons for them are still somewhat of a mystery. Because boys are subject to more birth damage to the nervous system, some have suggested this as the cause. Others point out that social and cultural expectations which promote differences in behavior start at a very early age, with boys permitted and encouraged to be more active and aggressive. Other scientists point to genetic evidence that these traits are strongly linked to male and female genotypes. One scientist even found evidence that mothers may have more allergic reactions to the male child in utero, becoming sensitized to males because of a particular immunologic reaction unique to males. Even very early differences exist in the rate at which brain neurotransmitter systems develop in boys and girls. So many social and biological conditions could explain differences in activity and aggression in boys and girls.

In a study of 100 normal fifth-graders from three different schools, researchers used measures of arithmetic and symbol manipulation (called a decoding task).[4] The children served as their own controls; that is, the same child received either an orange juice supplement or a placebo on different days. Improvement in performance on the tests occurred at 10:30 and 11:45 in the morning after the juice, but not after the placebo. Basic knowledge of arithmetic comes from instruction, not from foods. These tests, therefore, reflect the ability of the children to *attend* and to *apply* what they have learned, not their knowledge of arithmetic. Some of these children were regularly good breakfast eaters, while others usually skipped breakfast. There was no difference between these two groups of children in their response to the juice, suggesting that even if they missed breakfast, the added supplement was able to give the children a "boost."

Not all studies have been positive in showing the beneficial effects of morning supplements. For example, Dr. Joanna Dwyer, a prominent nutritionist, compared a supplement in the form of an "instant breakfast mix" to a control condition (no breakfast) in 139 first-grade boys.[5] This supplement contained a high-protein formula found in many "instant breakfast" mixes on supermarket shelves. No apparent effects surfaced on several tests thought to measure attentiveness. There was also no relationship of the effects to whether the children were regular or sporadic breakfast eaters. But this otherwise exemplary study did not measure what other things the children ate for breakfast before they came to school, and this may have affected the results. These students were also older than the children in the other studies.

Missing Breakfast

In a series of studies known as the "Iowa breakfast studies" (carried out at the University of Iowa in the mid 1950s), the authors concluded that omission of the morning meal "may result in the lowering of the mental and physical efficiency during the late morning hours."[6] Seven boys ate a controlled diet, with all meals taken at a university hospital cafeteria. They ate a basic cereal-and-milk breakfast for 4 weeks; then, over a 17-week period, they had no-breakfast periods of 2 weeks alternated with breakfast periods of 3 weeks. The only measures which seemed to show much effect had to do with physical work capacity (muscular tremor, grip-strength endurance, and reaction time). If the work was prolonged and demanding, breakfast had some effect.

Perhaps because of its focus on *physical* work capacity, this study had the effect for many years of causing educators and nutritionists to downplay the value of breakfast. Often overlooked, however, were the observations made by teachers who noted that "the majority of the boys had a definitely better attitude and a better scholastic record during the period when breakfast was included in the daily dietary regimen than when it was omitted."

PAYING ATTENTION

The studies we have discussed so far suggest an effect of breakfast on children's behavior in the classroom and on the playground. These are important effects, for children in calm classrooms learn better, and socializing on the playground is important to social growth and maturity. But equally important is the issue of what effect, if any, breakfast might have on learning processes themselves—the direct impact of breakfast on basic information processing and attention.

Psychologists have learned that paying attention is a complex process. Many changes in the body and the brain take place during the split seconds when we are attending and not attending. Trained athletes are quite familiar with some of these bodily changes and use them to improve their performance. For instance, when an Olympic marksman aims a rifle or bow at a target, he or she learns to notice when the heart rate speeds up (in anticipation of pulling the trigger) and to wait until the heart rate slows, only pulling the trigger or releasing the bow when the heart rate slows the most. (In his book, *Zen in the Art of Archery*, Eugen Herrigel gives a fascinating account of using archery in Zen as a form of attention training and for development of insight into the way the mind itself works.)

When the heart rate changes during attending, it is because the brain has sent a signal to the heart to slow down, perhaps, as some scientists have suggested, to optimize the intake of information during the state of attending. The brain first sends a signal to accelerate the heart—an arousal or alerting effect—followed by a slowing down and a general stillness in the muscles and reflexes. During this period, the brain too changes, with a slow electrical change being evident when scalp electrical recordings are made during the early phases of attending and preparation for responding. "Attention" then, is a dual process in which one is first alerted and aroused, then momentarily quiet; a moment of readiness for action followed by a "steady unblinking eye" and a state of focused awareness.

A simple method of studying attention is to record heart rate and brain electrical activity while a child does a warned reaction-time task. In this method, a warning tone precedes a visual target. The child attempts to respond to the target as fast as possible. Meanwhile, we record heart rate and brain response before, during, and after the warning period.

The acceleration of the heart rate begins shortly after the warning signal occurs, and it usually bottoms out just before the response is made, returning to normal shortly afterwards. Usually the more the heart rate accelerates and then decelerates, the better the performance. These changes are rather subtle, mostly averaging only two or three heart beats per minute.

We wondered what breakfast would do to these changes in the heart rate (and also to the associated brain changes) during a reaction-time task. One reason for selecting these measures is that studies of hyperactive children show that they are considerably more sluggish in these heart rate and brain changes when doing an attention-demanding task.

We asked 10 normal, 9- to 11-year-old boys to take this test on four occasions—two times after breakfast and two times following an overnight fast. We measured their responses three times during the morning, at 9:30, 11:00, and 12:15. The findings were clear cut: when the boys ate breakfast, their heart rates accelerated more after eating the warning signal and decelerated more just before their responses than when they did not eat breakfast. Their responses were also faster. This effect became progressively greater during the morning. Thus, if children missed breakfast, attention got worse as the morning progressed, compared with days when they ate breakfast.

In this same study we used another test of attention, a "continuous performance test," or CPT. In this test the child watches a screen on which a series of letters occurs and must press a key whenever the letter "X" occurs. In a more difficult version, the child presses the key only when the X precedes a "B." Because the letters occur every second and a half, and are only visible for a fraction of a second, the child must attend closely or miss a critical signal. If a child is impulsive, he or she is likely to press the key many more times than necessary, creating "false alarms."

At every period during the morning, the children got more hits and had fewer false alarms when they had eaten breakfast, though the effect was small enough in the group as a whole that one could not rule out chance differences between breakfast and no-breakfast days.

But this finding was deceptive, for the *averages* for the breakfast and no-breakfast days concealed some children who were having major lapses of attention, while others were virtually unaffected by missing breakfast. As a result, the *range* of errors was much larger during the no-breakfast days, with certain children contributing most of the errors.

The results strongly suggested that in situations demanding careful attention to a changing series of events over time, requiring regular alerting and anticipation, missing breakfast impairs normal children's attention, and some children are particularly vulnerable to this effect. We don't know why this should be so. Undoubtedly there are differences between the children who are easily disrupted by missing breakfast and those who are not; perhaps in the extent to which their bodies release nutrients to the brain; perhaps in their brain physiology itself; or perhaps in their attentional capacities and how easily disrupted they are. In any case, these studies of normal children showed that our psychophysiological measures were sensitive and could be useful in studying children with impaired attention.

Some people may wonder whether these laboratory changes have any significance for real-life activities of children. In our study we also included a series of arithmetic problems. A computer presented the problems, adjusting the difficulty level for the child's degree of proficiency. The computer kept track of both the number of problems attempted and the correct solutions. When the children missed breakfast they attempted fewer problems and got a smaller percentage correct than when they took the test after eating breakfast.

In addition, as the children repeated this task during the morning, they tended to do better. This is not surprising, since children are very good at "learning to learn"; practice with the task leads to more efficient performance. What was surprising was that breakfast enhanced this learning-to-learn effect. It seemed as though the children were not only responding more accurately and attempting more problems, but they got better at this activity during the morning—something that only happened after eating breakfast. It appeared as though the benefits of practice were much less when the children missed their breakfast than when these same children ate breakfast.[7]

BREAKFAST AND HYPERACTIVE CHILDREN

While we saw some evidence that simply omitting breakfast in normal children affects their attention, these effects are quite subtle, and there is reason to believe that, on the whole, normal well-nourished children are quite resilient in the face of occasional missed breakfasts. But what about children who have fewer mental reserves, whose attention is easily disrupted, and who are known to have "attention deficits"? In addition, missing breakfast is something easily corrected (at least in theory). Much more complex is the issue of whether *what* is eaten at breakfast matters.

We therefore decided to ask what effect different types of breakfast have on hyperactive children compared with normal children. Each group, normal and hyperactive, was randomly assigned to receive either a carbohydrate breakfast (two slices of buttered toast) or a protein breakfast (two eggs scrambled in butter). These two meals have about the same amount of calories, so any differences cannot be due to a simple energy effect or a difference in hunger pangs. (The butter tends to slow digestion, and we wanted the two meals to have their effects at about the same time.) A third group received no breakfast, but continued fasting.

In this study we measured attention by the same methods just described: heart rate deceleration, reaction time, continuous performance test (CPT), and changes in electrical activity of the brain. We collected these measures at different times during the morning.

The results were quite striking. For hyperactive children,

performance was significantly worse with the carbohydrate breakfast compared with the protein breakfast and even fasting conditions. Reaction time was slower, there were more errors of omission and commission, and the heart rate showed a slower onset of changes and less deceleration when the critical reaction stimuli occurred. For some of the measures (especially the CPT vigilance task), the effect became more substantial as the morning wore on.

The electrical changes of the brain were also markedly affected. Under the carbohydrate condition the children's brain responses were both slower and smaller when the target letters of the CPT occurred, showing that the brain was "paying less attention" to those stimuli. Carbohydrate, in the form of the toast, appeared to act much like a sedative does. These negative effects of the carbohydrate breakfast were always more apparent for the hyperactive than the normal children.

These results should not be taken to mean that toast is bad for children and eggs are good. These were not normal meals by any stretch of the imagination. But the most obvious implication is that there may be dangers associated with eating a meal that is *exclusively* carbohydrate, such as bread, pasta, or potatoes, and that children with attentional problems are especially vulnerable. Simply adding milk would avert this problem.

We might wonder why breakfast should be special in its importance. It may seem that any meal could have similar effects. But upon arising we have not eaten for at least 8 hours or so, the longest fasting period we are normally exposed to.

There are also certain bodily rhythms that are closely tied to the wake–sleep cycle, and several hormones and bodily changes occur in synchrony with these rhythms. For example, growth hormone shows an early-morning surge of activity and another one later in the morning. These changes are *circadian rhythms* (meaning "about a day" because they occur on a daily cycle). Very early in life, children become accustomed to a pattern of eating shortly after waking, and whether the body establishes its rhythms around this eating cycle, or vice versa, waking and eating become closely tied to one another.

Some of the hormones which show this rhythmicity are linked with nutritional metabolism. For example, growth hormone and cortisol help in the process of mobilizing energy stores. It seems likely, therefore, that breakfast may have a special place in preparing for the day's demands because breakfast coincides with some of the body's circadian rhythms, which in turn may become conditioned to the expectation of food.[8]

BREAKFAST AND HYPOGLYCEMIA

What accounts for the negative impact of carbohydrates upon children? One obvious answer might seem to lie with the elevated blood sugar that comes from carbohydrates. As blood sugar rises, the body secretes insulin in order to metabolize the sugar and lower it to the normal level. One theory that is commonly held is that this elevated blood sugar leads to a strong insulin reaction which then causes an "overshoot" of lowered blood glucose, leading to the condition known as hypoglycemia.

It is true that hypoglycemic reactions can cause many symptoms, including nervousness and jittery feelings, faintness, headache, dizziness and a spacey feeling. (We will encounter more about hypoglycemia in Chapter 5 when we discuss crime and aggression.) Physicians are commonly besieged with patients who claim that they are hypoglycemic because they experience some of these symptoms. However, most studies show that persons with these complaints do not have a hypoglycemic reaction. Studies of diabetics, whose blood sugars fluctuate wildly at times, show that impairment of learning and performance occurs with *both* low and high blood sugar levels.

However, in order to test the idea that blood sugar levels

affect behavior and brain function in children, we carried out studies on normal children who were given large doses of glucose. Glucose is the natural sugar used by the body for its fuel. Insulin and other hormones reduce complex sugars (like sucrose) to the glucose form. Again, we measured cardiac changes, attention, and brain electrical activity in a fasting condition compared to conditions in which large doses of glucose syrup were given.

Though there were some changes on these measures, they were unrelated to changes in blood sugar level; they didn't coincide with the peaks and troughs of blood sugar itself. These results suggested that something other than blood sugar was causing the changes in performance and brain activity. If sugar does not cause its effects though changes in blood sugar, what else might account for these effects?

In the following chapter we will look more closely at the carbohydrate–sugar–behavior connection and see that other, more complicated, processes are occurring whenever children eat sugar. Sugar affects attention and behavior, but not necessarily, as some have claimed, through hypoglycemia. For now, we can rule out hypoglycemia as an explanation of the attentional changes we saw in reaction to the carbohydrate.

CONCLUSIONS ON BREAKFAST

In earlier days, when children were often undernourished, there was little doubt that it was important to give them breakfasts or supplements in school. The federal fovernment sponsored many breakfast programs. But the general improvement in child nutrition in a more prosperous nation caused disbanding of most of these programs. Concern was primarily for physical nutrition, and that concern (except among the poor) seemed less pressing than other, equally expensive programs.

But studies in children show that breakfast is very important for both behavior and learning. Not all studies agree, but the preponderance of evidence suggests that regular breakfasts, or even supplements at school with milk or fruit juice, increase the likelihood of optimal mental and behavioral functioning in children. Normal children can miss breakfast without seriously impairing their mental functions, but they may do so at the cost of diminishing the probability of functioning *optimally;* and even among normal children, some are much more sensitive than others to missing breakfast.

Children whose attention is already impaired, who have learning and impulse control problems, are even more likely to suffer from missing breakfast than normals; and they are especially vulnerable to impairment in attention following a pure carbohydrate meal.

We have no conclusive evidence that particular nutrients, like calcium, vitamin D, and phosphorus, make any difference to children receiving ordinary well-balanced diets. But early studies, and more recent observations with hyperactive children, are consistent with an important role of these nutrients in mental and emotional functioning, and it definitely makes sense to watch for any signs of calcium or vitamin D deficiency. Children referred to mental health specialists for learning and behavior problems should have a thorough nutrition history and pediatric examination as part of the evaluation.

One should not run to the nearest health food store and begin supplementing breakfast with calcium, vitamin D, and phosphorus. These occur in adequate amounts in today's milk. The results may only apply to children with a real deficiency or inadequate intake, and one of the important things we will see throughout this book is that it is seldom necessary to supplement a good, normal diet with specific nutrients or vitamins. Under normal nutritional conditions for example, the body has adequate stores of calcium which it can draw upon, and additional intake beyond regular meals might actually cause some toxicity or unwanted side effects. The general belief that "more is better" is seldom true in nutrition, and as we will see in a later discussion of megavitamin therapy, it can be dangerous.

Our studies show that protein in breakfast is important. Normally, milk and cereal will provide enough protein to avoid swamping the child with too much carbohydrate, which, as we have shown, impairs attention. But many children will eat just waffles and syrup without milk. Many poor children eat either nothing or some convenient leftovers of potato chips, candy, or pasta. These are just the conditions most likely to further increase their disadvantages in life.

CHAPTER FOUR

Sugar and Its Effects on Behavior and Mood

Americans have a love–hate relationship with sugar. Consumption of sugar, whether in its naturally occurring form in plants, or as sweeteners derived from sugar cane, beets, corn, or honey and added to foods, accounts for almost 20% of the caloric intake of the average American adult. This represents almost 132 pounds of sugar per year for each individual. The public still can't get enough sugar, though articles in the press, popular books and magazines, children's cartoons and TV documentaries constantly remind us of the hazards of sugar. On the other hand, the messages are constantly subverted by TV commercials both overtly and subtly promoting sugar products.

One cartoon depicts a woman propelled out of a candy store, with her hair standing on end as if she had just stuck her finger in a light socket, running so fast she bends a parking meter. Contrary to this buzz theory, a popular book attributes the opposite effects of apathy and depression to the "sugar blues." Another popular cartoon series shows a character gradually escalating his needs for chocolate to the point where he is robbing a derelict, looking for money to support his candy habit. In these instances, sugar looks like an addictive substance, subject to abuse.

But it is not just popular culture that conceives of sugar as a dangerous drug. One well-known pediatrician believes that sugar contributes to bedwetting, aches and pains, and fatigue. Another pediatrician describes hundreds of hyperactive children whose behavior improved by removing sugar from their diet.

Some criminologists claim there is a link between sugar intake and violence, supporting their claims by observations that violent episodes decrease when penal institutions reduce sugar content in meals. Patients claiming to suffer from "reactive hypoglycemia"—low blood sugar levels caused by an excessive insulin response—plague many physicians. Some researchers also claim that some of the most violent offenders suffer from hypoglycemia. (We will discuss these theories of criminality in the following chapter.)

Is there any merit in these claims? If there *is* a relationship between sugar and mental functioning, is this a causal relationship in which the sugar elicits abnormal behavior; or do hyperactive, apathetic, or criminal types simply eat sugar as a *consequence* of their condition? Or is excess sugar intake a symptom that is intrinsic to the psychopathology, with something else causing both the abnormal behavior and the tendency to indulge in sweets?

As is often the case in a complicated scientific arena, answers to these questions are conflicting. Sometimes conflicting conclusions reflect differences in the methods used to study the problem; and sometimes apparent differences in findings are simply differences in the way the scientists choose to interpret their data. Still another reason study results may disagree is that sugar might be both harmful and helpful, depending upon special circumstances which are not carefully controlled. In this latter case, rather than ask "Is sugar bad for children?" it may be better to ask *"Under what circumstances* is sugar beneficial or harmful?" In this chapter we will see that the latter approach is correct.

WHAT IS SUGAR?

We tend to think of sugar as if it were a single substance. But sugar comes in a variety of forms (the table on p. 78 defines some of the terms used when discussing sugar and carbohydrates).

The body uses sugar in the form of *glucose* for basic processes which provide energy for cell metabolism. *Glucose* is the main fuel or energy source for brain activity. All other sugars and carbohydrates must eventually change into glucose to be useful for energy. *Sucrose* is often called "refined sugar," coming from the refining of vegetable and fruit products such as sugar cane and beets. Like sucrose, corn syrup (which comes from corn starch), corn sugar, and invert sugar are often added to foods for sweetening. These more complex sugars must be broken down to the glucose form before they can be used as nutrients by the body. Sucrose consists of a molecule of *fructose*, a sugar found in fruits and honey, and a molecule of glucose, and so this "double sugar" (disaccharide) must first be split before it can be used by the body. Invert sugar is a mixture of glucose, fructose, and sucrose. Corn sugar, or *dextrose*, is a crystalline form of glucose. When examining food packages, such as cereal, for sugar content, it is well to remember that sugar comes in these many guises.

Most people think of sugar as table sugar. Table sugar, or sucrose, is itself one member of the carbohydrate family. *Carbohydrates* are chemical compounds that have a 2:1 ratio of hydrogen and oxygen, and some carbohydrates simply consist of long chains of simpler sugars. Starches and sugars are merely different forms of digestible carbohydrates. Foods like pasta, bread, rice, and macaroni are often called carbohydrates, though they are foods *containing* carbohydrates, because these foods usually have other ingredients besides carbohydrates.

Carbohydrates, which are often confused with sugar, come in two main groups. *Complex carbohydrates* are mainly starch and

Sugar and Carbohydrates

Carbohydrate refers to a group of compounds containing carbon and water (carbo = carbon and hydro = water). There are three major types of dietary carbohydrates—starch, sugar, and fiber—all found almost exclusively in foods of plant origin. All three are similar in that they are chains of units called *monosaccharides* which are eventually converted into glucose, the primary metabolic fuel of life. The difference is in the number and nature of the linkage of these basic units. For example, starch, also called "complex carbohydrate," contains long chains of glucose molecules, whereas maltose, a "simple carbohydrate" contains only two molecules of glucose. Simple carbohydrates, or "sugars," contain either one (mono-) or two (di-) saccharide (from sacchar for sugar) molecules.

Glossary:

-ose: suffix used to identify carbohydrates (ex., glucose, fructose, sucrose).

-ase: suffix used to identify the metabolic substances or enzymes that break down carbohydrates (ex., sucrase, lactase, amylase).

sugar: a generic term usually referring to low molecular weight crystalline chemicals usually with a sweet taste. These are the smallest units of carbohydrate.

monosaccharides: (mono = one saccharide = sugar). The smallest units of carbohydrate. Examples include glucose, fructose, galactose, and mannose.

disaccharide: two units of monosaccharide. Examples include sucrose (glucose + fructose), lactose (glucose + galactose), maltose (glucose + glucose).

polysaccharide: multiple units of monosaccharides. Also called "starch." Examples include amylose, plant starch found in potatoes and grains; glycogen (called "animal starch"), found in animal muscles and seafood; and cellulose, a plant starch not digested by humans because of the nature of the glucose linkages, or bonds.

glucose: a monosaccharide which serves as the primary metabolic fuel of life. Primary food sources are fruits, honey, corn syrup.

fructose: a monosaccharide found predominately in fruits and honey. It is referred to as "fruit sugar" and absorbs more slowly than glucose but is eventually converted to glucose in the body.

Sucrose: A disaccharide containing glucose and fructose. Primary food sources are sugarcane or beets, molasses, and maple syrup. After refining, sucrose becomes table sugar.

Lactose: A disaccharide containing glucose and galactose. Found primarily in milk and milk products.

cellulose. Cellulose is not digestible (except by cows), but starch can be broken down into its simpler sugar forms. Some foods, like potatoes, contain a sizable amount of starch which must be broken down before it is useful as energy. *Simple carbohydrates* are made up almost totally of sugars, such as those found in most sweeteners and fruits.

Once sugars enter the body, they change into the monosaccharide form (single sugar, or glucose), and about 25% of the fructose converts to glucose in the gut. The monosaccharides are then transported to the liver and other tissues. Excess glucose gets stored in the muscles as fat or in the form of glycogen, a pool called upon for rapid mobilization of energy. These different forms of sugar might have different effects on behavior, for some, such as sucrose, have more powerful effects on the insulin response than others, such as fructose.

SUGAR, HYPERACTIVITY, AND ATTENTION DEFICITS IN CHILDREN

Anecdotes regarding sugar and hyperactivity appeared as early as 1929 in the scientific literature. A case report in the *American Journal of Diseases in Children* stated that:

> A boy, aged 12, had been termed by psychiatrists and psychologists a "nervous hyperkinetic child." To use his own words, "I have to keep on going and be doing something . . ." His diet was meager in meats and vegetables and rich in candy and cookies. This inadequacy of diet allied with hyperkinesis suggested the treatment . . .[1]

Mothers will often tell pediatricians or psychiatrists that they see a clear relationship between sugar and behavior. For example, one young parent stated to me:

> My 3¹/₂-year-old son is normally a pleasant and cheerful kid, no more active than other children his age. He plays well with his

> older sister most of the time, and will watch Sesame Street with
> rapt attention. I learned early, however, that if I give him a sugar
> snack or candy bar, his personality changes. He is like Jekyll and
> Hyde. He becomes boisterous, runs around in a non-stop manner,
> and becomes a real devil. He torments his sister and when she
> hides, he looks for the cat who has now learned to avoid him. He
> can't sit still for even his favorite shows, and he becomes cranky
> and says "no" to everything, just like he was at two. This reaction
> comes on within a few minutes and will last for an hour or more. I
> never see this pattern except after sweet snacks.

Another mother recently told me that she can always tell when
her son has eaten candy because his eyes become dilated and he
becomes unmanageable. I have heard many similar stories from
friends and colleagues, and even from pediatricians—who are
presumably excellent observers of child behavior—about their
own children. Pediatric allergists are also often asked by parents
whether their child's hyperactivity or explosive behavior might
be attributable to some form of sugar allergy. At a recent large
meeting of several hundred pediatric allergists in New York
City, I received many questions about the "hyperactivity–sugar
connection," from doctors inundated with patients believing
that their children were allergic to sugar products.

Scientists have approached the sugar–behavior problem in
two ways: by trying to correlate dietary sugar intake with behavior and by giving large amounts of sugar to children and
observing their reactions.

DIETARY INTAKE OF SUGAR AND BEHAVIOR
IN CHILDREN

Scientific studies on the role of sugar and behavior have
been accumulating since about 1980. Dr. Ronald Prinz and his
colleagues at the University of Florida, among the first to systematically study sugar and behavior in normal children, mea-

sured the amount of sugar intake among 91 4- and 5-year-old boys.[2] Many children were eating as much as 40% of their daily calories in the form of refined sugar, or almost double the level for the average *adult* consumer. When they compared children in the lowest 25% of consumption against those in the upper 25%, they found that the high-sugar consumers were significantly poorer on measures of attention. Differences between low- and high-sugar consumers weren't due to parenting skills, socioeconomic status, IQ, or parental education. Although these factors sometimes affect dietary patterns, they could not explain the differences in performance of the high- and low-sugar groups. Moreover, the pattern of sugar consumption was highly stable for individual children over a period of several months. Apparently, some children establish a pattern of high sugar intake very early in life, a pattern strongly associated with poor attentional skills.

As we have seen, poor attention is one of the hallmarks of the hyperactive child syndrome. Prinz's findings of high sugar intake in *normal* children with poor attention raise a suspicion that sugar might also affect attention in hyperactive and impulsive children with attention deficits.

The findings by Prinz and coworkers, of a relationship between attention and sugar in normal children, were further bolstered by a laboratory study in which they observed both normal and hyperactive children through a one-way mirror, counting aggressive behaviors and amount of movement.[3] They measured total carbohydrate intake and consumption of simple sugars. They found that activity level in both hyperactive and normal children was higher for those consuming high amounts of simple-sugar products and carbohydrates generally. In hyperactive children (but not normal children), they also found a high correlation of sugar intake with aggressive behavior. The more sugar these children ate (and the less protein), the higher their levels of observed aggressive behavior.

WHY SCIENTISTS DISAGREE ABOUT SUGAR
AND BEHAVIOR

Prinz's findings were quickly challenged. There are two issues. First, is there a correlation between dietary carbohydrate–protein intake and hyperactive–aggressive behavior as Prinz claims? One obvious flaw in Prinz's approach was that he measured sugar as a proportion of the *weight* of the foods, rather than as a proportion of calories. Another study correlating sugar and behavior, which used the appropriate measurement (sugar as a proportion of calories), did not find a relationship.

Second, even if there is a relationship, which is the cause and which is the effect? Does the high sugar and carbohydrate intake *cause* the hyperactivity; or does the hyperactivity simply lead to more intake of high-energy foods? Or is there some third cause linking the hyperactivity and dietary intake patterns and causing them to change together? Later we will see that this third alternative is probably the correct one, for some children have neurotransmitter defects that interfere with their regulation of sugar, and high sugar intake then causes further problems.

As with other issues regarding food and behavior, part of the disagreement about the effects of sugar reflects the innate conservatism and skepticism of some scientists, not just the factual issues involved. Some researchers take an ultraconservative stance, believing that they are more "scientific" when they can find reasons to demolish studies, even if they have to minimize their own findings. (This attitude was aptly caricatured by the Nobel Prize winner Albert Szent-Györgyi on the occasion of his 90th birthday. He asked, "How do you know when you have made a discovery?" and answered, "When all your colleagues object. You know it's a *serious* discovery when foundations refuse you grants.")

Sometimes the only part of a scientist's work that gets

quoted or noticed is what the scientist chooses to highlight in his or her abstract or summary. Those who write reviews of the field may then be aware only of part of the story. Review papers are important in science because they do much to shape the opinions of nonspecialists who may not examine the original studies.

One example of this burying of facts was a recent study in which the author chose to dismiss certain of his own findings showing a significant relationship between sugar consumption and hyperactive behaviors. The study itself was excellent in its execution. But the author felt that because several tests showed no positive results, the activity findings were somewhat isolated and probably due to chance. But another investigator, apparently unaware of these results because they were hardly mentioned, found the same activity changes, thus confirming something actually dismissed by the first author.

The problem was further compounded when another scientist, citing the first paper as agreeing with his results, decided to dismiss his positive findings which were also very significant (showing a strong relationship between intake of different sugars and hyperactivity). These positive findings were dismissed by the investigator, not because he doubted them but because he felt they were too small in magnitude to be of much clinical significance. In other words, the results were positive, but his evaluation was that they were not of clinical importance. But the question of practical significance is different from the question of *theoretical* significance. This latter researcher's data did support the connection between hyperactivity and excess sugar intake. But taking the whole picture into account, the investigator cautiously chose to minimize the findings. A different investigator looking at these same findings might choose to emphasize them rather than discount them, perhaps arguing that however small the effects they are real and show that sugar alters behavior. These conservative approaches to interpretation may be appropriate within a scientific context, but as consumers and caretakers of young children, anything that impacts upon the central nervous system, even in a subtle way, must be taken seriously. Subtle effects over a long period of time may end up being major influences on behavior.

Parents, educators, or others trying to make responsible decisions about children's mental health may find these conflicting opinions confusing. But in science there is a constant dialogue between scientists who may seem overly critical and those who appear not critical enough. Often the truth emerges out of this dialogue, though not always in the way either party expects. Many scientists prefer not to commit themselves to certain findings when there is the slightest possibility of being wrong. Other scientists may prefer to believe a finding if there is a reasonable chance it could be right, preferring not to risk rejecting prematurely something important that might be true. There are scientists who are strict conservatives and those who are on the liberal end of the spectrum. Risk-taking behavior and conservatism are not the sole province of gambling and politics.

THE CAUSE AND EFFECT PROBLEM

Findings reported by Prinz and others suggesting a relationship between sugar intake and behavior in normal children, and in mild cases of hyperactivity, are consistent with studies done by me and my colleagues at Children's Hospital in Washington, D.C., on more severely disturbed children admitted to a psychiatric ward. When we studied the diet diaries of these children, we found that about half had histories of binging on high-carbohydrate foods, such as candy, jelly, and sweet snacks, and that parents usually believed their child's behavior deteriorated after eating sugar. Many of the parents described a form of "sugar addiction," in which their child would sneak into the pantry or cupboard at all hours of the day or night and consume whole boxes of pure sugar. Just like drug junkies, these children would stash sugar in secret hiding places, lie about it, and use almost any subterfuge to get their daily "fix."

Many of these children qualified for a diagnosis applied to certain children with bizarre eating habits, who eat dirt, wallpaper, garbage, and almost anything else. This latter condition, known as *pica*, is sometimes the result of a specific nutritional deficiency, such as a sodium deficiency, which the child is trying to correct. But more often than not the bizarre pattern of eating is merely another aspect of a very unsocialized and impulsive style of life, resulting from abuse, deprivation of basic love, and a totally disorganized environment. These are such obvious causes of the hyperactivity in these children that disordered eating more reasonably seems like part of a general syndrome of deprivation and abuse than a response to the food. This type of eating behavior, then, is more a *symptom* than a cause of the behavior.

Likewise, many scientists prefer to believe that the high sugar intake is the result, not the cause, of the disordered behavior patterns or hyperactivity. In other words, children who are highly active and aggressive, or simply undisciplined and unrestrained, might be more prone to eat sugar as a means of gaining the quick energy they require to maintain their high levels of activity. Or perhaps undisciplined children simply follow any hedonistic path which lax discipline leaves open to them. Perhaps the "sugar junkie" is not addicted to the sugar but just to the pleasure it provides, much like adults who indulge their proclivity for chocolates, not because they are physiologically dependent but because of the pleasure afforded them by a delicious treat.

There is still another reason to be cautious about anecdotes involving the apparent increase in hyperactivity following sugar ingestion. Consider the following hypothetical scenario. Johnny is an 8-year-old boy who gets angry, restless, and aggressive when almost any stress comes along. For instance, he constantly fights with his older sister, who has a knack of irritating him to the point of an explosion and then skillfully disappearing into the woodwork when their mother comes along to find out what happened. Suppose Johnny also likes sweets and gets them more or less on demand. His mother might often see him eat sweets, but not see the immediate cause of his outbursts, and she therefore assumes that because eating the sweets often *precedes* these episodes, it causes them. She may be less impressed by the snacks that follow an outburst, even though they also occur often. Johnny's hyperactivity is *correlated* with eating sweets, but not *caused* by them.

In other words, the association of sugar and deviant behavior patterns cannot prove that sugar causes the deviant behavior. Therefore, a better way to study the problem is experimentally: to manipulate the amount of sugar and see whether behavior changes follow the ingestion of sugar, not just that poor behavior and high sugar intake correlate with each other.

People often fail to see the difference between these two approaches, of simply correlating two events as opposed to manipulating one event and studying effects on the other. It took scientists a long time to come to the realization that many things that fluctuate together are not causally related. You may always get over a cold when you follow grandmother's advice of bed rest and drinking chicken soup, but chances are the chicken soup (however good it makes you feel) has nothing to do with causing your cold to go away. The two events correlate, but are not causally related. On the other hand, if 50 people given chicken soup improved more than 50 people given fake chicken soup (whatever that might be), one would have better grounds for faith in this legendary remedy. By *manipulating* the presence and absence of chicken soup, *and nothing else* (such as taste, texture, or nutritional content), one gains control over the supposed cause. This is the logic that guided the challenge studies of sugar, and as we will see later, the challenge studies of food additives.

STUDYING SUGAR EFFECTS BY ADDING IT TO THE DIET

In nutritional research it is often informative to *add* a nutrient to the diet in order to study its effects. This approach is called a "challenge study," and is generally easier to interpret than a correlational study. One can then see the symptoms come and go, knowing that the food causes the changes in behavior because the food changes precede the behavior changes. Other potential causes are kept the same while introducing the food changes. Few such studies have been done with sugar in humans, even though it was shown some time ago that rats fed a chow high in carbohydrate and low in protein showed increased activity levels compared with regular diets.

In one such challenge study on children, Dr. Jane Goldman at the University of Connecticut gave normal preschoolers either a sugar or a placebo drink and then had them do a continuous performance task (CPT) to measure their vigilance and attentiveness.[4] The amount of sugar was about as much as found in a typical can of soda. The preschoolers who had the sugar drink showed a definite decline in their performance, compared with those on the placebo. The decline was barely apparent at 30 minutes following the sugar, but it became highly significant after 1 hour. These children made about twice as many errors after the sugar drink than after the placebo drink.

This study also examined how much the children moved around the room and how much they engaged in task-related behavior during free-play sessions. The "tasks" the children engaged in were different kinds of play with toys. When they focused on the task and were not moving about, they were behaving appropriately. After the sucrose the children engaged in more locomotion and spent less time behaving appropriately (referred to as "off-task behavior") than after the placebo. This effect was apparent about 1 hour after the sucrose, but not after 10 minutes or 1½ hours. In other words, the sugar challenge had created a "window of vulnerability"—a time when focused attention was poor, locomotion was high, and behavior was inappropriate. These effects, then, are similiar to most drugs, which tend to have a peak time when their effects occur maximally but which then diminish after a certain period.

However, studies with older children have not always shown such clear-cut results. For example, Richard Milich and his colleagues conducted a study of 16 hyperactive boys between 7 and 9 years of age.[5] They measured a variety of classroom, social, and behavioral responses following challenges of sucrose or a placebo, using observational procedures much like Dr. Goldman's. But they found no significant effects of the sucrose.

Similarly, a team at the National Institutes of Mental Health (NIMH) studied another group of school-age boys who were specifically designated by their parents as being "sugar reactive" (meaning that the parents believed that sugar caused hyperactivity in these children). Observations took place over a 5-hour period after a large dose of glucose or placebo, using actometers to measure movement.[6] (Actometers, as mentioned earlier, are small watch-sized devices that record locomotion electronically.) These children showed little change in their motor behavior, actually showing a tendency to have *lower* levels of motor activity after drinking glucose than after placebo.

Do these negative results reflect the older age of children in this study as compared with the children Prinz and Goldman studied? Or is there something else that explains differences in results between the studies? We believe that results from several of our studies support the latter interpretation.

My colleagues and I at Children's Hospital also noted the inconsistent effects of sugar in our own studies. For example, in our first sugar study we added sugar to the breakfast drinks of severely hyperactive children on our inpatient psychiatric unit and observed them in their classrooms during the morning for 6 days. The amount of sugar (50 g) was about the amount contained in a Hershey bar plus a piece of cherry pie. On 2 days the sugar was sucrose, on 2 different days it was fructose, and on the 2 remaining days the drinks were regular breakfast orange juice with no sugar added.

We had two observers sit in the hospital classroom which the children attended daily and count various types of behaviors, including gross motor activity (for example, running around the room) and fine motor or fidgeting activity (not getting out of the chair, but wriggling and constantly moving). Each 15 seconds the observers noted whether the children were attending to their work or moving about. The teachers also rated the behavior using a hyperactivity checklist. Both observers and teachers remained blind to the treatments. The observers did note significant increases in motor movements, but these changes were subtle enough that classroom teachers were unable to notice them with their less refined method of observation. This is an instance in which the findings differ depending on the measuring instrument. The effects of sugar were only apparent in detailed observations requiring much training to perfect accuracy, not in general impressions.

As is often the case, one study merely raises questions for further research. Our team was aware of several limitations of this study. The children in this experiment were of different ages, ranging from 6 to 12, which means that some were much larger in body size than others. In studies of drugs it is often important to adjust for total body size by giving the drug in proportion to body weight, since the drug's effect depends on its distribution into bodily tissues. Some of the children received three times as much sugar per body weight as others, so perhaps the different effects at different ages could be due to differences in the ratio of sugar to body size or to different reactions at different ages. We decided to see what happens when we adjusted the sugar according to body weight. This time the drinks contained either sucrose or fructose, and the placebo was an aspartame-sweetened drink.

Also, the earlier experiment was acute; that is, the children only received two exposures to the sugar. What happens when sugar is given over a longer period of time? After all, in the natural setting children develop long-standing patterns of higher or lower sugar intake. In animal studies chronic and acute sugar effects differ. For example, in one rat study researchers found that rats receiving a chronic high level of sugar became more active when the sugar was *reduced* to the normal level, suggesting that somehow the brain had adjusted to the high levels and became disturbed at the normal levels. This time, therefore, we decided to observe the children for at least a month, and some children were given the additional sugar or placebo for as long as 6 months. (Despite this increased sugar intake the children did not gain weight more rapidly than expected, probably because they compensated by reducing calories at other meals.)

Another important addition to this study was to collect 24-hour records of everything the children ate for as long as they remained in the hospital. We wondered what effect the contents of a child's breakfast might have on the sugar effects, so we kept a record of exactly how much of each food was eaten along with the sugar drink. This involved weighing the foods before they were eaten, weighing the remainder after the meal, and calculating the exact nutrient content of each meal.

When we examined the results of this long-term study, we found that on the average the children were slightly *less active* on their sugar days than on their placebo days. Recall that this was the result obtained by the NIMH team, using the actometer measure of motor activity after glucose challenges.

However, since we had measured the other things the children ate, we could look at the results against the background of the total calories, carbohydrate, protein, and fat which the children consumed at the breakfast meal. When we did this, it became apparent that *the behavior was quieter on days in which the breakfast was relatively high in protein but more active on days with relatively high carbohydrate intake.* Carbohydrate-containing foods, such as bread, waffles, and doughnuts eaten at breakfast, produced a worsening of behavior (more activity) in conjunction with the sugar drink. If the children ate eggs, meat, fish, or cheese, the sugar was beneficial.

Although the children were always served a balanced hospital diet, on certain days they might choose to eat pancakes and syrup, while on others they might eat bacon or eggs. On days in which they consumed a lot of carbohydrate but little protein, the sugar appeared to make them more active, but the opposite occurred if they had a moderate amount of protein. Apparently, the sugar effects depended upon what else was eaten along with it.

But admittedly, children in this study were much more severely disturbed than the outpatients and normal children studied by others. We wondered how our findings might turn out in normal children and in children who are hyperactive but not as severe as those requiring psychiatric hospitalization.

These questions prompted us to study the problem further. In the last chapter we briefly described this experiment involving a carbohydrate and protein breakfast in both normal and hyperactive children. The carbohydrate breakfast consisted of two slices of buttered toast, and the protein breakfast was two eggs scrambled in butter. (As we noted in the last chapter, the butter helps to slow digestion time.) After each breakfast the children received either a sucrose or placebo drink, on a random schedule.

This latest challenge study strongly supported the earlier purely correlational study: the sugar effects depended upon the carbohydrate and protein content selected at breakfast. Even the normal children who ate the carbohydrate breakfast did more poorly than normal children eating the protein breakfast. When the hyperactive children eating a carbohydrate breakfast received sugar, their attention was much poorer than on the placebo days. However, the reverse was true for the hyperactive children after eating protein: their attention was *better* after consuming sugar than after the placebo. Children who ate nothing did about the same after receiving sugar as after the placebo. (It is easy to see from this last result why studies that test sugar on a fasting stomach might come to the conclusion that it has no effect.) Sugar can either promote, hinder, or have no effect on mental functioning in children, depending both upon the type of child and the type of breakfast. The next question is what is different about hyperactive children that could explain why they respond so differently to sugar after a carbohydrate compared with a protein breakfast.

We noticed that the rise in blood sugar following the carbohydrate meal was significantly greater among the hyperactive than the normal children, so it was reasonable to wonder whether blood sugar accounted for behavioral effects in the two groups. But one fact arguing against this idea was the finding that sugar effects were the same throughout the morning; that is, the effect of eating sugar did not wane with time. This is somewhat puzzling if it is changes in blood sugar that are responsible, because we know that blood sugar rises rapidly after a meal and after the sugar challenge and then gradually returns to normal over a few hours. If blood sugar levels were causing the problems in attention, then the problems ought to decrease over time, in parallel with the blood sugar decline.

There was, however, no correlation of behavior changes with blood sugar changes. Moreover, blood sugar was already more elevated in the hyperactive children *before* they received any sugar challenge. Blood sugar was different in hyperactive and normal children, both at the start of the study and in the response to challenge. But blood sugar level was not itself directly accounting for the impact on attention of the sugar challenge which the children received. We had to look for some culprit other than blood sugar. A clue surfaced in the hormonal reactions to the meal and sugar challenges.

HORMONES, SUGAR, AND BREAKFAST

Some of the hormones we measured showed a pattern of change exactly like that of the children's behavior. These hormones went in opposite directions among the hyperactive children, depending upon whether they ate carbohydrate or protein. One of these hormones, cortisol, is one of the familiar "fight–flight" hormones. When the body reacts to an emergency, like preparing for a fight, escaping from a threat, or when almost any stress occurs, the brain triggers a series of events causing secretion of cortisol from the adrenal glands. The exact function of cortisol in these emergency states is not well understood, though it probably has many roles, such as repair of tissue damage and control of inflammation.

Scientists know, however, that cortisol helps regulate blood sugar levels. Low blood sugar stimulates cortisol, which helps promote the production of glucose. High blood sugar suppresses further output of cortisol. This seems understandable if cortisol helps prepare for emergencies requiring additional quick energy.

The normal children in our study reacted appropriately to the sugar challenge. Rising blood sugar levels suppressed further cortisol production. The hyperactive children, however, did not suppress their cortisol output. They responded as if the message from higher blood sugar levels did not reach the brain, telling it to turn off further production of cortisol. But this abnormal response occurred only when they had a carbohydrate, not a protein, breakfast. A similar pattern occurred for growth hormone, which like cortisol, acts to regulate blood sugar level by mobilizing sugar stores when blood sugar levels decline.

We cannot be sure at this point why the hyperactive children respond differently under the two kinds of breakfast conditions, but we can reasonably speculate that it has something to do with brain neurotransmitters like serotonin. Manufacture of brain serotonin increases when the insulin reaction to carbohydrates causes tryptophan to enter the brain. Elevated proteins, say from a high-protein breakfast, block this effect. In animals, serotonin inhibits cortisol release, so if the hyperactive children were failing to get the serotonin signal, they might continue to produce cortisol, even though their blood sugar levels were high.

The two breakfasts affected growth hormone in a manner similar to cortisol, further supporting the serotonin signal idea. Growth hormone, like cortisol, has many functions, and it is also involved in stabilizing blood sugar levels. We know that serotonin also inhibits growth hormone secretion, so the same reasoning applies: the carbohydrate breakfast normally causes serotonin to signal the brain to shut off further growth hormone release, and the hyperactive children appear not to be getting this signal.

SOME SPECULATIONS ABOUT BRAIN GROWTH AND SUGAR

We have noted that sugar and carbohydrate effects in children appear to have some relation to age. Dr. Goldman's study on attention and activity in preschoolers found that sugar affects behavior, whereas Milich's similar study on older children did not. Prinz noted particularly high levels of sugar consumption among 4- and 5-year-olds. In our inpatient studies there were some important differences in the effects depending upon age. Usually, the sugar effects were more pronounced in the younger children. Older and younger children also differed in the amount of carbohydrate and protein which they chose to eat, with younger children consistently eating more carbohydrate than older children. Subsequently we found that older, less active children were eating more protein, increasing their ratio of protein to carbohydrate. Perhaps, then, differences in response to sugar at different ages could reflect differences in protein–carbohydrate ratios at different ages. Since systematic studies of sugar effects for children of different ages have not yet been done, we can only speculate what differences in sugar reactivity at different ages could mean.

But there are some theoretical reasons why sugar may be more important at certain ages than others. After birth the main fuel of the brain is glucose, and children expend an enormous quantity of their daily calories just to supply the brain's energy requirements. Some estimates place the percentage of calories needed for brain glucose as high as 50% of the child's total caloric intake.

The total number of nerve cells in the brain peaks early in the child's development, and after age 3 or so there are few new brain cells added, compared with the enormous explosion of brain growth occurring shortly before and after birth. The 3-year-old already has almost all the brain cells he or she will ever have. Nevertheless, the brain continues to grow, mostly by elaboration of *connections* between the brain cells.

Head size, brain weight in relation to body weight, and electrical activity all continue to show signs of growth throughout childhood. But these changes do not occur in a simple, linear fashion like body size. Instead, there appear to be "brain growth spurts" during certain periods. During these periods one sees correlated changes in mental functioning, such as performance on intelligence tests.

Since the number of brain nerve cells does not account for these spurts, much of this increase in brain activity presumably reflects sudden increases in the number of interconnections among the cells. The brain's neurons appear like tree trunks, with more "arborization" developing in ways that allow for greater degrees of interconnectedness amongst the cells. Even though the number of brain cells remains constant, the number of interconnections increases dramatically during certain periods of renewed development.

One such brain growth spurt appears between 3 and 5 years of age, another from 9 to 11, and still another during adolescence, at about 12 to 14 years of age. These growth spurts in the brain appear to signal greater capacity of the brain for new levels of function. There are many more synaptic connections requiring neurotransmitter activity and thus new levels of energy supply. We have wondered what happens when a child has become adapted to a certain level of dietary intake of carbohydrates and sugar and then suddenly finds that the brain is calling for more fuel to carry out new activities which the larger network of nerve fibers now requires.

While no research data yet exist on this question, such brain growth spurts mean that children might suddenly begin changing the foods they are willing to eat. We have speculated that some children begin to crave more carbohydrates during these rapid growth periods and that some of these children will then overindulge, thus leading them into a chronic pattern of excess carbohydrate intake. In contrast, some parents might not permit their children to have enough of the new levels of carbohydrates, thus interfering with the brain's ability to make full use of its new capabilities.

Again, I am stressing the idea that high carbohydrate foods

by themselves are neither good nor bad but must be reasonably balanced in the diet. But what that balance is may fluctuate according to changing needs of the brain at particular ages, just as it fluctuates according to changing stresses and demands of the environment. Parents must be observant in noticing how a child's dietary needs change as he or she grows and flexible in meeting changed needs at the right time. In a later chapter I will give suggestions for ways to monitor a child's diet and behavior in order to optimize the child's functional capacities.

ARE ALL CARBOHYDRATES EQUAL?

Scientists have observed that as nations become more affluent, they tend to eat fewer complex carbohydrates (starches) and more simple carbohydrates like sucrose. All carbohydrates cause a rise in blood sugar and provide energy for metabolic and nervous system activity. But there has been a steady decline in the consumption of complex carbohydrates in the American diet since the introduction of large quantities of refined sugar in the early part of this century. Complex carbohydrates include foods like pasta, potatoes, rice, and grain-based cereals.

In the past, doctors who manage diabetes have usually recommended that patients avoid simple carbohydrates in favor of complex ones, because the simple carbohydrates cause a much more pronounced rise in blood insulin. But recent studies show that there are very large differences in insulin reactions, even among specific types of complex carbohydrates.[7] Each has a somewhat different profile of action on insulin and blood sugar, and some of the old myths about these foods have been revised. For example, glucose and insulin responses to cooked potato are much greater than to cooked rice. The peak effect of potatoes on insulin is just as large as the pure sugar dextrose (though the onset of the peak for the potato is somewhat slower by about 30 minutes). The insulin response to bread is about the same as for potato and dextrose sugar. These foods produce a much stronger insulin effect than rice and corn.

But these general differences are further complicated by differences among people in their individual reactions to carbohydrates. For reasons which are unclear, some people have a much stronger blood glucose response to simple sugars than others. When the "high reactors" are compared to the "low reactors," they also have a stronger insulin response to potatoes and bread. Thus, for some people who are *sensitive* to certain complex carbohydrates, eating them may be equivalent to eating a pure sugar, at least as far as the impact on blood sugar and insulin. These differences in individual response to carbohydrates lead us to wonder whether certain children might also be more sensitive in their *behavioral* responses to different complex carbohydrates, just as they apparently differ in response to sugar itself.

There is not enough evidence to answer this question now, but again the data provide "food for thought" when tracking the apparently random ups and downs of a diagnosed hyperactive child or even an apparently normal but rambunctious youngster. As we saw, even a simple meal consisting only of bread had significant negative impact upon the attention of both normal and hyperactive children. Adding sugar put the hyperactive children at a further disadvantage. Because each carbohydrate source can produce its own unique pattern of effects on insulin and blood sugar, there may also be unique effects of particular carbohydrates on behavior and mental functioning in children.

SUMMARY

Evaluating and interpreting the impact of sugar and carbohydrates on the mental function, mood, and behavior of children is a complex process. There are still important areas of disagreement among many scientists. Nevertheless, our research strongly suggests that sugar can be either negative or positive for children, depending upon their age, their diet, and their biology. We believe there is a good possibility that a child's changing brain may leave him or her vulnerable to sugar and carbohydrate at certain ages. But there may be a vulnerability to either too little or too much. The protein sources in food play an important protective role against overloading of the brain by chemicals which are under the influence of sugar and carbohydrates. This protective role of protein argues for generous amounts of it in the diet, especially when sugars or other carbohydrates are being eaten.

In this chapter we proposed the theory that some children have a deficit in the ability to manufacture or use certain basic neurotransmitters. This deficit in turn causes them to be hyperactive. Food plays an important role in this process, for we need proteins like tyrosine and phenylalanine to manufacture the neurotransmitters. We saw that sugar helped hyperactive children when they also consumed protein, suggesting that sugar helps the protein get to the brain where it can be useful. Carbohydrates, on the other hand, seemed to make the children worse when they received the sugar challenges, possibly because the greater insulin response produces a rise in brain tryptophan and serotonin, in effect slowing the children's thought processes down, much as serotonin does in natural sleep.

Speculations about the role of sugar, hormones, and neurotransmitters can become overwhelmingly complex. Yet, we cannot ignore the practical consequences of our findings. Children should not load up on carbohydrate meals and sugar at the same time, and some protein in the meal is always sensible.

None of the findings in sugar studies justify eliminating sugar from the diet of children. Nor do the positive effects of protein imply that one should load up the child on meat, cheese, and fish or, even worse, go to the health food store for gallons of pure tyrosine or other amino acids. Carbohydrates, including sugar, are essential ingredients in a normal diet, and a varied, well-balanced diet is still the best protection against adverse physical and mental consequences related to food. Any major changes in a child's diet should always be made with the guidance of a nutritionist, dietitian, or knowledgeable physician.

CHAPTER FIVE

Food and Violence

Despite a hundred years of study by anthropologists, psychiatrists, and criminologists, we still know little about the causes of crime and violence. We do know that there are several forces pushing a child in the direction of criminal or violent behavior.

We know that the social environment is important. Poverty, discrimination, poor education, family values, and general misery all contribute. We also know that disease or damage to the central nervous system plays a role in criminal behavior. Studies of prison populations show that many criminals have had serious head injuries, early bouts with viral infections, and encephalitis. Some have chromosomal abnormalities (such as an extra Y chromosome, allegedly associated with violent behavior). Many have minor anomalies of the face and hands, indicating early abnormalities in embryologic development. Sometimes disease or damage to the temporal lobes of the brain produces an explosive, aggressive personality and impulsive reactions to slight provocations.

Genetics plays some role in both criminality and alcoholism. Alcohol use often accompanies or precedes violence and antisocial acts. Investigators in Sweden and Denmark studying children of biological parents with criminal or alcoholic histories found a higher frequency of violence and court appearances, even among children adopted early by normal families. Off-spring of alcoholics adopted early in life are more likely to become alcoholics, despite growing up in normal environments.

In addition, low intelligence and reading failure abound among habitual offenders. This probably reflects both their environmental deprivation and abnormal brain function. But most poor readers or dull children do not become criminals or commit crimes of violence, so these associated features are not *intrinsic* to criminality but only predispose to it. Poor environments, brain injury, genetics, and alcoholism all make violence and criminal behavior more likely in children and young adults, but many with these same disadvantages lead normal lives. In the parlance of sociology, these are "risk factors," but not specific causes. We seldom understand why some children with those disadvantages become criminals or periodically commit violent acts, while others with the same risk factors do not.

Some have suggested that food and diet could tip the balance when other risk factors are present. Speculations about the role of food and diet in criminal and impulsive behavior have been especially popular since the so-called Twinkies defense case. Dan White, the confessed killer of the mayor and the city supervisor of San Francisco, gorged himself on Twinkies. One of the defense lawyers argued that if a susceptible person ate junk food it could trigger antisocial or violent behavior. This idea is reminiscent of the delinquent's line in the satirical song in *West Side Story* that says something like, "Don't blame me, Officer Krupke, I have a social disease." Is food anything more than a lame excuse for avoiding responsibility? Could it tip the balance toward a life of crime or violence?

In this chapter we will examine the claims that food, crime, and violence are somehow related. Some of the claims may not be as silly as they seem on the surface. But the truth turns out to be much more complicated than Dan White's defense, which in essence was, "My dinner made me do it."[1]

HYPERACTIVITY, AGGRESSION, ALCOHOL, AND CRIMINALITY

Hyperactivity, aggression, and antisocial behavior often occur within the same child. But sometimes only one or two of these symptoms are prominent. Some hyperactive children are aggressive, whereas others are sweet, happy-go-lucky, and mild mannered. Some children are aggressive, either verbally or physically, but seldom commit antisocial acts such as breaking laws or committing crimes of violence. Many children who indulge in antisocial acts are not at all hyperactive.

A common denominator of hyperactivity, aggression, and alcoholism is impulsivity—the tendency not to look before leaping, to obtain immediate gratification of a temporary urge or need. This tendency can be apparent very early in life, and anecdotes often implicate food as something which exaggerates impulsive and aggressive behavior.

For example, one mother of a very hyperactive 4-year-old gave the following account of her experiences:

> When I was carrying Richard I was amazed at the vigor of his kicking, and after he was born he was the same way—always kicking or hitting, even when I fed him. For no apparent reason he would pound me or his father when he was held. From the time he could walk (or rather run, because he never really walked), he would suddenly strike out at his brother Arthur who is 3 years older and much bigger. He has a violent temper and it seems to be set off for no apparent reason most of the time, or else will flare up at the most insignificant frustrations. . . . This reaction is something I notice whenever Richard gets into candy.

Children who are impulsive and aggressive very early in life have a surprising degree of stability in this pattern. Long-term studies of such children show that they often become aggressive adolescents and adults, often ending up in trouble with the law. Retrospective studies (looking back at past records) of violent offenders also show that a majority were already known as troublemakers by their kindergarten and grade-school teachers. About a third of hyperactive children followed into adulthood lead normal lives. But two-thirds still show signs of the restless, impulsive, and inattentive characteristics they displayed as children. They have more auto accidents, suicides, academic failure, and job instability.

The youngster who starts life with many accidental self-injuries, goes on to be a reckless driver who drinks, explodes in anger over minor frustrations, gets involved in daring gang activities, and is prone to violence, is a frequent type seen in most juvenile and prison populations.

Family studies show that first- and second-degree relatives (parents, siblings, aunts, and uncles) of hyperactive–aggressive children have a much higher than normal incidence of hyperactivity, antisocial behavior, and alcoholism than the relatives of normal controls. This association is probably not just familial but genetic as well. The families of hyperactive children adopted before the age of 3 months may be no different from normal families in their histories, but even though they are adopted early, these children go on to become hyperactive. This shows that not all hyperactive behavior is simply learned from one's family (though learning surely plays an important role too) but has a genetic cause as well.

The association of the hyperactive–aggressive pattern with alcoholism is well established. Hyperactive children have a much higher tendency than nonhyperactive children to become alcoholics, and their family histories contain many more relatives with alcoholism. Hyperactive children's involvement with alcohol probably contributes to their later tendency to commit violent acts, since alcohol both releases inhibitions and increases aggressive urges.

Part of the association between drinking in parents and drinking in their offspring may be due to the effects of maternal drinking during pregnancy. Very small amounts of alcohol in early pregnancy cause subtle damage to the nervous system development of the child in utero. Even a moderate amount of alcohol during pregnancy may result in a child with a lower IQ and abnormal physical features, characterizing the "fetal alcohol syndrome." Such children are often grossly retarded and malformed, but scientists suspect there is a continuum of effects from very subtle to more extreme impairment. Children with the more subtle variations may not look physically different or be mentally slow, but they still lack some of the control and inhibitions of normal children.

The search for the causes of alcoholism has led to possible links with diet. First, alcoholics are often malnourished. This is not surprising, for heavy alcohol use itself causes dietary deficiencies and disposes alcoholics to eat poorly. Many alcoholics are hypoglycemic (have low blood sugar), again possibly the direct result of heavy drinking and its effects on sugar and insulin metabolism. But animal studies reveal a possible link between diet, alcohol, and brain neurotransmitters which may be an intrinsic biological link that exists early in life.

DIET AND KILLER MICE

Accustomed as we are to thinking of mice as benign little creatures like Mickey Mouse and his family, there are certain strains of mice that are killers. These "muricidal" animals will often devour their own young or viciously attack other mice in their neighborhood. These mice differ neurochemically from nonkillers. They have unusually low levels of the neurotransmitter serotonin. Moreover, some normally peaceful mice can be made into killers by altering their diet. Mice fed a diet low in tryptophan become muricidal. Recall that tryptophan is an amino acid found in protein food and that it has a unique tendency among amino acids to get into the brain when sugar and other carbohydrates stimulate an insulin response.

Studies of tryptophan and serotonin in killer mice have led

scientists to consider whether aggressive and violent behavior in humans might also have some connection with tryptophan and serotonin. The neurotransmitter serotonin plays a crucial role in modulating aggression, and as we have seen, under certain conditions tryptophan in the diet causes the brain to make more serotonin.

HYPOGLYCEMIA AND CRIME

In his book *Diet, Crime, and Delinquency*, A. G. Schauss popularized the notion that crime is due to hypoglycemia—an abnormal fall in blood sugar level, which can be determined from a glucose tolerance test (GTT).[2] The GTT involves drinking a large dose of a glucose syrup and then measuring the changes in blood levels of glucose over a period of several hours. The insulin reaction to the glucose is sometimes excessive. This causes blood sugar levels to fall well below normal to a state of hypoglycemia ("hypo," meaning too little, and "glycemia," referring to sugar). Low blood sugar in turn can cause mental symptoms. Some scientists claim that ingestion of sugar or carbohydrate meals (such as pasta or bread) produces a temporary neurologic abnormality of heightened impulsivity and poor self-control.

Most scientists reviewing these claims insist, however, that the subjects in these studies seldom meet the *medical* criteria for true hypoglycemia. Rigorous standards for true medical hypoglycemia include all the following criteria: a fall of blood sugar to below 40 mg per 100 mL of blood accompanied by mental symptoms; a regular fall in blood sugar to this level after carbohydrate meals; and a relief of symptoms within 10–20 minutes after eating food. Even then, about 40 to 50% of the normal population has this large a fall without any accompanying symptoms.

The list of mental symptoms experts cite to characterize true hypoglycemia include the following:

Crying	Mental confusion
Irritability	Guilt
Nausea	Hostility
Depression	Cognitive loss
Weakness	Restlessness
Palpitations	Drowsiness
Visual disturbances	Dizziness
Fatigue	Headache

One scientist looking at this list noted how these non-specific, subjective states reminded him of the anecdote told by Mark Twain: "He [Twain] said that he read a textbook of medicine, and then concluded that he had every disease except housemaid's knee." These symptoms surely do occur in *some* cases of true hypoglycemia, but there has been a temptation to attribute them to hypoglycemia even when other medical criteria are absent. The frequency of self-referral by patients requesting a GTT for these symptoms led one physician to characterize hypoglycemia as "an epidemic of nondisease." It is easy for depressed, psychosomatic persons to attribute their vague array of symptoms to "hypoglycemia." But objective clinical tests usually fail to support such a medical diagnosis.

Nevertheless, without becoming hung up on the medical label, if it turns out that criminals have *any* degree of overreaction to carbohydrates compared with normal people, the effect still requires explanation. An abnormal reaction to sugar (or other carbohydrates) might not meet criteria for true hypoglycemia, but it nevertheless could be evidence of some metabolic or physiological abnormality which predisposes a person to impulsive behavior. This could be significant in persons with poor self-control and aggressive tendencies, even if it is irrelevant for normal people.

A frequent reason for dismissing the hypoglycemia idea is that a large proportion of the normal population has similar degrees of response as those reported for criminals. But no one would argue that a stronger reaction to sugar is the only cause for criminal behavior or that it inevitably leads to crime. Surely criminal behavior and an impulsive personality are multifactorial problems. If there is any degree of excessive reaction to sugar and carbohydrates, even though small in comparison with true hypoglycemia, it could act to increase the risk of impulsive or violent behavior. Even a small degree of abnormality in sugar response might represent the tip of the iceberg of some abnormal hormonal or neurotransmitter function.

Anger is a mood state that disposes one to violent behavior. Even though most normal people get angry without becoming violent, given the right conditions, anger increases the likelihood of violence. If low blood sugar disposed one to anger, it could become a trigger that culminates in violent behavior.

Particularly with children, who must learn early to cope with their frustration and anger, and whose parents must mete out appropriate consequences, early bouts of repeated anger could set up a cycle of conflict that could shape a child into a violent pattern. A food reaction that leads to anger might be especially significant in the early development of children's personalities. Some surprising data emerging from human studies support this idea.

SOCIETIES THAT KILL

High in the Andes of southern Peru lives a group of Qolla Indians renowned for their violent way of life.[3] Dr. Ralph Bolton, an anthropologist, studied this group because "the forms of conflict in Qolla society are legion, ranging from petty insults through theft and homicide." Murder is a common occurrence in this isolated community, often sparking long-standing family feuds.

But the community itself recognizes that there are marked individual differences in the propensity to violence. They designate the active, abusive members "los abusivos," while the humble, passive men who fight only to defend themselves are known as "humildes."

After reviewing hundreds of cases of violent conflict, Dr. Bolton recognized that much of the violence was set off by the most inconsequential acts, which often appeared as irrational and unmotivated by the participants themselves. He wondered whether there might be some dietary feature which set the "abusivos" apart from the "humildes." One clue about the group as a whole is that unlike many neighboring communities the Qolla rely on potato agriculture rather than on mixed agriculture centered on maize.

Blood glucose concentrations appear to be lower in high-altitude natives than in the lowlanders of the Andes, and their metabolism of glucose is more rapid. Strong craving for sugar and an insatiable hunger are other traits found in this community. All these considerations led Dr. Bolton to administer a GTT.

Using a finger-prick to take a single sample of blood for analysis 4 hours after the challenge, Dr. Bolton found that almost 43% of the male population reacted with moderate hypoglycemia. (He defined moderate hypoglycemia as a blood sugar level of 10 to 25 mg below the fasting glucose level.) More important, he found a strong correlation between the level of hypoglycemia and rankings of aggressiveness made by independent key informants. As he says, "the very high aggressors were almost [invariably] moderately hypoglycemic. And it is the behavior of these men that determines the high levels of aggression in the village as a whole, since other villagers must to some extent behave aggressively out of self-defense."[3]

But aggressive behavior was not the only thing related to the larger decreases in blood sugar level. Using translators, the natives answered an incomplete sentences test. Incomplete sentences are often used in psychology to sample the thought contents of a person. The stem of the sentence—perhaps a phrase like "My favorite activity is"—gives respondents a chance to fill in the rest of the sentence, presumably with something that is meaningful about themselves.

The Qolla Indians responded to incomplete sentences such as "I am angry because . . ." or "A family . . . ," and so forth. The responses were then categorized according to the presence and amount of aggressive content (independent of knowledge of the blood sugar results on each person). Aggression would be shown in answers like "I am angry because others are out to get me," or "A family needs to fight in order to survive." The amount of aggressive thought content had a high correlation with the level of hypoglycemia. The greater the hypoglycemia, the more aggressive the content of the answers. Thus, in both their behavior and their thought content, the more aggressive natives of this village had the lowest levels of blood sugar after the glucose challenge.

Dr. Bolton carefully addressed possible alternative explanations, building a reasonable case that hypoglycemia (as here defined) has a causal relationship to the violence among the men of this culture.

While such an explanation for violence in a whole society may seem farfetched at first, it fits well with much of what we know about aggressive and predatory behavior in all mammals. The hungry lion will charge a water buffalo but when sated will lie next to its prey in pacific bliss. A fall in blood sugar level may be a universal trigger for brain centers that regulate aggressive and predatory instincts. Low blood sugar occurs when there is hunger. Perhaps it signals the animal to attack potential sources of food or potential sources of threat to its territory. Among a marginally surviving agricultural society, subsisting on a carbohydrate-rich, protein-poor diet, people with some innate propensity to have sharp drops in blood sugar level might be the most irritable and combative in the group. Their problem may not be lack of food but an unusual response to carbohydrate-containing foods.

It is important here to realize that individual differences are important. For reasons which are largely unknown, some people have a much sharper drop in blood sugar than others following a carbohydrate challenge. This does not mean that they are hypoglycemic in the medical sense; that is, such people may still fall well within the normal range of blood sugar. (Actually, a large proportion of people within the normal range of blood sugar would fall in the "moderate range" of hypoglycemia in Bolton's study.) This does not mean, however, that slight differences are unimportant. These slightly exaggerated carbohydrate reactions could interact with other predispositions (such as a genetic tendency toward aggressiveness or a hostile family environment) to weight the outcome toward violent behavior. Even mild hypoglycemia leading to more anger or aggressive thought content could become important when other conditions are ripe for impulsive and violent acts.

BLOOD SUGAR AND AGGRESSIVE FANTASY IN NORMAL ADULTS

The reader may wonder whether such a remote and unique culture as the Qolla Indians can provide any basis for explanations of violence in our own culture, where, presumably, most people are well-fed and nutritionally intact. A study of normal university males addressed this question.[4] These young adults were carefully screened to rule out medical, drug, or psychiatric conditions that might confound the results.

Measuring *overt* aggression in such a generally well-behaved group poses a problem. Like Bolton, however, the researchers wondered if the thought contents and fantasy of normal men would vary with their blood sugar response. They gave questionnaires about aggressive behavior, hostility, experiencing anger, and approval of aggressive acts, to the students. Another technique used by psychologists is one in which subjects project their own interpretations onto cartoons depicting various frustrating situations. Like the incomplete sentence test, these "projective tests" presume that some unpleasant or forbidden feelings or ideas are more readily expressed in an indirect way than by direct questioning.

One especially interesting measure was what the researchers called "the approval of aggressive acts." They presented eight aggressive acts of different intensities; for example, killing, hitting, or shouting angrily. The subjects indicated how justified these were in various situations.

Unlike Bolton's study, these investigators measured blood sugar after a glucose challenge every half hour to an hour over a 5-hour period. They used the two lowest points of the glucose curve as a measure of the hypoglycemic reaction, comparing it with the level just before the glucose challenge. Thus, their measure was more in accord with standard medical procedures for the GTT and was more accurate because of the larger number of samples obtained.

Again, strong relationships emerged between several of the measures and hypoglycemia. The approval of violent acts and outwardly directed aggression was particularly strongly related to the fall in blood sugar. Thus, in these normal university males, those whose blood sugar fell the most were also the most likely to have a general attitude of approval and justification of violent acts in response to threat.

An experiment with normal 9- to 11-year-old children showed that they too became more impulsive when blood sugar fell.[5] By maintaining careful control of their diets on a metabolic ward, researchers achieved control over other dietary factors. Observations took place after the children had breakfast on some days and after the children skipped breakfast on other days. When the children skipped breakfast their blood sugar levels fell (because they had no food convertible to glucose).

One of the tests required the children to inspect a group of drawings that were very similar and to indicate which one exactly matched a target figure. This "matching familiar figures test" is widely used to measure impulsivity. If a child impulsively makes an incorrect response, his or her response time is short and errors are high. If the child is "reflective," he or she will take a longer time but make more correct matches.

Impulsive children measured in this way tend to be poor readers and poor achievers, even when IQ is taken into account. When children skipped breakfast their blood glucose levels tended to fall, and the *extent* of this fall correlated with their impulsivity. Again, it is important to realize that there were big differences among the children in the extent to which their blood sugar levels fell. Thus, some were much more likely to become impulsive after missing breakfast than others.

Another test in this study involved remembering target items in a memory test compared with nonrelevant items in the test. This "incidental learning" task measures whether a child is paying more attention to the central (required) items or to the peripheral items which appear on the same pages. Children whose blood glucose fell on the no-breakfast days were *superior* in recall of the irrelevant items. This may seem paradoxical, but as the authors point out, normal children tend to recall fewer of the nonessential items because they are paying more attention to the target items.

Anxious children also tend to scan the environment more during these tasks and recall more irrelevancies than nonanxious children. Whereas normal children tend to recall fewer incidental items as they get older, anxious children do not. Thus, there is more focus on the important than the unimportant items during normal development. Anxious children, however, continue to scan their environment and to pick up useless irrelevant information at the expense of other information. In effect, then, the drop in blood glucose made these normal school-age children more susceptible to distracting items in the test. This caused them to lose focus on the central, relevant aspects of the test. They behaved more like anxious, impulsive children than normal children of the same age.

How such decreases in blood sugar operate to affect mental function is unclear. The mechanism is probably not a direct effect on brain glucose, because the supply of glucose to the brain takes place within very tight limits. But the fall in blood glucose may trigger other changes in the brain, such as a change in brain serotonin; or possibly, as some studies have suggested, insulin receptors in the brain are directly altered by the effect of dietary sugar on peripheral insulin response.

One rat study shows how lack of sugar in the brain—true brain hypoglycemia—could paradoxically occur from eating too much sugar. Rats ate high-sugar diets for several weeks, and then the sugar intake reverted to the normal level eaten by the control rats. This change back to normal levels caused the experimental rats to have a sudden drop in brain sugar (glucose). The authors speculated that chronic high levels of sugar in the diet caused a loss of sugar from the brain by altering the membranes in the blood vessels that sugar has to pass through to get into the brain. In any case, regardless of the specific mechanisms involved, the initial link in the chain of effects on behavior appears to start with a blood sugar reaction to what is eaten.

HYPOGLYCEMIA AND VIOLENT OFFENDERS

True hypoglycemia, as we have noted, is a rare occurrence. But there are wide variations in the extent to which blood sugar falls after a carbohydrate challenge. A Finnish investigator, Dr.

Matte Virkkunen, wondered whether these differences might be important among violent and impulsive criminals.[6] He noted that these severe offenders fell into two groups: those that committed their acts in an impulsive, unpremeditated way, and those who were generally antisocial but acted with premeditation. He found that the impulsive criminals had a sharp drop in blood sugar compared with normal men, but a quick return to normal levels. The antisocial group, on the other hand, also had a greater than normal drop in blood sugar after the glucose challenge, but took a long time to recover. Thus, he found two different patterns of response to sugar associated with two different patterns of criminal activity.

Review of past records revealed that several childhood characteristics of these criminals also correlated with a large drop in blood sugar level: truancy, uneven intellectual function, tattoos and slashings, and crimes against property, including stealing from one's own home in childhood. Tattoos are almost a hallmark of prison inmates, with a surprisingly large number of incarcerated offenders having them. They are "marks of distinction" and signs of an impulsive act leading to a permanent alteration of one's appearance. Slashings, too, often represent sudden, impulsive acts. Of course, many people get tattoos on an impulse (often regretting it later), so the tendency to get them only takes on a special meaning as part of a pattern of aggressive and impulsive behavior.

One problem in interpreting blood sugar as a catalyst or instigator of crime in these men is that alcohol use accompanied all their violent acts. Alcohol increases insulin secretion during the usual glucose-caused insulin reaction. Even though testing occurred several months *after* any alcohol use, one cannot be sure that chronic alcohol use had not permanently altered blood sugar response to glucose. Perhaps chronic alcohol use permanently alters the insulin reaction, and therefore alcohol is the main culprit, not sugar or the insulin response to sugar. Possibly persons predisposed to have a sharp hypoglycemic reaction have the effect aggravated by alcohol.

Many of the fathers of the criminals also were alcoholic, so in addition to contributing to the child's violent pattern by being abusive at home, there is a possible genetic link between the alcoholism of the fathers and the sons. The physiological deficit in these criminals may involve activity of the hormones that counterregulate the insulin reaction (such as growth hormone, cortisol, adrenaline, and noradrenaline). A genetic pattern of hormonal response could pass from father to son, making them prone both to an abnormal response to sugar and to violence. (It is not clear whether the higher incidence of alcohol and aggression in males compared to females is cultural or genetic.)

Thus, as we have seen so often, it is virtually impossible to disentangle the web of causes and effects involved in a food and behavior connection. Nevertheless, the correlations of blood sugar response with behavior extend to early childhood. This implies that adult criminal behavior is unlikely to be simply a manifestation of greater alcohol use. Rather, it suggests the possibility that very early in life there are some children whose unusual response to carbohydrate-induced changes in blood sugar level interacts with their aggressive predisposition.

Brain serotonin, known to be readily influenced by the carbohydrate–insulin reaction, correlated with violence in another set of studies. A team at NIMH studied a group of murderers and attempted murderers.[7] Again, they divided them into those who committed impulsive acts and those who showed premeditation. A careful history revealed that all the impulsive violent offenders had exhibited disturbed behavior at school. They showed many signs of attention deficit and aggressive conduct disorder, and they started using alcohol in their early teens. A large percentage of the impulsive offenders also had a history of impulsive suicide attempts.

One of the methods for gaining information about brain neurotransmitters involves studying the breakdown products of serotonin—the chemicals that result from metabolism of the neurotransmitter. Spinal fluid washing through the brain cavities provides these breakdown products, giving a direct measure of brain neurotransmitter activity. This circumvents many of the problems in interpreting the breakdown products from the blood or urine, since other parts of the body besides the brain influence the results. Spinal fluid is withdrawn by a needle inserted into the lumbar portion of the spine (the lower back). Although the procedure itself is safe and painless, a severe headache may result afterwards.

From samples of spinal fluid taken from the violent offenders, researchers found that the impulsive offenders had significantly less by-product coming from the brain's serotonin. The authors of this important NIMH study conclude that "there may be some persons in whom a defect in central serotonin metabolism is present, who start to abuse alcohol in their early teens and later become violent psychopaths."

Other studies of spinal fluid confirm that there are low levels of the brain serotonin breakdown product in people attempting violent suicide. There is often a connection between feelings of rage and suicide, and it often happens that the same people who commit violence on a spouse or child will turn their rage against themselves in a suicidal act. (Other methods of suicide in people with serious depression may reflect, to the end, the person's abhorrence of violence.) It does not seem farfetched to conclude that an abnormality of brain serotonin lies behind both the violent behavior toward others and toward oneself.

One implication of the NIMH studies on impulsive violent offenders is that serotonergic drugs (such as certain antidepressant medications) might be useful in treating adolescents prone to drink and violence. These drugs are useful with some types of depressed, suicidal people. Another possibility is that diet might help prevent these problems. Several studies looked at this question of diet effects on aggressive behavior among incarcerated criminals.

DIET AND AGGRESSION IN PRISON

In 1977, Barbara Reed, an Ohio probation officer, testified before the U.S. Select Committee on Nutrition and Human Needs. She claimed that modifying diets of her probationers produced amazing rates of improvement and decreases in recidivism (returning to a life of crime). Her diet was low in refined sugar and flour, food additives, coffee and coffee substitutes, soft drinks, grapes, prunes, dates, raisins, figs, all refined starch foods, caffeine, and alcoholic beverages.

There are many problems with Ms. Reed's reports.[8] Most of her evidence consisted of anecdotes, with little supporting documentation. From a nutritional point of view, the diet is such a hodgepodge of changes that it is hard to know what was important (just stopping alcohol, for example, might be the entire key). But the dramatic nature of the claims was sufficient to interest criminologists and prison researchers in the idea.

In one early study, 44 jail inmates received a diet low in refined carbohydrates (for example, table sugar, white flour) and either vitamin supplements or a placebo over an 8-week period. A control group had no diet modification. Most of those receiving the diet low in refined carbohydrates showed improvements on their psychological test scores, appearing brighter, more alert, and more emotionally stable. Unfortunately, for administrative reasons over half of the subjects dropped out of the study, leaving only seven in the control group. This study, like most carried out in the unfriendly confines of prison, suffers from other major methodological flaws. For example, giving different diets to some prisoners would be likely to mark them as special. They might receive different treatment as a result, or feel that they ought to act differently to comply with the expectations of the authorities.

Another investigator looked at the disciplinary records of 34 boys in a juvenile detention center after they started a diet low in refined carbohydrates. He compared these records with a different group seen *before* the dietary change was made. He found a 45% reduction in disciplinary actions in the group on the special diet compared with the control group. Unfortunately, the study did not record the actual consumption or changes in dietary sugar or other refined carbohydrates. Additionally, the control group was not carefully matched with the experimental group, so conditions may have been different for the control group. Several other studies by this same author gave similar results but shared similar methodological problems. Most critics have therefore been skeptical about the results because of the flaws in the research methods.

A somewhat better experiment took place in a Florida center for drug dependency offenders. Over 100 inmates volunteered for the study. After measuring their carbohydrate intakes, the researchers divided the inmates into "hypoglycemic" and "nonhypoglycemic" groups. After one month of a diet low in refined carbohydrates, the hypoglycemic group showed a significant reduction in various indices of maladaptive behavior, such as fighting and breaking rules. One important flaw of this experiment was that those receiving the special diet wore armbands identifying them as people who should not receive any candy and other refined carbohydrates. This marking of a special group destroys any double-blind aspect of the study and sets those inmates apart, making objective evaluations of their misbehavior unlikely. Other flaws were of a dietary nature; for example, the diet allowed table honey instead of sugar, which still provides a large dose of sugar in the form of fructose. This carelessness in designing experiments is justly criticized, but unfortunately, those who know better often fail to do the experiments themselves.

CONCLUSIONS

Various studies appear to support the idea that a greater than normal fall in blood sugar following a carbohydrate challenge (the glucose tolerance test) correlates with impulsive violent crime or impulsive suicidal behavior. The impulsive criminals in these studies were almost always impulsive and hyperactive as children.

Scientists who review these studies have many well-founded criticisms: that the impulsive and violent actions are usually intertwined with alcohol consumption in some way, making it difficult to know how the sugar reaction is causally connected to the behavior; that the so-called hypoglycemia standards are such that a large proportion of normal people get mistakenly classified as hypoglycemic; that there are flaws in the design and execution of studies of dietary change.

The evidence for hypoglycemia as a cause of violence is complicated and contradictory. One should not, therefore, jump to the conclusion that one's aggressive child has a problem with blood sugar and is doomed to become a violent psychopath. Nevertheless, there is a strong pattern of intertwined facts: in a culture known for its violence, the most violent men have the greatest drop in blood sugar and the most aggressive thought content; normal adolescents who have more violent thoughts and approve more of violence have the lowest blood sugar in response to a GTT; normal children whose blood sugar level falls the most after missing a meal are more impulsive and inattentive than peers whose blood sugar levels react moderately; there are significant differences in blood glucose changes to sugar challenges in impulsive offenders compared with nonimpulsive offenders; a key brain neurotransmitter, serotonin, is deficient in adult impulsive offenders and people attempting violent suicides; serotonin levels correlate with levels of aggression in animals and is modifiable by diet.

Just how diet, sugar intake, blood sugar response, serotonin, and impulsive, violent behavior influence one another is not clear. All we see is a suggestive pattern of interrelationships whose causal path could take many different forms. The brain neurotransmitter serotonin may be a key link between all these facts. Some genetic defect in this neurotransmitter system could account for both the behavior and the response to sugar. Equally, chronic overload with sugar could alter the system; or deficiencies in handling blood sugar could be at fault.

Based on the information presented in previous chapters, we would expect that a high chronic consumption of carbohydrates would lead to an *excess* production of brain serotonin, resulting in calming or somnolence, but killer mice, impulsive suicide attempters, and violent criminals are thought to have a *deficiency* of brain serotonin. This paradox is not difficult to rationalize, for the body has a homeostatic system, much like a thermostat, that may be set to different levels depending upon the typical state. Perhaps a high, chronic consumption of carbohydrates leads the brain's neuronal receptors to adapt in such a way that it turns off the serotonin signals.

Another possibility is that the brain itself, for whatever reasons, has inadequate ability to produce or use its serotonin. Since brain levels of serotonin must tell the body when to eat more carbohydrates, the individual might experience a constant state of carbohydrate craving. Here, the cause-and-effect cycle reverses: low brain serotonin causes higher intake of carbohydrates (to raise the brain levels of tryptophan for manufacture of more serotonin). In this interpretation, excessive carbohydrate intake is a *symptom* of an abnormal brain state, not its cause.

One way to resolve these alternative explanations about the role of food and violence is with adequately designed studies that treat criminals with alternative diets, and to date, good studies have proved elusive. But better studies could, and must, be done, since the importance of the issue for public policy and the public's general welfare is so great. To be able to curb crime through diet should be a tantalizing enough possibility to stimulate further studies.

Future studies should also determine what the effects of chronically high intakes of carbohydrates in children are on the brain's neurotransmitter systems. Nobody has yet prospectively studied the effects of diet in children prone to anger and aggressive outbursts, but such studies, while expensive and difficult to conduct, could reveal important causes of violence and crime.

In the meanwhile, it seems obvious that individual parents have a responsibility to avoid conditions which lead to a fall in blood sugar, like missed breakfast, and to provide diets that are nutritionally balanced, adequate in protein and other essential nutrients. Glucose tolerance tests are inappropriate for most children unless there are clear signs that mental symptoms regularly occur over a few hours after a high-carbohydrate meal. Even then, a desirable approach is first to see that the child eats enough protein to block the reaction.

CHAPTER SIX

Diet, IQ, and Learning

Popular culture has always held the belief that certain "brain foods," like fish, improve mental functioning. Many pregnant women throughout the world believe that eating special foods will ensure delivery of a brighter, more capable child. Religious traditions have always prescribed certain foods for enhancing communion with the divine and proscribed other foods thought to hinder achievement of higher consciousness. On the other hand, many people assume that intelligence is completely fixed by heredity, and that children's genes completely determine their capacity to learn as well as their other talents. Here we will look at the ways scientists have addressed the possibility that diet and foods influence intelligence and learning capacity.

WHAT IS IQ?

There are two points of view about the nature of intelligence. While neuroscientists search for the biological mechanisms which determine intelligent and nonintelligent behavior, psychologists and naturalists usually focus on features of the environment that promote or inhibit learning, memory, or problem-solving skills.

One point of view is that the biology of the brain determines intelligence. In contrast, others claim that interaction with the environment and experiential learning determine intelligence. If "nature" completely determines our intellectual destiny, then there is little room for modification of basic intelligence by diet, while if intelligence is something created by instruction and opportunities for learning, food is also irrelevant.

But this extreme distinction between nature and nurture does not hold up under close analysis, for both are important. Intelligence is not a fixed capacity, but a dynamic changing state that reflects both biological and cultural limitations. The basic wiring of the brain is itself greatly influenced by the social and physical environment, and the brain's organization and biological capacities in turn alter the manner in which people explore and experience their environment. Food is part of the physical environment of the developing brain, but diets are largely determined by social and cultural habits, by where one lives, and by affluence or poverty. In this sense, diet has both biological and cultural influences on intelligence.

The genes from a child's parents set broad limits on how intelligent that child will be, but intelligence is not fixed. Most scientists now believe that intelligence is some combination of the limits set by one's biology and the opportunities afforded by one's environment. Even biological aspects of the individual, determined by the body's intricate genetic mechanisms, are subject to modification by the environment. For example, the genes from our parents largely determine how tall we will become, but body height is still modifiable within certain limits by nutritional patterns (as evidenced for example, by the progressive increase in height of successive generations of immigrant Japanese in this country). Though intelligence is strongly influenced by heredity, it too can be enormously modified by the environment, including the nutritional environment which begins in the womb of the mother. That a trait is hereditary does not mean that it is unchangeable. There is good reason for believing that social and environmental effects may be even more difficult to change than biological effects. (Poverty and war are social and cultural, yet mankind has been unsuccessful in getting rid of them.)

Intelligence is a very broad term for the set of capacities that allow organisms to adapt to their environment and cope with its challenges. But exactly what intelligence is has eluded analysis. Nevertheless, scientists have adopted working methods that sidestep the conceptual issues of defining intelligence and enable them to ask many questions.

Beginning with Alfred Binet in 1905, a French psychologist who wanted to develop a measure for predicting whether children would be successful in the school system, psychologists have compiled batteries of tests involving problem-solving, reasoning, memory, classification, language, and visual–motor skills. While imperfect, these tests do provide broad guidelines of how successful a child will be in negotiating the complex demands of schooling.

Binet began the tradition of the "intelligence quotient," or IQ, by expressing the test results as a ratio of the "mental age" to the chronological age. Mental age is a score based on the average performance of normal children for a given age. If a child has a mental age of 12 but a chronological age of 10, he or she has an IQ of 120 (12 divided by 10 times 100). Mental age increases in most children as they grow older, but it maintains a constant average relationship to their chronological age, allowing IQ to be a more or less stable estimate across the age span. Before 2 years of age, it is possible to measure basic reflexes and motor skills, but while important in themselves, these measures are practically useless for predicting later IQ. After age 2, however, standard tests of intelligence are very useful in predicting success in learning, especially academic success.

Most of the separate specific measures in the IQ tests (such as vocabulary and reasoning by analogies) tend to have a lot in common. People who do well in one measure also tend to do well in the others. This fact has led to the idea that there is a central, common core of intelligent behavior, a general pervading capability that underlies all the separate abilities—a "g" factor, as psychologists call it. While genetic studies show that this general ability has a large component determined by heredity (some say as much as 80%), studies also show that IQ can be greatly modified by experience.

Apart from the "g" factor, there are some special abilities that seem to form specific clusters or *types* of intelligence. One of these is language-related abilities. Individual children may be particularly gifted in one aspect of intelligence, such as language, but be quite ordinary in another, such as musical talent. Other abilities have more to do with nonverbal, primarily visual–motor or visual–spatial abilities. One way of thinking about these two different aspects of intelligence is that the verbal abilities reflect sequential, linear aspects of information processing, while the spatial abilities reflect information processed in patterns. We reason in sequences, but we grasp pictures, maps, and melodies as wholes, or "gestalts."

These aspects of intelligence reflect brain organization. For example, verbal abilities are predominantly governed by the left hemisphere of the brain in most people, while spatial abilities are more tied to the right hemisphere of the brain. Right-brain functions determine emotions and feelings, such as sadness. This has been shown by putting part of the brain to sleep with the sedative drug sodium amytal and then noting the changes in mood. Depressed patients show more impairment of right-brain functions, while schizophrenics, with their typical disruption of thought processes, are thought to have more left-brain impairment. When the brain is split by disease or surgery, it is as though there were two separate brains, each specialized for different functions.

This specialization of the two hemispheres is easily seen for handedness. Motor dexterity in right-handed people shows that the motor areas of the left brain are more in charge (the motor fibers cross completely to the opposite side of the body). The left brain apparently becomes dominant for language abilities in most right-handed people, as is shown by aphasias (deficiency in understanding or producing speech). Head wounds on the left are more likely to produce aphasias than wounds on the right. Damage to the right side of the brain may result in a very specific loss of recognition for patterns, such as the ability to recognize human faces. Damage to the left-frontal speech areas may result in the inability to produce speech, while damage to the left posterior portion of the brain may result in problems in perception and understanding of written or spoken language.

While somewhat oversimplified, this picture of hemispheric specialization is important in understanding how diet might influence brain function. We found, for example, that when a carbohydrate breakfast together with sugar impaired hyperactive children's vigilance, it also produced a diminution in brain electrical activity that was larger on the right than the left side. Just as some drugs have different effects on different parts of the brain, related to the organization of neurotransmitter pathways, so foods might have selective effects upon certain functions, depending upon their specific neurotransmitter effects.

These broad aspects of intelligence, verbal and spatial, can be further broken down into even more basic processes. For example, before a child can solve a block design puzzle involving joining segments to match a pattern, he or she must be able to discriminate the different shapes and colors involved, remember the information, integrate the visual and tactual information, and have the requisite visual–motor integration skills to complete the design.

Some language processes require recognition of the speech sounds (speech perception), while other language functions involve retrieving information from storage and expressing it verbally (verbal memory). Conceivably, then, food might alter verbal memory while not altering other language-related functions, just as damage to the brain sometimes affects memory without affecting recognition or perception. Although these subskills make up broader dimensions of intelligence, which in turn make up a general core of intelligence, they can be individually influenced or altered, and so they might be individually affected by certain nutritional or pharmacological influences.

It seems reasonable, therefore, to consider the possibility that nutrition influences quite *specific* aspects of intelligence because it affects brain processes involved in particular skills. Nutritional influences might be especially important during times when a part of the brain controlling a particular skill is developing. Nutrition might also affect very *broad* aspects of intelligence because of its widespread impact on many parts of the brain at once. Later in this chapter we will see some examples of both kinds of effects, specific and general, caused by nutritional influences.

STUDYING FOOD AND IQ IN CHILDREN

There are two ways that scientists study the problem of dietary and nutritional influences on intelligence and learning in humans. One is by "experiments of nature"—natural disasters such as famine—that severely limit calories or availability of certain foods, such as protein, or that produce radically different diets in certain villages or habitats. The other method is by attempting to alter mental functions through direct manipulation and experimentation with the diet. The latter approach has the advantage of controlling for many things that the former cannot. But ethical limits rightfully exist on what can be done with deliberate human experiments.

Usually then, the disasters of nature tell us more about drastic harmful effects, while the controlled experiments tell us more about possible beneficial effects. Animal research has been helpful for studying both the loss of intelligent behavior and its improvement, but, especially in regard to higher cognitive and language functions, the final judgment on many questions can only be made after humans themselves have been carefully studied.

Although the extreme experiments of nature, such as starvation among children and their mothers, may seem remote and even largely irrelevant to the concerns of the citizens of well-fed Western industrialized countries, this is not so. For one thing, though we may choose to close our eyes, malnutrition is still a frequent fact of life, even in America.

A recent survey examined children among poor urban households several years after the families had been given federal food assistance. While there was considerable improvement over their original nutritional status, there remained a substantial portion of children who were deficient in vitamin A, vitamin C, and iron. Iron accomplishes its function of transporting oxygen from the lungs to the tissues by attaching to the protein substances hemoglobin and transferrin. As many as 18% of children studied in this survey were deficient in these iron-related proteins. We will see that these deficiencies may be important to urban, well-fed children as well, affecting their IQ scores, attentional abilities, and behavior.

Severe malnutrition has also been instructive in showing the importance of the level of social and intellectual stimulation the child is receiving from the family at the time malnutrition occurs. Nutritional deprivation has more profound effects against a general background of social deprivation than when the child is otherwise well cared for.

The lesson from these studies seems to be that nutritional effects compound preexisting problems created by the social environment. It seems reasonable to expect similar interactions with less profound alterations of the diet. Perhaps, for example, the apathy and irritability of the iron-deprived infant becomes more significant if there is already apathy and irritability due to other causes, such as occurs in a neglected or understimulated infant. Interpreting studies of food and diet effects on learning and IQ is difficult because of this entanglement of social and biological effects on the brain.

MALNUTRITION AND IQ

The stark facts of severe malnutrition are clear. It is the largest cause of death in the world. For the survivors, the severe restriction of calories, particularly calories from protein, leads to abnormality in virtually every bodily system. When starving mothers themselves have too little protein, and their milk dries up, their children suffer since that milk is the main source of their own protein. In children under 1 year of age, the effects are devastating on intellectual function of every kind. Not only is IQ severely depressed, often to very retarded levels, but more basic processes on which learning depends are markedly impaired, seldom returning to a normal level.

For example, consider one of the most basic abilities involved in learning, the ability to transfer information from one sensory modality (or channel) to another—for example, recognizing something visually that one first explored by touch. As humans achieved greater levels of intelligent behavior over animals, they did so not by multiplying the number of senses or their acuity but by greater elaboration of the *connections* among the senses. This "intersensory ability" is severely compromised by early nutritional deficiencies.[1] Children severely malnourished in infancy are significantly behind well-nourished children in how well they can link information between the senses—a deficiency that remains long after vigorous nutritional interventions and successful physical rehabilitation. The same is true of basic motor skills, reaction time, and visual–perceptual tasks such as drawing and copying. Severe malnutrition, then, is likely to result in impairments of virtually all aspects of intelligence.

There is considerable debate about just how permanent these mental effects of severe malnutrition are. It is clear, however, that simply restoring good nutrition at a moment in time, although important, does not guarantee a good long-term outcome. One reason for this is that malnutrition is almost always intertwined with severe poverty and lower educational status, and correcting the nutrition without attending to the rest of the environment only partially corrects the deficits and basic causes of intellectual impairment. Deficiencies in parental stimulation and nurturance *prior* to the malnutrition seem to play just as important a role as the malnutrition *per se* in the long-term outcome. The combination of environmental deprivation and food deprivation is much more devastating than either by itself.

Observations of mothers and children during the period when the child is severely malnourished reveal how intertwined the mother's and child's behaviors are with the physical changes caused by the malnutrition. For example, mothers of malnourished infants, even when not malnourished themselves, sit farther away from the children, respond less often to their cries, and provide less eye contact and other stimulation. As the infant becomes weaker, its own diminished behavior provides even less stimulus to the mother to interact with the child. Training mothers in basic parenting skills turns out to be as important for the mental development of the child as restoring good nutrition. Studies with animals show that environmental stimulation produces changes in the brain which are almost exactly the opposite of the destructive influence of malnutrition upon the brain's structure, size, and complexity. To some extent there is a protective factor here: environmental enrichment stimulates the brain to grow, protecting it against nutritional deficiencies and accomplishing many of the same functions as nutrition itself. Environmental deprivation acts much like malnutrition, reducing the brain's growth, complexity, and general efficiency.

In a sense, then, the lasting effect of severe malnutrition is a nutrition–*behavior* deficit, not just a food deficit. It is tempting to think that it is merely the poverty of resources that is to blame for the wasted intellects and the wasted bodies. But in order to grow, the brain seems to crave stimulation, especially social cues, as much as food, and one of the indirect effects of brain malnutrition is the limiting of the child's interactions with the environment. The listless, apathetic, undernourished child fails to get the social stimulation it needs, and because it gives off fewer cues to caretakers, the caretakers may give up and cease providing the cuddling, talking, and stroking that the brain also needs.

MOTHER'S DIET AND IQ IN HER CHILDREN

Nature provides tremendous nutritional safeguards to the developing embryo, because the embryo uses nutrients supplied by the mother, even at the expense of the mother's own nutritional requirements. The fetus will usually get most of the nutrients it needs, even in a severely limited maternal diet. But there are definite limits on this safety mechanism, and dietary deficiencies in the mother can have an impact on the mental capacities of the child.

One study illustrates how maternal diet can affect later mental functioning in children.[2] This study divided pregnant inner-city women into three groups. The first group (the supplement group) received two daily eight-ounce cans of beverage containing 40 grams of protein, 470 calories, and an array of vitamins and minerals. The second group (the complement group) received two daily eight-ounce cans of beverage containing 6 grams of protein, 322 calories, and a vitamin and mineral supplement similar to that of the first group but lower in calcium, magnesium, iron, zinc, copper, iodine, vitamins A, D, E, and niacin. This latter vitamin and mineral supplement was the same used in the standard clinic supplement. The third group (control group) received only the standard supplement without the protein.

Mothers who entered the program early (within the first 3 months of pregnancy) delivered babies who were heavier than those who received supplementation later in pregnancy. But this effect was due almost entirely to smoking mothers in the supplement group, who delivered larger infants than smoking mothers in the control group. Thus, early supplementation appeared to protect smoking mothers to some extent from the lower birth weight usually associated with smoking. A year after birth, however, the other groups caught up, and there were no longer any differences in weight.

The effect of the protein supplement on *intellectual* function, however, had an impact that lasted up to the time of the measures taken at 1 year of age. The investigators found that supplementation affected a very basic form of early learning important for the development of IQ. The babies sat in their mothers' laps and saw a screen on which a figure appeared. Most babies will look at the screen when a novel figure occurs but gradually lose interest with repetition of the figure. How rapidly the baby habituates to (that is, gets used to) the stimulus is a good measure of simple learning or attention. After the baby has habituated, a different figure is shown, and most babies will then have renewed interest in looking at the screen. This renewed interest (dishabituation) reflects the child's awareness of novelty and attention to the changing stimuli. The curiosity of normal infants is apparent in their renewed interest in events that change, and their ability to learn is shown by their rapid adaptation to unchanging, repeated events.

At 1 year of age, the supplement group was significantly superior to the other two groups in habituation and dishabituation. Because this basic capacity for attention was noticeably improved by the high-protein supplement, these babies would explore their environment more, be more aware of changes, and eventually accumulate more information. It would not be surprising, then, if much later they tested out as having higher IQs. Unfortunately follow-up tests beyond 1 year are not available.

Another, more obvious measure of attentiveness is length of play time. Observers watched the children through a one-way mirror while they played with toys placed around the room. The length of time the child played with toys was significantly higher in the supplement group compared with the other groups. The complement group was no different from the controls on any of the measures. Thus, early persistence, attentiveness, and alertness are strongly influenced by maternal diet. We can't know for certain what mechanisms lead to these effects. Perhaps the mothers were simply healthier and therefore they played with their babies and were more responsive to them, and this in turn altered the babies' behaviors. Perhaps the better nutrition of the rapidly developing brain in the womb allowed more complete brain development. In any case, the babies were the beneficiaries of an improved maternal diet.

DIET AND IQ IN YOUNG CHILDREN

As suggestive as the above study is, one must wonder what the effects of a good early diet would be on classical IQ tests and on actual school learning when the children reach school age. Another study provides evidence on this question.

The government food supplement program for women, infants, and children (WIC) provides nutritional supplements for low-income mothers and their children. Infants under 1 year receive iron-fortified formula, iron-fortified cereal, and fruit juice rich in vitamin C. Older children and their mothers get milk, eggs, cheese, iron-fortified cereal, and fruit juices rich in vitamin C. Researchers studied children in the first grade who received the WIC program in the first year of life and their siblings who received the program only after their first year. Because these children came from poor families, special care was taken to use IQ measures adjusted to their particular ethnic and social class background.

The results were striking: children who received the food supplements in the first year of life outstripped their siblings who did not get the early supplement on almost all the measures, including verbal and nonverbal IQ, visual–motor skills (drawing a human figure), and grade point average. There was a 17-point advantage in verbal IQ and a 13-point advantage in nonverbal IQ for the early supplementation group. There were also far fewer aggressive conduct disturbances among the early-supplemented children than among their later-supplemented siblings. Even though both groups continued receiving supplements up to school age, the earlier access of the experimental group gave them a lasting advantage over their siblings.

We cannot know from this experiment whether any particular food was crucial in the outcome. The improved diet from the supplementation increased available protein as well as iron and a variety of minerals and vitamins. Perhaps all are important and act to synergize each other; perhaps only the iron made a difference. What is important, however, is that *adequate nutrition from a variety of foodstuffs* was available during a critical phase of development. Without the supplements these children could become undernourished in any number of ways, slowing brain growth, or diminishing their energy level and their capacity to benefit from the environment. The best guess is that improving total nutritional state optimized total brain growth, and this in turn started a cycle of more learning from the environment.

Low IQ and behavior problems go hand in hand because both depend upon the state of the brain, and these studies show that good nutrition has a significant role in preventing both.

DIET AND IQ IN OLDER CHILDREN

Most of the rapid brain growth in children takes place just before they are born and during the first year of life. It seems reasonable, then, to expect that children's basic intelligence would be little affected by diet later in life, short of the catastrophic malnutrition we touched upon earlier or in undernourished poor children. But a recent experiment in Britain calls this assumption into question.[3] The experiment is all the more important because the children were about as well-nourished as the average British child, and they did not come from deprived homes or poor educational backgrounds.

Ninety 12- and 13-year-olds kept a diet diary for 3 days. Records were kept of the amounts and content of everything they ate, allowing calculation of vitamin and mineral intake. On average, most of the children were at or above the recommended daily allowances (RDA) for vitamins and minerals, but many *individual* children were below the RDA.

The children received an intelligence test and then assignment to three different groups. Over the course of a school year, one group received no special treatment, one group received a placebo, and the other received a standard multivitamin and mineral supplement of the "one-a-day" variety. They took the pills in school on a daily basis (an important feature for ensuring compliance). They got another IQ test at the end of the year.

To the surprise of the researchers, who expected to find no differences, the supplemented group showed a significant rise in IQ. The IQ test, like most standard tests now used, had a separate component which measured verbal intelligence and one which measured nonverbal intelligence. It was this latter aspect of IQ which showed the change. The rise in nonverbal IQ was about 10 points, well beyond the 1 or 2 points that occurred just with practice.

Usually it is easy to find a major flaw in the methodology of a study like this, leading one to discount its outcome. But this study appears to be very rigorous in design, execution, and analysis. How is it possible that vitamins and minerals could achieve such an effect, particularly in apparently well-nourished children?

Unlike verbal IQ, nonverbal IQ depends much less upon the child's exposure to information, language, and unique cultural environment, and it is therefore often considered a more "culture-free" and fluid form of intelligence; unlike verbal IQ, which develops rapidly very early in life, nonverbal IQ appears to continue developing through adolescence.

We noted above that some believe these nonverbal abilities involve much more of the right hemisphere of the brain than the left. Since the two hemispheres develop at different rates, the *timing* of nutritional insults or benefits could be important. A recent study of a large number of children from birth through adolescence measured the electrical activity of the two hemispheres of the brain and found that the right hemisphere showed a spurt in development that was much later than the left hemisphere. Whereas the left hemisphere reached most of its adult level within the first 3 years, the right hemisphere did not do so until age 10 or 11. These neurophysiological studies suggest that the brain's right hemisphere could be more vulnerable to nutritional deficiencies later in childhood and therefore also more likely to benefit from optimal nutrition.

Another point to consider is the importance of individual variations in nutritional needs among children. The authors of the supplement study make a very important point about the RDA for vitamins and minerals. Although large surveys in developed countries usually show that the RDAs are adequate, these figures are averages for populations, and there are many individual children who will be below this average for specific vitamins and minerals. They found that a sizable minority, usually about 10%, were deficient in vitamins, mostly vitamin D and folic acid. There were more cases (as many as half) who were deficient in one or more of the minerals. Especially among girls, iron, riboflavin, and thiamin were often deficient.

In the British study, almost 16% of the children were deficient in thiamin. A study of 11-year-old children in an American orphanage in the 1940s also found that, despite an apparently well-balanced diet, the children were deficient in thiamin. After several years of supplementation with thiamin compared with a placebo, the supplemented children showed a significant improvement in intelligence, visual acuity, and reaction times. That experiment was not well controlled and received a lot of criticism.

But thiamin is particularly important to the central nervous system because it helps regulate the functions of nerve cell membranes. Thiamin is abundant in only a few foods, including lean pork, wheat germ, liver and organ meats, poultry, egg yolk, fish, dried beans and soybeans, and whole-grain enriched breads and cereals. Irritability and lethargy are common effects of thiamin deficiency.

From these studies it appears that IQ may be modifiable in a substantial way by the nutritional environment, not only prenatally but in infancy and childhood as well. The interpretation of these studies, however, is complicated, for many nutritional changes are occurring together. Moreover, we don't know whether the effects only occur for nutritionally deficient children or for well-nourished ones as well. Even defining what is adequate intake for a particular child is difficult because nutritionists compute RDAs for large populations, and there are large individual differences in the needs of particular children.

Are there particular nutrients that are especially important, or is there some general pattern that determines the optimal growth environment for the brain? Learning and adaptive behavior are too complex to assume that there will be a single "brain food" that affects IQ and learning, but there may be specific foods at critical times which enhance (or even impair) brain function. One of the most well-documented nutrients known to affect brain function is iron, to which we now turn.

TIRED BLOOD AND IQ

Perhaps the most universal dietary problem is iron deficiency. Iron is present in every cell of the body and is important in many of the body's most fundamental processes. Because of its role in activating and carrying oxygen, we might expect that iron would be especially critical in the functions of the brain, since the brain uses oxygen in order to convert glucose—the brain's main fuel—into energy.

In developing countries iron-poor diets are further aggravated by a variety of diseases and parasites which cause loss of iron. But even in well-nourished Western countries, subtle and not-so-subtle iron deficiency is common. Recent studies show that 20% of women and 3% of men had no reserve iron stores. Over 8% of women are clinically anemic. A U.S. Department of Health Survey in 1972 found that 20% of children are probably iron deficient.

While the newborn full-term infant usually has enough iron stored in its body to cover its iron requirements during the first 4 to 6 months, within the first year the full-term infant almost doubles its body iron and is therefore dependent upon dietary intake for adequate iron.

Breast milk, the most complete nutritional substance known, is hard to improve upon, but it may not be adequate to meet the child's iron needs during the first year. Mothers who don't breast feed their child may mistakenly rely on iron-rich cow's milk. But cow's milk lacks an essential iron-binding protein necessary for utilizing iron, so iron in cow's milk is much less readily absorbed than iron in the mother's breast milk. This is why overfeeding with cow's milk may dispose a child to iron deficiency. The protein in cow's milk is also much less digestible than protein in breast milk. In later childhood daily need for iron decreases, but then it increases again during the growth spurt of adolescence. Therefore, an iron-adequate diet in infancy is no guarantee of continued adequacy later when dietary needs change.

A 6-month-old infant absorbs about 0.5 to 0.8 mg of iron in a single day, which is very high in relation to its energy intake. Since breast milk only supplies about 0.25 mg per day, iron supplements are usually recommended. Within the first year, these requirements are almost doubled. In later childhood, children need about 0.2 to 0.3 mg per day, but this requirement again goes up in adolescence to 0.5 to 1.0 mg per day. Since a good diet in Western countries usually supplies 10 to 20 mg per day of iron, this is usually enough to cover children's needs.

But the metabolism of iron is complex. Iron comes in two forms, called heme and nonheme, with heme iron coming mainly from animal protein and nonheme iron from plant sources such as beans, rice, corn, and cauliflower. The two forms differ greatly in the way they are absorbed. The absorption of nonheme iron is markedly affected by the iron status of the subject (greater absorption if the subject is iron-deficient). Some foods, like meat, fish, poultry, and ascorbic acid (vitamin C), enhance absorption; while certain substances, like phytates (found in plants such as cereal grains and soybeans) and tannin (found in tea), inhibit iron absorption. (The inhibiting effects of soy products on iron absorption is usually offset by the high iron content of these products themselves, so soy milk is not a problem for baby formulas.) Some cereals, wheat bran, coffee, and certain vegetables also inhibit the absorption of nonheme iron. Tea is a very strong inhibitor of absorption, while orange juice is at the other extreme in enhancing it. Because some wines have a high iron content they will tend to increase availability of iron. Antacids also reduce absorption. Thus, though readily absorbed, the nonheme iron is easily altered by other dietary factors. While heme iron is plentiful in meat, only about 25% of it is readily absorbed. Nonheme iron from plants is much more readily available and is thus usually the main source of iron in the diet.

Thus, regardless of the amount of iron in the raw food, the particular contents of a meal can markedly affect iron absorption and, hence, its availability to the body. For example, about five times as much iron gets absorbed from a continental breakfast (toast and jam) with orange juice as the same breakfast with tea. The practice in some parts of the world of giving young children tea with meals is decidedly a hazard that should be avoided. A vegetarian meal of navy beans, rice, corn bread, and an apple will provide only one-sixth the amount of iron in hamburger, mashed potatoes, and string beans. More of the iron from the meat-containing meal gets absorbed because it is less affected by other foods.

Because of these considerations, nutritionists generally recommend including meat, fish, or poultry and some source of vitamin C *at every meal* if possible; and that one avoid drinking tea or coffee with meals. Having a leisurely dessert with coffee served a half-hour later would allow more time for iron absorption before the coffee's inhibiting effect takes place. The food preservative EDTA (found in many meats) is also a potent inhibitor of iron absorption and needs to be carefully screened on package food labels.

Cooking can also have an effect. For example, overcooking may destroy the enhancing effects of vitamin C on iron absorption. Though cooking in iron pots can increase iron content of foods (especially during boiling of vegetables), this iron may not be well absorbed.

As with other dietary deficiencies, iron deficiency is often compounded by poverty and neglect and by other nutritional deficiencies. An increased proportion of calories from fat and refined sugar in poor households usually decreases the density of iron in the diet. Low household income may also force parents to leave the baby on the bottle for long periods of time while the mother works, leading to inadequate iron because of poor absorption from cow's milk. Sometimes the neglecting parent simply finds the bottle the easiest way of avoiding an irritable crying infant who is colicky (often precisely because it lacks the iron its body is demanding).

Many studies now document that anemic infants and children do more poorly than nonanemic children on a wide range of intelligence tests, measures of attention, motor coordination, speed, and neurologic development. These children also suffer from many more behavior problems, particularly of the aggressive type.

Many of these studies took advantage of "natural experiments," by comparing groups of children who were anemic with those who were nonanemic. Such studies always raise the problem that there may be other important differences between the groups which account for their learning and IQ differences. But several studies have now been done in which children were randomly assigned to iron supplements and placebo, and most of these studies found marked improvements in intellectual function in the iron-supplemented children.

These effects are important in infancy and in middle childhood and adolescence as well. The form of temporary insanity known as adolescence may be partially the result of these nutrition–environment interactions. At most risk are adolescent girls, who, because of the combination of growth spurt, loss of menstrual blood, and quirky eating habits, tend to be the most prevalent among iron-deficient groups, with as many as half estimated to have inadequate iron stores in their body to meet their needs.

Adolescents often choose food as one form of expressing their independence, and they will often indulge in many of the foods previously forbidden by parents, such as coffee and tea or high-carbohydrate snacks. When an adolescent girl begins to lose considerable amounts of her iron stores from menstruation, she may eliminate just those high-protein foods that could replenish the stores and, instead, consume foods that inhibit iron absorption, such as coffee and tea. A subtle iron deficiency then adds to the general irritability and fatigue that accrues from an expanded pattern of activity. A high intake of caffeinated drinks may then become necessary to pep her up, possibly interfering with sleep patterns and continuing the cycle of fatigue and irritability. Concentration suffers and tolerance of parental demands lessens.

One of the important findings of these studies is that the child does not have to be *severely* deficient; that is, does not have to be clinically anemic, before these detrimental effects occur. Because iron is intimately involved in reactions of many body enzymes, subtle changes in these reactions can occur well before a condition of frank iron-deficiency anemia. This is why it is important to have a pediatrician check the child's blood levels for iron throughout childhood.

Studies of brain electrical activity by Dr. Donald Tucker confirmed that iron (and to some extent ferritin, a form of iron stored in certain tissues) correlates with brain function. A finding of particular interest was that iron appears to influence some brain areas more than others. For example, low iron levels correlated with lower activity in the right posterior hemisphere of the brain, and in the left frontal lobes.

Again, a chain of events connects diet, the brain, and intelligence. How and what we eat determines whether we absorb sufficient iron. Iron in turn affects neurotransmitter systems governing particular parts of the brain. These parts of the brain are responsible for certain intellectual functions.

These studies by Dr. Tucker employed men whose daily variations in iron levels were broadly within normal limits. In a later study with truly iron-deficient men, he replicated several of the important findings, such as asymmetries of the effects of iron deficiency on the posterior portion of the brain. While based on a small number of men, and therefore preliminary, these studies raise the possibility that selective nutrient deficiencies have very selective effects upon the brain and hence upon the cognitive functions mediated by the brain. As before, the later development of the right hemisphere means that iron deficiency might affect intelligence depending on that portion of the brain well into adolescence.

HEAVY METAL

This discussion is not about the dangers of rock music (that's another story) but about the relation between diet and metal. Some minerals, like zinc and iron, are present in very small amounts in foods (hence their label as micronutrients), but they nevertheless play an important role in the body's metabolism; other minerals, like lead, mercury, and cadmium, which get into food unintentionally, have no known use by the body.

Heavy metals and diet interact in two ways. First, foods are often a medium through which heavy metals get into the body. Raw, unprocessed foods often contain significant quantities of metal pollutants, and metal composition of food is also increased by canning and packaging processes. Second, some nutrients in foods and the body counteract and/or reduce heavy metal toxicity by altering the absorption and excretion of the metals. The food-refining process, often involving heating, chemical purification, or pasteurization, often reduces the content of many of these protective micronutrients. It has long been known from animal research that some of the body's micronutrients, such as zinc, iron, and calcium, will offset the effects of exposure to heavy metals such as lead and cadmium.

Lead

A typical scenario for a young couple—let us call them John and Mary—might go somewhat as follows. John and Mary have been living in a small apartment, saving their money for a house. When Mary happily learns that she is pregnant, they purchase an older house which they can afford, knowing that between them they can fix it up to the standard they want. They plan to move in shortly before the baby is born. Among the first things to receive their attention is the old lead-based paint, which most well-informed couples now know constitutes a hazard to themselves and their children.

They begin the tedious process of stripping off the old paint, even sanding the walls and woodwork and burning the residue to remove every vestige of the dangerous surfaces. What they may not know, however, is that they have liberated a large amount of lead dust and fumes that may infiltrate the attic, crevices, and air-conditioning system, exposing them and their newborn child to just the hazard they were trying to avoid. If the plumbing does not leak, they may also be unaware of the original lead pipes often used in older housing. Precisely because lead pipes last a long time, they may give many years of untroubled service and, therefore, go unnoticed as a continuing source of lead traces in the drinking water. Even worse, modern plumbing sometimes uses soldering techniques in which lead infiltrates the water as it passes through the plumbing joints.

This could lead to a sense of false security about the problem. (It is therefore desirable to run the water tap for a minute or two before filling the coffee pot or the baby's formula bottle.

Like many young mothers or professional women, Mary may choose to work to help support the new mortgage and extra mouth to feed. As soon as she stops breast feeding, Mary hires a sitter and the child goes on the bottle. Reassured by the high mineral content in the supplemented formula, they don't know that it is much less well absorbed than the minerals from breast milk. Meanwhile, their baby is doubling its needs for iron, which is important as an inhibitor of lead absorption. Unless they have a good pediatrician who suggested baby iron supplements, the dull, irritable child on their hands might puzzle them.

Because lead is one of the most deadly neurotoxic substances known to man, even in minute quantities too small to produce overt symptoms of toxicity, it damages the central nervous system, perhaps permanently altering neuronal functions. Unfortunately, lead is also one of the most pervasive toxins in our society, thanks to the automobile and to the widespread use of lead in manufacturing, paint, and water pipes.

Lead is also often found in glazes applied to pottery, and though regulated in this country, tourists or import companies may slip such goods past customs. Occasionally, safeguards over manufacturing fail, as in a recent incident in which souvenir glasses honoring the Washington Redskin Super Bowl champions contained high quantities of lead in the painted emblem on the glasses. Many cribs still have lead paint, despite prohibitions banning its use. An area of paint as small as a penny can contain 50 or 100 times the amount of lead believed safe for consumption. Eaten over a few month's time by a baby, the paint could cause severe damage to the brain or kidneys. Scientists estimate that in the United States nearly 600,000 children below the age of 6 have elevated blood lead levels, and some studies show that as many as 30% of preschool children have elevated lead levels. The Environmental Protection Agency (EPA) monitors and regulates pollutants to our atmosphere. But in recent years they have often been unable (for political and economic reasons) to control the tide of heavy metals pervading our cities. Funds to the EPA for removing lead paint from homes only covered cases of confirmed lead toxicity (where blood levels are measured and found beyond the presumed safe limit). Recently, a Washington, D.C., television station conducted its own tests on the national capital's water supply and found an alarming amount of lead, well beyond EPA standards for safety. Like many cities, Washington D.C. has many older water pipes made of lead.

An interesting observation was made by some hyperactivity researchers during a large study of schools in the city of Ottawa, Canada. Dr. Ronald Trites and colleagues gave our teacher rating scale for symptoms of hyperactivity in the classroom to teachers, who rated over 14,000 children in their classrooms. In order to see the distribution of hyperactivity in the city, they created topographic maps which, instead of showing the height of mountains, plotted the peaks of hyperactivity. The map that resulted showed a large corridor of hyperactivity peaks running through the center of the city. This corridor exactly corresponded to the path of the Queen's Highway through Ottawa. They suspected that the airborne lead from automobiles was the cause. Studies of lead content in the soil confirms that it is much denser near the highway. Thus, homes situated near major freeways or highway arteries may be particularly at risk for higher lead content. Standards for lead in gasoline have undergone many flip-flops during the course of a continuing battle between automobile manufacturers and public agencies and interest groups.

Children pick up lead from soil, from auto fumes, or from contaminated foodstuffs. The lead is then partially absorbed into their teeth. The relation of lead to classroom learning and behavior was strikingly uncovered in a 1979 study of the lead deposited in the teeth of 2,000 lower-middle income Boston school children.[4] Teachers answered the following questions about the children (without knowing the results of the lead examinations):

1. Is this child easily distracted during his work?
2. Can he persist with a task for a reasonable amount of time?
3. Can this child work independently and complete assigned tasks with minimal assistance?
4. Is his approach to tasks disorganized (constantly misplacing pencils, books, etc.)?
5. Do you consider this child hyperactive?
6. Is he over-excitable and impulsive?
7. Is he easily frustrated by difficulties?
8. Is he a daydreamer?
9. Can he follow simple directions?
10. Can he follow a sequence of directions?
11. In general, is this child functioning as well in the classroom as other children his own age?

For every question there was a dose–response relationship to lead levels in the dentin of the children's teeth; that is, for every question, the higher the number of endorsements, the higher the lead level in the children.

The role of lead in hyperactivity was also documented in studies of children in New York City. Researchers found that in a sizable sample of hyperactive children, for whom there were no known sources of their problem, lead levels in the blood were much higher than in nonhyperactive control children. When the lead was flushed from the body by chemical means, the childrens' hyperactivity diminished. Many hyperactive children have had birth trauma, infections or illnesses, or some known injury to the brain which adequately explains the origin of their problems. But most children's hyperactivity is unexplained. This study shows that a sizable portion of these unexplained cases may have brain impairment due to lead.

Known dietary influences on lead absorption, excretion, and toxicity include iron, calcium, zinc, and thiamin (vitamin B_1). These nutrients, which prevent lead from entering the bloodstream and retard its absorption in the gut, are often deficient in growing children. In animal studies, thiamin supplements caused a rapid excretion of lead from the body, suggesting that thiamin-deficient children may be at higher risk for accumulation of lead in the tissues over time. Despite this knowledge, programs for supplementing diets in children most at risk for lead intoxication are scarce.

Zinc and Cadmium

From our discussion of iron above, it seems obvious that children most at risk for iron deficiency are also those most at risk from the harmful effects of lead. The same is true for children with inadequate zinc and thiamin in their diets.

A large study carried out in rural areas of eastern Maryland illustrates the complex influence of diet on metal toxicity.[5] The investigators measured the dietary intake of several hundred children, and also measured their IQ with a standard intelligence test. Somewhat to their puzzlement, they found that children who ate whole wheat bread tended to have higher IQs than those who ate white bread. The investigators were careful to examine variables—such as socioeconomic status and education—that might be accounting for the IQ differences, and they ruled them out as the explanation. They speculated that the lower levels of zinc in the white bread (the zinc contained in the part of the wheat kernel having been lost in processing) led to more toxicity from heavy metals. Other nutrients, such as thiamin, are also lost during the milling process of wheat but are usually added back as supplements.

In this study researchers also found that the intake of refined carbohydrates showed a strong correlation with the amount of cadmium contained in the childrens' hair. Although hair is often an unreliable source of exposure to metals, they took particular care to overcome the limitations of usual testing methods. Cadmium is a metal with no known nutritional value, and like lead, is neurotoxic. It is often a by-product of industrial manufacturing, and a major source is thought to be cigarette smoke.

Even when the cadmium levels were controlled by statistical means, there was still an inverse relationship between refined carbohydrates and IQ; that is, higher carbohydrate intake correlated with lower IQ. They noted that the ratio of zinc to cadmium was much lower in the refined grains than in whole grains. Thus, something about the refining process may have either raised the cadmium levels or lowered the zinc levels. They pointed out that certain carbonated colas contained higher concentrations of cadmium than the allowable limits set by the EPA for ordinary drinking water. In accord with the IQ data, they also found that reading levels were significantly lower in children with lower zinc levels, again, probably because the zinc protects against the adverse effects of cadmium exposure. *The dietary factors accounted for almost 20% of the variation in reading levels.*

A significant source of cadmium is the smoke from cigarettes. Pregnant mothers who smoke probably don't contribute cadmium directly to the child in utero because cadmium does not cross into the placenta. But parents who smoke in the presence of young children may be directly adding toxic cadmium to their child's body. Because the body excretes cadmium very slowly, cadmium tends to accumulate over time, thus being a particular hazard to younger children. Because cadmium also increases the toxicity of lead, it represents a special hazard to children of smoking parents who live in high-lead environments.

Zinc is an essential molecule in over 70 of the body's enzymes, and it is essential for rapidly growing tissues. Deficiencies cause impairment of cellular growth and division and retardation of amino acid utilization. Paradoxically, cadmium (which competes with zinc for absorption in the body), is a by-product of zinc refining processes. How the cadmium gets into the food supply is still something of a mystery, though cigarette smoke and the practice of dumping manufacturing wastes into waterways are good bets.

As with iron, fiber in cereals retards zinc absorption, and people with high cereal, low-protein diets may become zinc deficient. In normal diets this is not usually a problem, but some extremists, alarmed by the Surgeon General's call for more fiber in the diet to avert colon cancer, end up consuming a virtually all-fiber diet. Food processing and cooking can also alter the availability of zinc. Also like iron, zinc deficiencies are greater in inner cities than in suburban households.

Like most nutrients, zinc interacts with other nutrients in the diet. Scientists believe that the levels of phosphorus and nitrogen (found in protein and amino acids) in the diet play a critical role in determining zinc requirements. For example, if protein intake is high and phosphorus intake is low, the bodily requirement for zinc is almost doubled compared with a low-protein, low-phosphorus intake. (Peanuts, turkey, fish, pork, milk, and chicken are particularly high in phosphorus; and because calcium helps absorb the phosphorus, milk is an especially good source.) Because zinc is an essential molecule for insulin, low zinc levels may dispose one to hypoglycemia.

NUTRITION AND IQ: WHAT SHOULD WE DO?

We have seen that the nutritional environment dramatically affects both verbal and nonverbal forms of intelligence. Nutrition also modifies basic subskills making up general IQ. Beginning with the early stages of brain development in the womb and extending through adolescence, the quality and quantity of nutrients affect general IQ and development of its constituent parts. Good maternal diets counteract some of the known hazards to the fetus, such as maternal smoking (and probably the passive smoke provided by others). Adequate intake of nutrients like iron, zinc, calcium, and the B vitamins lessens the impact of many unavoidable toxic environmental hazards. One may not be able to move to a smoke- and pollution-free idyllic environment, but a good diet in childhood may reduce the harm of exposure.

Should one therefore supplement the regular diet in children with vitamins and minerals? Most nutritionists and pediatricians say that this is unnecessary if the basic diet is adequate. One exception is iron, which is usually given as a supplement to young children by pediatricians, especially when they first begin to eat solid foods. Since breast milk contains nonheme iron, other foods affect its absorption. For example, one study showed that introducing solid foods to the breast-fed infant reduced iron stores to zero. Another exception is vitamin D—the sunshine vitamin. Because polluted environments filter out sunlight, and many mothers live totally indoor lifestyles, they often require supplements. Finally, the fluoride content of human milk is quite low, so breast-fed infants need some tap water and perhaps supplements, depending upon the fluoride content of the local water supply (well water in rural areas is a problem).

Adequate nutrition for brain functions may not be the same as those for general health. But what is adequate nutrition for brain function? The guidelines for adequate intake of nutrients (the RDAs) unfortunately are poor guides for individual children. Many of them come from values extrapolated from adult studies, and many of those come from other countries with very different conditions. Almost all reflect the relation of nutritional ingredients to purely physical, not mental, growth.

An important recent study from India illustrates the problem of relying upon RDA values as a guideline here. A large number of vitamin-deficient children got supplements of B vitamins or a placebo. Although at the end of a year there was improvement in their *biochemical* status, more than half were physiologically deficient, according to standard RDA criteria. Nevertheless, the children still showed improvement in measures of *behavioral* function, such as sensory–motor tests. Thus, as the authors say, "functional impact of vitamin supplements may be seen even in the absence of clear-cut clinical or biochemical change." We saw above that a well-nourished group of British youngsters had an impressive nonverbal IQ gain after supplementation with vitamins and minerals for a year, even though they were not deficient by conventional criteria.

As far as *mental functions*, we do not yet know what the optimum levels for nutrients really are. Supplementation with vitamins and minerals would seem to be a rational course, though relevant data are mostly lacking. Even with macronutrients like protein, we cannot be too glib in stating that more is necessarily better. Earlier in this chapter we described a study in which pregnant mothers produced children with better cognitive function when the mothers took a high-protein supplement early in pregnancy. We did not mention, however, that the high-protein group *also had a higher mortality* in those mothers who delivered prematurely or had past problems with shortened gestation. This special, high-risk subgroup may have been unable to cope with the bodily stress incurred by a sudden increase in their habitual intake of protein. Once again, it looks as if tinkering with mother nature may entail some risks.

There is no mental disorder or cognitive function known that cannot arise from severe nutrient deficiencies of one sort or another. Frank dietary deficiencies are still common, particularly among the poor, but these severe deficiency states are avoidable by good nutritional practices. However, this says little about what is optimal for the brain and its functions. We still must admit our ignorance when it comes to the ideal diet for mental as opposed to physical functions.

One thing is clear from the available information, however. Large national surveys show that there are certain *patterns* of eating which are more associated with impaired mental function, including apathy and irritability (though typically, behavior gets short shrift as an outcome measure). The worst diets tend to be high in diet drinks ("nonsugary beverages") and low in dairy products; the best are high in dairy products and soups and lower in sugary foods and beverages. (By implication, poor eating patterns include high consumption of both diet and sugary beverages.) The studies described in this chapter give only a hint, but perhaps an important one, that variety and avoiding *restricted* diets may be more important than trying to contrive a chemically ideal diet.

Americans are becoming much more diet conscious, both for esthetic and health reasons. But there is a danger that all this raised consciousness about food will backfire. It is easy to mistakenly extrapolate good nutritional ideas for adults to improperly restricted diets for children, or go to extremes when changing the diet in accord with new knowledge about cancer or heart disease.

A common mistake, for example, is to interpret the Surgeon General's advice of lower fat and cholesterol in the diet in a way that causes children to get too little of the essential fats required for brain growth. Feeding skim milk to infants in the interest of cholesterol restriction is one such mistake. A Washington, D.C., television station recently showed proud mothers with their babies taking aerobics classes and sharing a low-fat diet. Retarded brain growth in the service of healthier hearts seems like a poor trade-off.

Many pediatricians now recommend breast feeding for the first 6 months or year, followed by 2%-fat milk in the preschool child. Dietary requirements for cholesterol in infants and children are not known, though the cholesterol in breast milk is higher than in whole cow's milk. Some have suggested, though not proved, that some cholesterol in the infant diet is important in being able to properly handle cholesterol later. Cow's milk, whether whole or low-fat, is not as adequate a source of usable protein as breast milk.

Less well known is the tendency of some parents not to allow fish or shellfish in the diet (for fear of allergies), thus eliminating the main source of omega-3 fatty acids, an essential nutrient for the brain and retina. (Soybean oil is much richer in this type of essential fatty acid than safflower oil, so that restricting cooking to the latter could also seriously limit adequate intake of omega-3 fatty acids.)

Every effort should be made to eliminate exposure to toxic metals and insecticides in the food and environment of children. The emasculation of the funding to the EPA needs reversal. The role of the federal government is crucial, and more, not less, action is required. The policy of restricting lead removal only to homes of people already identified as having lead toxicity is a dangerous limitation that seriously hampers removal of undetected sources of lead in homes where there are children with significant but subclinical problems (such as learning disorders). In the long run it is a false savings of human resources.

"Behavioral toxicity" should become as important as physical toxicity in the FDA's evaluation of food product safety. The Soviet Union and Eastern bloc countries are well ahead of us in this regard. In the tradition of their great Nobel Prize winner Ivan Pavlov, they often use tests of learning and behavior in dogs to screen foods and drugs. It is only very recently that the threats to mental growth and development of environmental hazards like lead, pollutants, pesticides, and herbicides have received any attention at all in this country. Until the public insists on committing more resources to scientists willing to study nutritional effects on *mental* processes, specific guidelines for optimal behavioral nutrition in children will elude us.

CHAPTER SEVEN

Food Additives and Food Allergies

FOOD ADDITIVES

We have already seen how food additives *unintended* for human consumption, such as heavy metals, pose a considerable threat to children's health, mental growth, and development. Much more controversial are *intentional* food additives, used for cosmetic purposes, flavoring, texturizing, and preserving foods. Most people agree that the unintentional additives are harmful and require elimination wherever possible, even when their role in health is uncertain. But there are sharp disagreements about the harmfulness of intentional food additives, with the food industry generally arguing for their safety and their value in the esthetics of food choice; while consumer advocates and some scientists regard them as either toxic or, at best, as worthless frills with a potential for harm in special circumstances or excessive amounts. A key difference between these two kinds of additives, unintentional and intentional, is that the former are difficult to control and eliminate, while some choice is possible with the latter, both in terms of labeling and outright elimination. In this chapter we will ask whether the intentional addi-

157

tives do pose a threat to the mental health of children and whether diets eliminating them work.

FEINGOLD'S THEORY OF FOOD ADDITIVES
AND HYPERACTIVITY

A charismatic, white-haired, brilliant and persuasive advocate, Dr. Feingold was in his 70s when he first proposed a link between food additives, behavior, and learning in children. Feingold had already published observations on food additives as a cause of allergy in 1973, but in 1974, before the American Medical Association, he broadened this idea to include the role of food additives as a cause of hyperactivity and learning disabilities. While recovering from life-threatening surgery in 1975, he wrote a best-selling book, *Why Your Child Is Hyperactive*. He summarized clinical observations of many years from his practice of pediatric allergy, basing his theory that additives cause hyperactivity and learning disorders upon his success with an additive-free diet.

Feingold's hypothesis about children originated in his observations of an adult. The patient was a young woman who was allergic to the yellow food dye tartrazine. She happened to be in psychotherapy at the time for various emotional problems. After placement on a tartrazine-free diet for her allergy, she reported that she was suddenly improving in her psychological symptoms as well. She was better able to concentrate and felt less restless. The symptoms reappeared when she went back to her regular diet. This case sparked Dr. Feingold's idea of a connection between food additives and hyperactivity in children.

This case also suggested something about the composition of the diet. A small number of people allergic to tartrazine are allergic to aspirin as well. Aspirin is a salicylate (acetylsalicylic acid), and salicylates, found in many fruits and vegetables, are naturally occurring compounds similar to aspirin. Because of the chemical similarity of natural salicylates to aspirin and tartrazine, and because some people are allergic to these compounds, Dr. Feingold concluded that he should also eliminate *natural* salicylates. Thus, he reasoned that people may have unsuspected allergies to those fruits and vegetables containing salicylates, just as they sometimes have for aspirin and tartrazine.

The weight of his authority at first caused Feingold's theory to be taken seriously by scientists. He had already made some fundamental discoveries in allergy and had written a well-regarded textbook of pediatric allergy. Many years earlier he had published studies showing a correlation between allergic symptoms in young women and emotional disturbance as shown by their psychological tests. But unlike the earlier observations, dismissed as simply showing that chronic illness causes psychological disturbance, his hyperactivity book was a best-seller, appealing particularly to those parents who suspected that their children's behavior was food related.

Dr. Feingold appeared before the Senate Select Committee on Nutrition and persuaded many congressmen that food additives pose a serious hazard to the mental health of children. He appeared on radio and television and tirelessly spoke before national groups concerned with child mental health and learning disabilities. Before long there were hundreds of local chapters of the Feingold Association, a movement that is still strong today. The persistence of these mutual support groups, despite strong scientific criticisms of the theory, attests to the firm convictions which Feingold's style and message elicited.

Parents were less concerned about the supporting data for the theory than about the potential for harm which Feingold emphasized. With children, there was the possibility, he pointed out, that additives could accumulate in the body over time and damage the nervous system. The message fell on receptive ears. It focused attention on a problem people already vaguely suspected from living in an increasingly polluted environment.

Time and again he noted that children referred to him for allergies, because they had constant rhinitis (stuffy nose), tearing, puffy eyes, or other allergic signs, were also hyperactive and having trouble in school. He noted with astonishment that these behavioral symptoms often "dramatically improved" in as many as 50% of the children treated with an additive-free diet.

It was no secret among scientists that a huge number of additives litter foods, put there for a variety of reasons, some cosmetic and some nutritional (for example, to preserve the foods or retard bacteria). Feingold pointed out that simple inspection of government figures reveals a frightening list of chemicals added to foods (see table below).

Classification of Intentional Additives in Foods[a]

Additive	No. of kinds
Preservatives	33
Antioxidants	28
Sequestrants (agents to bind unwanted materials)	45
Surface active agents	111
Stabilizers, thickeners	39
Bleaching and maturing agents	24
Buffers, acids, alkalis	60
Food colors	34
Nonnutritive and special dietary sweeteners	4
Nutritive supplements	117
Flavorings	
Synthetic	1610
Natural	502
Miscellaneous	
Yeast foods, texturizers, firming agents, Anticaking agents, enzymes	157
Total number of additives	2764

[a]Compiled by the National Science Foundation in 1965.

Looking at this list, Feingold drew some obvious conclusions. First, there are some additives that do have a valid food-related purpose. For example, distribution and storage of foods in the Western world would be difficult without preservatives and antioxidants. But the largest number of additives—synthetic colors and flavors—are merely cosmetic. They add nothing to the food value and have often come under fire as potential carcinogens (cancer-causing agents).

People like pretty foods, and food manufacturers are well aware that bright colors and more intense flavors sell better than pale or bland "natural"-tasting foods. Even dog food has to be attractive to dog owners or they won't buy it, though dogs are color blind and wouldn't know the difference. (I once whimsically suggested to Dr. Feingold that I intended to publish a book called *Why Your Dog Is Hyperactive*, and he responded that it was no joke—dogs *did* calm down with additive-free food.)

Feingold saw the progressive increase in the presence of additives in the food supply paralleled by an increase in behavior and learning problems among children. He thought the two trends were causally related. Critics argued that increases in the GNP and many other changes of modern society followed the same course as hyperactivity, without being its cause (see table on p. 162 for Feingold's diet).

The salicylate part of the theory caused controversy and presented problems from the start. First, the diet eliminated a great many natural sources of vitamin C, which could affect many aspects of body growth and metabolism, including the ability to resist disease. Early studies confirmed that strict adherence to the diet did lead to reduced intake of vitamin C. Second, scientists pointed out that there were no reliable measures of the amount of salicylates in foods—Feingold's list came from old German data based upon unproven methods. Finally, authorities in the field of allergy doubted the so-called cross-reactivity between natural salicylates, tartrazine, and aspirin.

Feingold's Elimination Diet

Part I:
Artificial colors and flavors
Butylated hydroxytoluene (BHT)
Butylated hydroxyanisole (BHA)

Part II: Selected foods with natural salicylates

Almonds	Peaches
Apples (including cider and cider vinegar)	Plums or prunes
	Tangerines
Apricots	Cucumbers and pickles
Berries	Green peppers
Cherries	Tomatoes
Currants	Cloves
Grapes or raisins (including wine and wine vinegar)	Coffee
	Tea
Nectarines	Oil of wintergreen
Oranges	

Therefore, Feingold dropped the salicylate part of the diet and agreed that the reactions were not allergic in nature (we will discuss allergy later in this chapter). But he felt that the salicylate part of his diet was not essential anyway and that synthetic food dyes and flavors remained significant causes of hyperactivity and learning problems, and, most importantly, that these symptoms disappeared after eliminating artificial dyes and flavors. Even if it turned out there was no true allergic mechanism involved, success in reducing symptoms by eliminating additives from the diet stood on its own.

Feingold agreed that one can be *sensitive* to a food without being allergic. But changing the hypothesis from allergy to sensitivity made it much more difficult to prove. For there are no tests or predictors of food sensitivity reactions, whereas immunologic tests can detect allergy. Allergies, as we shall see later, are reactions of the immune system in attempting to defend the body against invading substances (allergens). Sensitivities can reflect the irritation from foods or substances on the stomach or mucosal tract. For example, some people are sensitive to aspirin because it irritates their stomach lining. Others are truly allergic to aspirin because it evokes a reaction from the immune system.

One reason for singling out the food dyes was their checkered safety history. Most of the food industry's artificial colors come from coal tar and have a low molecular weight, which allows them to cross cell membranes easily. Although recognized as safe by the FDA, coal tar derivatives (not to be confused with the tar in cigarettes) had long been of concern because of possible cancer-causing effects. As a result of new data at about the time Feingold was proposing his theory, the FDA banned some of the dyes (for example, the red dye no. 4), claiming they were possibly carcinogenic. Because of their sheer numbers in the food additive list, the synthetic dyes seemed like the most obvious additives to exclude from children's diets.

Testing Feingold's theory was not easy.[1] First, any strict diet in children requires considerable effort to get compliance and cooperation. Neither children nor parents find it easy to maintain the level of vigilance required to avoid occasional infractions of a diet, especially when trying to exclude so many foods. Even though he dropped the allergic theory of the reactions, Feingold still maintained that symptoms might recur from even the tiniest amount of the offending food, and this explanation could always account for failure of the diet to work in children treated for hyperactivity. People tended to forget that toothpaste, chewing gum, and even vitamins are often artificially flavored and colored. This ubiquity of additives makes the theory difficult to falsify.

Second, the very act of changing the diet, of giving the child a lot of attention, and of being openly gratified when behavior changes for the better are themselves factors in changing behavior. Reinforcing positive behavior and ignoring unwanted behavior is the cornerstone of behavior therapy. If the effects were created by placebo response and parents praised the changes, then this might set up a cycle of improved behavior.

Dr. Alan Zametkin, a scientist at NIMH, proposed that the Feingold diet effects were explainable by "the carrot hypothesis."[2] This hypothesis states that diet therapy is a subtle form of operant conditioning commonly used in behavior modification programs. Considering the child "ill" instead of "naughty" makes the food rather than the child the culprit. Punishment for deviant behavior often makes behavior worse because of the attention paid to it. Parents develop an attitude that the environmental setting is at fault instead. This new attitude makes them change things that contribute to the hyperactivity rather than just punishing the child.

Second, since restricted food items in the diet are often things that children like to eat most, such as colas and candy, removing them takes away reinforcement (reward) for bad behavior. Even if there is no improvement in the child's behavior due to the change in diet, parents may see changes which they attribute to the diet.

Finally, because Feingold was an allergist and not a psychiatrist or psychologist, he did not use any standard criteria for describing behavior patterns in his patients, making it difficult to know just what types of problems they had. Some critics wondered whether his patients were truly hyperactive and learning-disabled or whether they were simply mildly irritating or anxious children who got better with a little attention or from the treatments for their allergies.

But despite these limitations, Feingold's observations of dramatic responses to the additive-free diet persuaded him that whatever was happening, the effects were important. Over half of the parents who tried the diet were thrilled with the results, so he reasonably assumed that the diet therapy deserved the credit. He often noted that the ability to turn the symptoms on and off with the diet and challenges (or infractions) was the best scientific proof of a causal relation between food additives and the behavioral symptoms.

But scientists are more skeptical. Turning the symptoms on and off by adding and removing the suspected causative agents is only one part of the reasoning process about the efficacy of a treatment. It is always possible that the symptoms come and go because of observer bias in favor of the treatment; or that the patient turns the symptoms on and off to please the doctor; or because of unconscious needs to comply with expectations. There is an old adage in psychopharmacology which says "Use a new drug quickly while it is still effective," because many new treatments initially produce remarkable placebo effects in the hands of hopeful therapists and patients, only to wane over time. (Hope, as Jerome Frank showed in his seminal studies of psychotherapy, is one of the most important contributions that a good psychotherapist provides.)

Case Studies

The Feingold hypothesis of food additives was especially appealing because it pointed the way, not only to possible causes of hyperactivity but to a simple and effective treatment as well. Therefore, when people heard of Dr. Feingold's theory, they took it seriously. Taking nothing for granted, the first step in testing it was to see if the basic observations of improvement on the diet were correct. I was eager to see whether I could find carefully diagnosed cases that showed the dramatic cures, documented with daily measures of the children's behavior before, during, and after the diet. Our team included child psychiatrists who could confirm the diagnosis by careful interviews with the families and by physical and psychiatric examination of the children. The parents rated the children's behavior with daily checklists of hyperactive behaviors rather than giving a single global summary after the treatment was over.

A week or so before a child started the diet, we asked the parents to keep a record of what the child ate and to begin recording his behavior (most were boys, as is most often the case for hyperactive children). The parents continued these observations for 2 weeks or so while the child followed the diet and again for a period when the diet returned to normal. Thus, these case studies provided an off–on–off manipulation of food additives, and if being on the diet produced changes, they ought to be apparent compared with the beginning and ending periods, when the regular diet was in effect.

In practically every case of a dozen or so children, the results confirmed Feingold's observations of a significant decrease in the level of hyperactive symptoms. Symptoms were high during the regular diet, dropped off substantially during the additive-free diet period, and returned to their pre-diet level when the diet ended. In several children the effects were "dramatic," just as Feingold claimed. The children showed symptom decreases (that is, in restlessness, inattentiveness, aggressiveness, inability to get along with others, etc.) that were often from a very abnormal to a completely normal range. This part of the experiment was therefore a complete success and convinced us that the idea was worth studying further. The symptoms did turn off with the diet, and they turned back on again after resumption of the regular pattern of eating. The results were often just as impressive as those with psychoactive drugs, and if they were real and not just placebo effects, there would be a good argument for abandoning drug therapy altogether.

As Feingold had already discovered, I found that these initial data were quite persuasive to lay audiences, without further adornment by double-blind trials. These early results convinced most parents (and even many doctors) that Feingold's diet was effective. Many parents felt that there was no need for further study. They enthusiastically accepted the findings at face value.

This enthusiasm was quite evident when Dr. Feingold and I accepted invitations to speak to an audience of parents and educators at a meeting of the ACLD (Association for Children with Learning Disabilities) in 1976. This parent and professional support group was having its annual meeting in New York City. An unusually large number of people packed the hotel ballroom to hear Dr. Feingold's new theory.

He spoke without notes and showed just two slides (the tables given above). His speech was powerful, moving, and convincing. His concern for children was obvious; his impatience with the federal government and the food industry for their foot-dragging drew immediate sympathy from everyone. His scientific background in allergy and his knowledge were impressive. When he sat down the applause was thunderous.

I showed my slides of the case studies I had carried out with my colleague, Dr. Charles Goyette. They seemed to support Dr. Feingold's case, but although I said I hoped Dr. Feingold was right, my main message was: be careful, we don't yet have *double-blind studies*, and these findings of mine and those of Feingold might be placebo effects.

Pseudo-Diet Studies

It was inevitable that scientists would require more foolproof evidence. The federal Office of Education gave our team, then at the University of Pittsburgh Medical School, funds to carry out a controlled study comparing the Feingold diet with a dummy or comparison diet. Dr. Feingold helped us in composing the diets and with advice about what to look for. The dummy diet is equivalent to a placebo—a treatment that looks and tastes like the real thing without the key ingredients found in the real diet.

Well-diagnosed hyperactive children stayed on each diet for a month, half getting one diet first, followed by the other diet. One diet was Feingold's additive-free diet, and the other (taken from Feingold's allergy textbook) had many of the nonspecific features of the real diet; that is, it was a diet that required careful reading of labels in shopping, was difficult to follow, and was vaguely familiar as a diet prescribed by allergists for some children (it was an egg- and mold-free diet). We measured how difficult each diet was to follow by questionnaires given afterwards to the parents (they turned out to be equally difficult to follow), and we measured the children's hyperactive behaviors by both teacher and parent observations. We carefully interviewed the parents about the effects and made our own independent judgments about improvement.

After a month on one diet, the patients switched to the other one. We had told parents there were two Feingold diets, and they would have an opportunity to see which was best. (This was true; both were Feingold diets, but our instructions contained a little white lie of omission since only one diet was the real diet for hyperactivity.) We made them feel that the egg- and mold-free diet (the control diet) was potentially just as good as the other one. This was still early enough that parents were familiar from publicity with the name of the diet's author, but not its contents. After 4 weeks on each diet, we analyzed the results.

The results were promising but not clear cut. Although the improvement in the two diet conditions was no different for parent observations, there was a greater improvement as measured by teacher ratings on the hyperactivity diet. However, this effect was only true for the group that got the real diet second. This weakens the results considerably because an effective treatment ought to work whether it comes first or second.

But this difference between parents and teachers is not all that different from some trials of stimulant drugs, where teachers will often see effects missed by parents, either because of their better conditions for observation or because the drug wears off by the time the children get home. Still, the results were disappointing as far as revealing consistent effects.

There were 2 children out of the 13 studied, however, whose responses proved especially interesting. Both exhibited substantial reductions in symptoms that changed in parallel at home and school. When we followed up the entire group 2 years later, these were the only two children whose parents had kept them on the experimental diet, and both sets of parents felt the changes in these children were still substantial, tending to get worse when the children were taken off the diet temporarily or when they committed infractions.

Hearing of these findings, a group from the University of Wisconsin, headed by Dr. Preston Harley, spent a day going over our methods and results and decided to carry out a better-controlled study themselves. We were all aware of some of the flaws in our study—most importantly that the parents were not blind to the diets and might have been subtly biased in favor of one or the other. The small size of the sample (13) was another problem.

The Wisconsin group carried out a meticulous and heroic study improving and enlarging upon our study. The participants were 36 hyperactive school-age boys and 10 normal preschoolers. They studied younger normal children because it was felt they might be especially vulnerable to food additives. The measurement of changes during the diet periods was much more comprehensive. They included our parent and teacher ratings, but they also added direct classroom observations from trained observers and a battery of neuropsychological tests.

The most important feature of this study, however, was replacing *every item of food in the households* and supplying everything the families ate in coded packages. They removed all other foods from the pantry to minimize the possibility of diet infractions. Parents could not tell in any way which foods in the coded packages contained artificial colors and flavors and which did not. They even had foods that were made to look like they were on the forbidden list by coloring them with natural rather than artificial colors.

In addition, whenever the child attended a birthday party or had a meal away from home, the experimenters supplied all the food. If the child's class had snacks or birthday parties, they supplied the food for the whole class. Thus, they answered the most important criticism by Feingold of other studies—that violations of the diet were not controlled for—by insuring that the children always got the prescribed diet. The study also maintained a very effective double blind, because parents asked to guess which was the real diet could not do so better than chance.

The results of this study were also mixed. This time, it was the parents who noticed a significant improvement but, once again, only in the group that received the real additive-free diet second. Teachers saw no differences in behavior during the two diets. None of the direct observations of behavior in the classroom or psychological tests showed any effects of the diet. Given these limitations, it is not surprising that the Wisconsin group concluded that Feingold's hypothesis was disconfirmed.

However, there was one significant finding that was difficult to dismiss: in contrast to the results with the schoolchildren, all 10 of the mothers of preschoolers rated their children's behavior as worse while on the regular diet than while the children were on the additive-free diet. The probability of this result occurring by chance was astronomically small. There could be only two possible interpretations: either the parents somehow broke the double blind and were unconsciously biased in favor of the real diet; or the additive-free diet did reduce symptoms in the preschoolers, much as Feingold's hypothesis predicted.

Since the experimenters' superior methods argued for the validity of the findings with the older children, the argument ought to apply equally to the preschoolers.

But why would improvements occur only in the preschoolers and not the older children? After all, Feingold had never claimed there was any age limitation on the effects of the diet in his own practice. If the order effect, of improving on the Feingold diet only when it came second, was due to placebo, then why did this not happen with the preschoolers? If the effects on parent ratings in the older children were real and not placebo effects, then why did not similar effects occur for the direct observations by trained observers? Since consistent results across different measures and in different laboratories is the sine qua non of scientific respectability for a hypothesis, most scientists simply concluded that the Feingold diet was unproven. This was the interpretation of the Wisconsin group, though they were at a loss to explain the surprising effects on the preschoolers.

Challenge Studies

Because of the inconclusive findings and unanswered questions from the elimination diet studies, investigators realized that a different approach was necessary. Several research groups decided to carry out challenge studies, in which the children would remain on the elimination diet the whole time (nonblind) but be randomly peppered with known doses of food additives or placebo in a double-blind fashion. In this way, they avoided the difficulties of matching a whole diet with the experimental diet, and food additives were introduced in a known amount. Perhaps making the children *worse* after they improved on the diet would be easier than maintaining a double blind between two very different diets.

The "dose" of artificial colors chosen for the challenge was set at the 90th percentile for the average intake of children; that is, only 10% of the population would be likely to ingest more than this in a single day. If the artificial colors made children worse than the placebo challenges while on the diet, this would be evidence that the colors caused the symptoms. By eliminating additives from the diet as far as possible, and knowing that infractions would sometimes occur, but also knowing when, it would be possible to control just how much food additives they were getting, not relying entirely on the elimination diet.

The Nutrition Foundation arranged to develop an appetizing (though somewhat large) chocolate cookie containing either artificial colors or no additives. Since the cookies looked and tasted alike, we could carry out a study that was unquestionably blind. Moreover, since we would only use children already confirmed as responding to the elimination diet, there was little likelihood that nonresponders would be masking the results. The Nutrition Foundation arranged for Nabisco to make, package, and code the cookies. They kept the code a secret so that there was no chance of our team peeking through the double blind until after the experiment was over.

Hyperactive children included in this study had to be on Feingold's diet for 1 month and to show at least a 25% reduction in their symptoms while on the diet. After this period they continued the diet but ate two cookies every day for 2 months. Every 2 weeks we switched the cookies from the active ones containing additives to the placebo ones (without the parents, children, or us knowing which was which). Some children got active cookies in the first 2 weeks while others got placebo, and then we reversed the order so that there would be no consistent order across the whole group.

About this time, an engineer had adapted a task used for testing attention in pilots for testing with children. He suggested that it might be a good measure of attention in hyperactive children. The child had to control a cursor on a moving chart with one hand and push a button with another whenever a warning light went on. The difficulty of dividing attention between the two tasks seemed like a good test of the distractibility and limited attention so often evident in hyperactive children. The test was brief enough that we could measure the children's performance several times over a few hours after they had taken one of the loaded or placebo cookies, and not have to rely on parent measures of activity level which might not be accurate or sensitive.

The effect of the challenges on parent and teacher ratings produced nothing. This was the first clear-cut negative result in the several studies to that time. The children did not behave worse at school *or* home after eating the loaded cookies. But the tracking task showed us why that might be the case.

Several of the children showed a clear deterioration in their tracking performance after the loaded cookies, and not after the placebo cookies, *but only within the first hour.* Thus, perhaps the effects were there all along, but since parents and teachers were looking at effects across the whole day, they failed to see the sudden spurt of hyperactivity that lasted only for a short time. The first cookie was taken with breakfast, and the effects may have dissipated by the time the children got to school. The second was taken at dinner, but if the effects were short-lived, parents might miss them. This would be just like a pharmacological effect with a short-acting drug.

To many, including us, this explanation seemed like grasping at straws. It wouldn't explain the so-called dramatic effects which parents were supposedly able to see; but we decided that we could not ignore the possibility of a transient, druglike effect.

Therefore, we repeated the challenge study, confining parent observations to the hour immediately after dinnertime. To our surprise, this time the results were statistically significant: during the loaded-cookie days, parents did rate the children as worse than on the placebo days. Unfortunately, the Pittsburgh winter caused so many school absences that the teacher data were largely unusable, but this only further strengthened the possibility that because the kids were home more often, parents could better appreciate the changes in behavior.

The results of this study were encouraging enough to try one more attempt at replication. But by now we were running out of hyperactive children and parents who were willing to put up with our experiments. We had screened hundreds of children, just to get a small number we could be sure were clear-cut cases of hyperactivity. We stretched our entrance criteria, allowing some children into the study who were not as definitively diagnosed as previously. The outcome of the study was clear: once again there were no significant effects, though we had to wonder whether our change in entrance criteria had something to do with this. But since other experimenters found similar results, in the late 1970s the case appeared closed. A consensus conference of scientists, held under the auspices of the NIMH, concluded that the Feingold diet was largely discredited and due to placebo effects.

I have gone through this series of tantalizing and disappointing studies to give some flavor of just how difficult it is to turn a plausible diet theory into confirmed fact. When I last reviewed the Feingold diet studies from around the world, not counting the case reports and poorly controlled trials, the box score was 9 for, 9 against. In baseball or hockey we would probably say the series was dead even, and insist on a rubber match. But scientists play the game differently. Without clear and *consistent* evidence, they reject the theory.

But the finality of this rejection may have been premature. The best study, from the Wisconsin group, had shown a clear advantage of the Feingold diet over the regular diet *for the preschoolers*, a finding never explained. Most of the studies had dealt with older children.

Additionally, another group headed by Dr. Bernard Weiss,

an outstanding psychologist and toxicologist in collaboration with an excellent nutrition department at the University of California at Berkley, saw two important flaws in most of the studies. First, they felt the dose of food colors used in the challenge studies was too low. Second, they argued that there should be enough challenges for each child that a complete experiment could take place *for each individual child*. The previous studies were group results, and averages might mask a few children responding well to the diet.

Weiss's group carried out a study on 22 younger hyperactive children (most were preschoolers, though some were 7-year-olds) over a period of 77 days, with many random double-blind challenges using a much larger dose. They measured the particular symptoms that parents had identified as being unique for their child by direct observations with trained observers, by ratings taken over the telephone, and by counting of specific behaviors from the mothers.

One child, a 3-year-old girl, consistently showed worsening of symptoms on the challenge days compared to the placebo days. In absolute numbers the results might seem insignificant, *but for this one child*, the problem was real and important. Whether this child's problem was a true allergy or some other form of sensitivity does not matter from a practical point of view. Scientists might discount the significance for the population at large, but if the child were *my* 3-year-old, it wouldn't matter. I would still choose to eliminate the artificial colors.

Another recent study used a similar method of repeated challenges. From 55 children originally studied, 8 entered a double-blind challenge with tartrazine (yellow food dye) over a period of 18 weeks. Two of the children showed a confirmed reaction. One of these, in a 12-year-old boy, was quite dramatic and extreme. Interestingly, both of the confirmed responders to the challenge had asthma and other allergies.[3]

Despite some encouraging findings, the large number of

well-controlled studies finding no effects or contradictory ones leaves most scientists feeling that food additives are of little consequence in the diets of most children. Most doctors are now loath to prescribe the Feingold diet. However, before rendering a final judgment on this approach to dietary management, we will consider some related studies dealing with food allergy.

FOOD ALLERGY

The concept of food allergy is quite different from the concept of sensitivity to additives. Food allergy refers to an *immunologic* reaction to ingestion of a food, a reaction much like allergy to the more common allergens such as dust, mold, or ragweed. One can be sensitive to or unable to tolerate a food or additive without being allergic. Some children are sensitive to cow's milk, but not because they are allergic; rather, because the milk is irritating to their stomach lining.

Allergy, as allergists use the term, is a much more specific and well-defined problem than sensitivity. In the most well-defined type of allergic reaction (classified by allergists as Type I), a specific substance (the allergen) causes certain cells in the skin and mucosal tracts (for example, in the throat or lung) to release histamines, which then produce the allergic symptoms (this is why antihistamines are often effective against allergic symptoms). These symptoms include coughing and wheezing, skin rashes (urticaria), and stuffy or runny nose (rhinitis). There are other types of allergic reactions, allegedly involving different mechanisms, but these are more controversial.

One recent study found that 50% of a group of 81 children with confirmed allergy (atopic dermatitis) also had attention deficit disorder. The authors suggest that a disturbance of the body's production of the neurotransmitter norepinephrine might underlie both the attentional and allergic problems. Some evidence indicates that immune deficiencies (the cause of allergies) impair the body's production of norepinephrine.[4]

That food *additives* act by an allergic mechanism has been a debatable issue; but there is agreement among researchers and practitioners that allergies to certain *foods* do occur in children and adults. The debate concerns whether these effects have any connection with learning and behavior, other than as minor irritants. Some practitioners have claimed that true food allergies are quite common and directly involved in affecting brain function. While not denying the existence of food allergies, most allergists think they have little relevance to mental and behavioral disorders, being no different than any intermittent, chronic illness.

Food allergy is quite common in the population at large, occurring in 2–3% of the adult population and 10–15% of children, with perhaps as many as 30–40% showing minor manifestations of the problem. Allergies are most common to animal and plant proteins, inhalants, and drugs. Among foods, cow's milk, chicken, eggs, and cereals usually lead the list. The symptoms that usually occur include nasal stuffiness, hives, eczema and other rashes, migraine headaches, nausea, diarrhea, asthma, and sometimes anaphylactic shock.

Despite several decades of suspicion, however, very little solid evidence supports the idea that food allergies cause behavioral and learning problems. Many of the studies are biased or flawed in obvious ways. Particularly suspect are studies involving placing a food under the tongue and measuring heart rate and behavioral changes to the food. Some allergists continue to use this test, despite the fact that no satisfactory double-blind experiments have ever confirmed this method.

However, one rather convincing study by Drs. Helen Tryphonas and Ronald Trites in Canada, does give some support for an association between allergy and behavior.[5] Using an objective measure of allergy (the so-called RAST, or radioim-

mune-allagosorbent test), the investigators tested 90 hyperactive children, 22 nonhyperactive learning-disabled children and
8 emotionally disturbed children. They found that 77% of the
learning-disabled group were allergic, compared to about 40%
in the other groups. Also, the higher the hyperactivity score on
the parent's ratings, the more allergies the child had.

When the allergic children ate diets eliminating foods for
which there was a confirming allergy test, there was no difference in behavior for the group as a whole, but some individual
children showed marked improvement. These children showed
improvement in both learning and behavior, suggesting that a
few strong responders to certain foods were in the larger group
of nonresponders. Some recent studies also give further support
to a link between food allergy and behavior, both involving
children with many allergic symptoms

The Oligoantigenic Diet

This tongue twister refers to a diet containing few varieties
of foods. Some scientists have long suspected that certain foods
in combination can cause behavioral symptoms, though until recently there was little objective evidence to support the idea.
When a group of allergists and immunologists were carrying out
a double-blind trial of foods suspected of causing migraine
headache, they noted that many of the children were also hyperactive and that the hyperactivity improved with food avoid-
ance, sometimes for foods not usually suspected as causes of
migraine. (People with migraine often learn to avoid cheeses,
alcoholic beverages, and chocolate because they provoke or
worsen migraine headaches.) They decided to study this diet
more carefully in a large sample of severely hyperactive children.

The children in their study were probably not typical of
most hyperactives, for a large proportion also had neurological

disorders (including seizures), allergic conditions, or other physical symptoms such as headaches, abdominal discomfort, chronic rhinitis, aches in limbs, skin rashes, and mouth ulcers. About half of the children came from poor home environments (where there was parental conflict, neglect or overinvolvement of parents, psychiatric illness in the family, stress at school, etc.).

In the first phase of the study, lasting 4 weeks, the researchers introduced the oligoantigenic diet. This diet restricts foods to two meats (for example, lamb and chicken), two carbohydrate sources (such as potatoes and rice), two fruits (for instance, banana and apple), a vegetable, water, calcium, and multivitamins. Patients who show improvement in symptoms then continue to the second phase.

The second phase reintroduces foods previously eliminated, for a week at a time. If behavioral or physical symptoms recur, the food is withdrawn again. Otherwise it remains as part of the diet. The yellow food dye tartrazine and the preservative benzoic acid (used as an antibacterial agent in pickles, sausages, and soft drinks) were given separately in an orange squash and in capsules, respectively. Of the 76 patients, only 14 did not respond adversely to a suspected offending food reintroduced in phase two, confirming the improvement that occurred when eliminating it the first time.

The third phase was a double-blind, placebo-controlled trial testing one of the specific foods that had caused a behavioral reaction in a child when reintroduced. Of the 31 children who entered this double-blind phase, 28 completed it.

All observers—parents, physicians examining the children, and the psychologist observing the children during psychological tests—found the children improved during the double-blind active phase, compared to the placebo phase. One of the psychological tests measuring impulsivity showed a reliable worsening in the active compared to the placebo condition.

The most common offending foods (in 79% of the children)

were benzoic acid and tartrazine, which were usually involved together. But over 50% also reacted to cow's milk, chocolate, wheat, and grapes. Only cabbages, lettuce, cauliflower, celery, goat's cheese, and duck eggs showed no confirmed reaction in any child.

The degree of improvement was not trivial. Forty-seven children ceased having headaches, and 13 who previously had seizures became free of them. Those who had been taking anticonvulsants and became seizure-free on the diet remained seizure-free after discontinuing the anticonvulsant. Although improvement on the diet was less in the families with poor home conditions than in better conditions, it was still significant (71% in the poor versus 90% in the good showing some improvement). Our hyperactivity checklist (filled out by parents) was significantly improved by the diet.

Benefit from this oligoantigenic diet study appears to have been substantial, not just in the number of children shown to be responsive to removal and reintroduction of offending foods, but in the level of improvement after eliminating offending foods.

The study was very ambitious and complex, and as the authors admit, it needs replication. They also point out several important drawbacks of this approach. It may not apply to most hyperactive children, it is difficult to carry out, and there are no diagnostic tests that identify likely responders. A trained medical and dietary staff must administer this diet,

> which is complicated and, unsupervised, potentially dangerous. The diet is expensive and disruptive to the social life of the children and their families. There is a danger that parents who are hostile to their children may use the diet as a means of punishment or that parents may attribute all alteration of behaviour to diet. (p. 544)[6]

While the study strongly supports the idea that there may be ordinary foods to which children are allergic, finding out what those are, keeping a well-balanced diet, and avoiding other hazards is quite difficult. Nevertheless, despite the effort and expense involved, over 90% of the families elected to stay on the diet. With such severely impaired children not helped by other methods, one can understand the diet's great appeal to desperate parents.

The Back-to-Basics Diet

The study just described differed from other elimination diet studies in that a wide range of foods and additives were individually tested. This is important because differences among children in the foods they cannot tolerate means that a narrow elimination diet might miss the mark for many children. That study also used children with many signs of allergy. None of the challenge studies of the Feingold theory involving food dyes included a broad range of foods or other additives. None used a sample with clear signs of allergy, and most used older children. A very recent diet study by Dr. Bonnie Kaplan and colleagues in Canada corrected several flaws of previous studies and added important refinements.[7]

Dr. Kaplan had noticed that poor sleep habits and allergic symptoms often go together and that these problems would sometimes improve when a change of diet occurred. She assessed a large number of 1- to 3-year-old hyperactive children who had sleep problems or other physical problems (such as stuffy nose, cramps, rashes) and were not on a special diet. From an original pool of 196 children referred for hyperactivity, she ended up with 24 who met criteria for attention deficit disorder with hyperactivity and also had the other symptoms.

The children's regular diet over a 10-day period was the basis for constructing an "equivalent" diet for comparison with the experimental diet. The experimental, or back-to-basics, diet, eliminated food dyes, food flavors, preservatives, monosodium glutamate (MSG), chocolate, and caffeine. Children received a multivitamin supplement containing no sugar or artificial colors or flavors. The researchers eliminated most sugar from the diet. The amount of protein was kept the same as the baseline and equivalent diets. They eliminated all milk and dairy products for 15 children whose parents suspected that those foods might be a problem. Instead of milk and dairy products, those children received a supplement of calcium with their food.

As in the Wisconsin studies, all food for every meal came in coded packages for use by the entire family and for the child on any special occasions. This "family affair" approach helped to maintain good compliance during the diet, and debriefing sessions after the study showed that the children were very compliant and that no parents deciphered when the equivalent and experimental diets were in effect. Blood samples were taken at the end of each dietary phase to check biochemical changes.

The results of this study were positive and clear. They showed first that carbohydrates, sugar, and total calorie intake went down during the experimental diet, but protein intake remained equivalent to the regular diet. Blood studies showed a significant increase in 9 of the 11 vitamins assayed (vitamins A, D, C, B_6, B_{12}, folacin, thiamin, niacin, and biotin) for the experimental diet compared with the equivalent diet. These changes show that the experimental diet did result in better nutrition and accomplished its purpose of reducing sugar and carbohydrates (and presumably additives).

There was a very strong improvement in daily ratings of hyperactivity and in sleep (quicker falling asleep and fewer night awakenings). There were also significant improvements in physical signs and symptoms: bad breath, chronic rhinitis, and headache all improved (though the latter two were marginal in degree of improvement).

This was an excellent study providing very strong conclusions. The back-to-basics diet definitely had an important effect on this group of preschoolers, particularly with problems that often plague parents when the doctor has found nothing wrong. Nighttime fussiness and trouble going to sleep, which are among the most common concerns of parents of young children, appear to have lessened noticeably during the experimental diet. For many parents this alone would be worth the trouble of carrying out the diet.

The problem with the study is that it is hard to know how applicable the diet is to most children. Of the 24 children, 11 showed a substantial change (25% or more reduction) in hyperactivity symptoms. These were the good responders. This amounts to about 5% of the original sample of 196 children, who themselves may represent at most 10% of the general population (some estimates place the incidence of hyperactivity that high). This means that the overall number of diet responders is small (possibly as few as five in a thousand if we accept these figures as generally valid for the whole population).

While small compared to the total pool of hyperactive children, about 50% of those children studied were "good responders." This could mean that if the child is hyperactive, is under 4 years of age, and has sleep problems or allergic-type symptoms, then there is a reasonable chance the back-to-basics diet could prove useful.

Some qualifications are necessary, however. First, no parent in the study just described found that the diet "cured" their child; they became better, but not normal. Second, we cannot be sure which components of the diet are relevant to which children. There is no way of knowing whether it was the addition of vitamins, reduction of carbohydrate, elimination of caffeine, and so on, that was important. Perhaps different food items are important for different children. There are no tests or measures which predict which children will respond well. It would require a systematic elimination, as in the oligoantigenic diet, to determine which particular food (such as chocolate) might be causing a problem, and this, as we have noted above, is a tricky and sometimes dangerous process, especially when not supervised by a dietitian or nutritionist.

On the other hand, the success of this diet is encouraging. It is notable that many of the items causing problems in the oligoantigenic study described above (such as oats, peanuts, wheat, grapes, and bananas) were not excluded in the back-to-basics diet. This suggests the possibility that eliminating them might have resulted in still more improvement.

ADVICE ON CHANGING BEHAVIOR WITH DIET

I have to admit that I have changed my mind about the Feingold idea since the 1970s. I sympathize with pediatricians and mental health workers who find the zeal of some parents for dietary treatments to be an impediment to other good treatments. I do not want to add to their burden. But my judgment is that the evidence is strong enough, at least for preschoolers, and especially those with confirmed allergic symptoms, that one should eliminate a broad range of unnecessary and possibly harmful ingredients from these children's diets.

I often hear the question, "If the risks of the Feingold diet are small, why not just place all young children on this diet anyway, even if it happens not to work for most of them?" One problem is that strictly maintaining the diet is next to impossible. Our food environment is too cluttered with additives; and labels on food packages are either microscopically small or nonexistent. Under the present circumstances, shopping for an additive-free diet becomes a chore. In his last years, Dr. Feingold pleaded for better, clear-cut labeling on foods as a partial solution. It is hard to disagree with this approach, and legislation to bring it about seems of paramount importance. But when parents have a hard time sticking to a rigorous diet, they feel guilty or discouraged and usually lose hope that anything further can be done.

Another problem is more attitudinal. Many parents neglect *obvious* reasons for their child's hyperactivity and fail to get proper treatment or change their own behavior which is causing some of the problem. I am often told by parents that all they want is Feingold's diet, even if many other priorities seem more pressing. Some parents strongly resist the idea of an "unnatural" treatment like drug therapy, despite its proven effectiveness and safety with many hyperactive children. Others feel no need to engage in family therapy while convinced that changing foods will do the job.

My first advice usually is to seek the family counseling, medical, educational, and behavioral treatments the child needs and then follow a modified version of Feingold's diet if it helps. In the following chapter, we will include an elimination diet that seems sensible and appears to work. Some useful books on basic nutrition are listed at the end of Chapter 10. Taken with the caveat that diets do not cure, there seems good reason to try them as part of a total therapeutic effort including medical, educational, and behavioral treatments. But no diet should be undertaken without proper supervision, for, almost always, inadvertent side effects will crop up (such as the lowered vitamin C we found by monitoring daily food intakes).

It certainly cannot hurt to eliminate all unnecessary additives, most chocolate and candy, and to lower sugar and carbohydrate intake for most children. (But even here one should remember that children need carbohydrate, and the levels should be in accord with age requirements.) The evidence we presented in Chapter 6, regarding multivitamin supplements, also suggests that such supplements may be valuable in combination with a low-carbohydrate, high-protein diet.

CHAPTER EIGHT

Megavitamins

It is easy to understand why many people turn to vitamins as an explanation or a cure for mental and behavioral disturbances. There is virtually no mental symptom—from minor lassitude to major psychosis—that does not result from severe vitamin deficiencies of one sort or another. For instance, consider vitamin B_3, or niacin, which is abundantly present in cereals, legumes, oilseeds, and flesh foods. Niacin deficiency can ultimately lead to a severe disease state known as pellagra; but it often results in apathy, depression, irritability, emotional lability, memory loss, delirium, and sometimes seizures—often well before appearance of the more extreme physical and mental manifestations (the so-called three Ds of diarrhea, dermatitis, and dementia). Common reasoning assumes that if vitamin deficiencies can lead to mental symptoms, then they may cause those symptoms, and therefore the opposite state—vitamin *excess*—may be curative.

This manner of thinking leads to an extraordinary consumption of vitamin supplements by people seeking improved mental function, longevity, or general well-being. The amounts consumed are far greater than those recommended by most nutritional authorities. For example, surveys estimate that the United States produces enough vitamin C in 1 year to meet the total daily requirements of half the world's population.

But *is* more better? Are there dangers associated with too much of a good thing? Some answers to these questions are now available, and in this chapter we will look at how effective mega-doses of vitamins are for treating symptoms of schizophrenia, hyperactive-attentional disorders, mental retardation, and childhood autism. We will also look at the risks of these treatments.

WHAT ARE VITAMINS AND MEGAVITAMINS?

Vitamins are nutrients that are essential to growth and development and to practically every aspect of bodily function, including the brain and its functions. The body does not manufacture vitamins, so they must be taken in with food. Yet vitamins are present in foods in such microscopic amounts (often a few millionths of a gram) that their potent effects seem miraculous. Their potency comes from their role as key elements in virtually all metabolic processes in the body.

People have known for centuries that certain patterns of illness occur when particular kinds of foods are unavailable. The condition of scurvy was known to ancient Egyptians and to Greek medicine. But not until 1747 did the British physician Lind show that oranges and lemons could prevent and cure the disease. Almost 2 centuries later, two Americans isolated vitamin C (ascorbic acid) from lemon juice, and Europeans extracted it from oranges and cabbage. This simple crystalline chemical, found in certain foods, is the essential ingredient that prevents scurvy. This pattern, of noticing that the absence of certain foods leads to a disease and its presence prevents it, and then isolating the critical chemicals involved, took place many times, with the last true vitamin (B_{12}) being discovered in 1948. (It is interesting that until then, strict vegetarians often unknowingly developed a B_{12} deficiency since the vitamin is not present in plants—a problem now correctable by supplements. It is also interesting to note that megadoses of vitamin C can cause a B_{12} deficiency since vitamin C apparently destroys B_{12}.)

It is now known that in the normal amounts required by the body, most vitamins function in chemical processes as cofactors for enzymes; that is, enzymes require vitamins to complete their normal functions. Enzymes are chemicals that facilitate certain chemical reactions. A coenzyme is like the last piece of a puzzle that makes the picture complete. Processes of synthesis or degradation of certain chemicals are interrupted when coenzymes are absent. Unwanted substances accumulate, or reactions needed for bodily work fail to take place. Some vitamins, such as B_6 (pyridoxine), are so intimately involved in the synthesis and destruction of neurotransmitters in the brain that it seems logical to expect them to be important in mental illness. (The best sources of this vitamin are yeast, wheat germ, pork and other meats—especially liver—whole grain cereals, legumes, potatoes, bananas, and oatmeal.)

Since many of the functions of vitamins are unknown, their possible role in psychiatric disorders, either as causes or cures, has become a fertile field for speculation. When vitamins are present in much greater amounts than needed by the body, they can exert chemical effects that are different from those that nature intended, and this has been a source of hope regarding their possible benefits as well as concern regarding their toxic effects. Megavitamin doses usually refers to doses that are 10 times or more than the RDAs (recommended daily allowances), and, often, amounts several hundred times normal requirements are given.

ORTHOMOLECULAR PSYCHIATRY
AND BIOCHEMICAL INDIVIDUALITY

The use of megavitamin therapy came into public prominence in 1968 when Linus Pauling, a Nobel laureate in chemistry, proposed that megadoses of vitamin C would be useful in curing many illnesses, including the common cold. Pauling developed a general theory for treating mental illness called "orthomolecular" ("ortho" meaning to put straight or correct), the basic idea of which is "the treatment of mental disease by the provision of the optimum molecular environment for the mind, especially the optimum concentration of substances normally present in the body."[2]

The notion of providing an optimum molecular environment is similar to another idea, that of *biochemical individuality*. This notion, propounded by R. J. Williams in 1956, comes from the observation that everyone has a unique pattern of bodily structures and functions. Just as no two snowflakes are identical, so no two bodies are the same. It is true that the average size, shape, and position of bodily organs, for example, is remarkably similar from person to person in our species. The pictures found in medical textbooks are a reasonable guide to what one can expect for most people. But any particular person will vary from the picture in many ways. This is why surgeons must have experience with many different cases; the picture in the textbook is only approximate for any given person.

Biochemical individuality is also a general rule. There is always a range of different normal values for enzymes, proteins, blood chemistries, liver and kidney measures, and the like. All of these values vary across a range—sometimes very wide—in normal persons. Moreover, the pattern or profile of these biochemical measures varies in many different ways within a sample of persons from the normal population. Genes are thought to determine each person's specific chemical profile.

Thus, everyone has his or her own biological fingerprint, largely determined by his or her unique genetic endowment. There is no disagreement among scientists about this aspect of the theory of biological individuality, which forms the foundation of modern genetic theory. Without human variability there could be no natural selection and evolution of species.

Williams' theory of biochemical individuality led to the logical conclusion that each person has individualized nutritional requirements. He stated that "although every nutritionally important mineral, amino acid, and vitamin is needed by every individual, it follows, if biochemical individuality exists, that the needs are quantitatively distinctive for each individual."[2]

The orthomolecular school (sometimes called the human ecology approach) adopted the notion of biochemical and nutritional individuality, proposing that by supplying nutrients in the required amounts, a person achieves optimum function. Treatment with this approach often involves measuring the levels of many nutrients and juggling their values by changing the diet in various ways, particularly by vitamin and mineral supplementation.

The most obvious problem with this approach is the question of how to measure each individual's particular needs. If a patient shows up with certain symptoms—say a headache—and the human ecologist or orthomolecular psychiatrist believes a particular mineral deficiency causes symptoms, how does he or she define the optimal level *for that person?*

One solution is just to give more of everything, particularly vitamins, on the assumption that swamping the system will correct any deficiencies. Then the only questions remaining are, Does it work? and, Is it safe? Most of the proposed treatments suggested by human ecologists were not tested by them, leaving it to others to carry out the double-blind trials. When the advocates of the program *do* carry out studies, critics claim they use biased and nonscientific methods:

> The real problem seems to be that the megavitamin proponents do poor science. They generate interesting hypotheses, but they have not accepted the responsibility of being self-critical and conducting the experiments that would rigorously test their hypotheses . . . [publishing] papers that fail to meet the scientific and editorial standards of international medical and scientific journals. (p. 252)[3]

The problem of verifying the orthomolecular theories becomes even more complex when considering the question of the nutrient profile or pattern. The effect of a zinc deficiency, for example, may depend upon the profile of other nutrients. If there are many possible unique profiles, there is unfortunately a lot of room for endless juggling of a pattern until the symptom remits. Critics of this approach argue that it is a perfect setup for endless manipulations of the diet, often at considerable expense. If it works, no doubt patients will be grateful, but then one has to wonder what would have happened to the symptom *without* treatment? Suppose instead of the megavitamin supplements that appear to produce a behavioral change, the capsules contained placebo; would the symptoms remit anyway?

The orthomolecular theorists usually argue that placebos are unnecessary, either because the condition is so severe and unchanging (as in autism) or because there is a long baseline of other failed treatments to compare megavitamins with. But this is asking hardheaded scientists who are familiar with many dramatic placebo "cures" to take too much on faith. So the only solution is double-blind, placebo-controlled experiments. The idea is appealing, but such studies are very difficult to pull off in practice. Schizophrenia was the first mental condition to illustrate this point.

MEGAVITAMINS AND SCHIZOPHRENIA

Schizophrenia is perhaps the most severe and untreatable form of mental illness, for both children and adults. Patients have grossly impaired cognitive functions and reality testing, including hallucinations and delusions, often accompanied by bizarre behavior and affective displays.

The physician who coined the term "megavitamin" therapy, A. Hoffer, carried out a series of studies over a 10-year period (1952–1962), treating schizophrenics with very large doses of vitamin B_3 (nicotinic acid and niacinamide being the active biological forms of this vitamin). The doses were about 150 to 300 times the daily recommended amounts (3 to 6 g vs. recommended doses of about 20 mg).

Hoffer speculated that niacin would prevent the overproduction of certain by-products of neurotransmitter synthesis within the brain. Some of these by-products, such as dimethyltryptamine (DMT), can act as natural speed or as a hallucinogenic. Hoffer's hypothesis, then, was tantamount to the idea that schizophrenics are tripping on their brain's own amphetamine-like and hallucinogenic-like by-products. He proposed that large doses of vitamins could compete in the brain for certain of the building blocks required for the formation of these hallucinogenic-like chemicals.

Thus, vitamins were supposed to act like certain drugs, and it was their *pharmacological* rather than their nutritional effects that Hoffer felt might be important. In other words, he was not proposing the simplistic idea that schizophrenics are simply vitamin deficient in a general sense; usually they are not, or they would show the physical signs of deficiency, such as pellagra. Rather, he was proposing that for genetic reasons schizophrenics were overproducing (or underexcreting) certain hallucinogenic by-products and that vitamins in much larger than normal doses would minimize these effects.

Hoffer's work, though supported by his own double-blind trials, was generally greeted with skepticism. Controlled trials by others failed to support his conclusions. Eventually, a thorough review by a task force of the American Psychiatric Association concluded that there was no merit to the hypothesis.

But Hoffer's son reexamined the critiques and pointed out that most of the attempts at replication were done with *chronic* schizophrenics—people who are "burned out" and whose long-time illness has compromised their nutritional and brain functions to a point where no intervention could work. The original studies used *acute* schizophrenics, those having a sudden onset of their symptoms. Critics countered that these so-called acute schizophrenics were a mixture of all kinds of patients, including manic depressives and others whose acute psychotic episodes spontaneously got better much of the time.

There is some merit in these criticisms, but according to more recent methods of diagnosis, inadequate diagnostic methods plagued both the original studies and attempts to replicate them. It is only recently that rigorous diagnostic research criteria for schizophrenia have evolved. Getting a homogeneous group for these early studies would have been very difficult, no matter who was carrying them out.

Most of the original treatments by Dr. Hoffer and his associates took place along with other therapies, especially shock therapy. Shock therapy is usually reserved for severe biological depressions, and the claims of improvement for combinations of shock therapy and niacin raise the suspicion that the diagnostic criteria may have been flimsy enough to include many depressed patients. It would still be important if vitamins plus shock therapy was curative for some subgroup of psychotic disorders, although this is quite different from the original claims about schizophrenia. Nevertheless, only using niacin and not the other treatments was a significant omission in replication studies.

Critics contended that every time tests were done and found to produce negative results, the orthomolecular theorists made additional changes to their treatment program, adding some treatments and subtracting others, so that there was never any one testable theory, only a moving target that could always prove too complex for validating studies. The orthomolecular advocates, on the other hand, could point to the rigidly simplistic tests, carried out without the sensible flexibility that all good medicine requires for individual patients.

Thus, the real impact of megavitamins on schizophrenia remains somewhat unresolved, though mainstream psychiatry by and large discounts the value of this treatment. The testing of this theory has been useful, however, for it was an important stimulus toward a biological theory of schizophrenia. It raised the possibility that nutrients may either help create or cure mental illness.

The episode also highlighted some of the inherent difficulties in testing complex treatment programs by conventional double-blind, placebo-controlled methods. There is considerable merit to the observation by the orthomolecular practitioners that controlled trials tend to oversimplify the real requirements of good treatment, such as individualized combinations of treatments, drug levels, and nutritional supplements. On the one hand, critics are right in arguing that if someone proposes a key *ingredient* in therapy for mental illness, they have the responsibility of proving that it makes a difference, not simply presenting testimonials and case studies that may reflect the bias of the practitioner. On the other hand, careful review of the countering studies shows that they are not without many problems themselves and fail to address some of the key issues in megavitamin therapy.

Despite the uncertain status of this hypothesis of adult mental illness, it prompted several investigators to extend the idea to children.

MEGAVITAMINS AND HYPERACTIVITY

Dr. Alan Cott, one of the proponents of the orthomolecular approach for treatment of hyperactive and learning-disabled children, says that a regimen of vitamins in large doses results in "decreased hyperactivity and the improved concentration and attention span, [leading to] improved capacities for learning."[4] This idea was put to the test by Dr. Eugene Arnold at Ohio State University, who used a treatment recommended by Cott in a double-blind trial (1 g of niacin, 1 g of vitamin C, 100 mg of vitamin B_6, 200 mg of calcium pantothenate, and 500 mg of glutamic acid, all given twice daily). Thirty-one carefully selected hyperactive children were randomly assigned to either a placebo or the vitamin supplements for 2 weeks.

Dr. Arnold reported that only two children showed enough improvement to warrant continued treatment (as judged from rating scales). Both were on placebo. There was some diminution of irritability in the vitamin group as judged by teachers, but this isolated finding was thought to be a chance finding.

But others recognized that this experiment ignores one of the main tenets of orthomolecular psychiatry, *the individuality of each person's response pattern*. A better approach would be to try various vitamins at high doses, and then if a positive response occurs to one of them, to test the response further by more controlled trials. Dr. Arnold Brenner, a pediatrician, carried out such a trial with 100 hyperactive children.

Dr. Brenner's approach was to expose the children, in sequence a day or so apart, to thiamine (100 mg four times a day), placebo, calcium pantothenate (218 mg twice a day), and vitamin B_6 (100 mg three times a day). If the child was thought to have improved on any of these challenges, then a further trial occurred over another week, followed by a placebo trial for a week. If the improvement was "dramatic," and relapse (worsening) occurred during the placebo phase, then treatment with the vitamin continued over a longer period, with occasional periodic withdrawals to test the response. This method is similar to the one used in testing the oligoantigenic diet described in the previous chapter. Sometimes the effects were allegedly synergized by additional vitamins added in these longer trials; that is, additional vitamins or trace elements were thought to enhance the effectiveness of the original supplement.

Of the 100 children, 38 showed no initial response to the vitamins. The rest responded as shown in the table on page 197.

Response of Hyperactive Children to Vitamin Therapy[a]

Thiamine		Calcium		Vitamin B$_6$	
Improved	Worse	Improved	Worse	Improved	Worse
26 (11)	22	23 (4)	9	18 (9)	16

$n = 100$.
[a]Numbers in parentheses are those children who showed a dramatic response and relapsed when given placebo.

From this table it is easy to see that although about two-thirds of the children showed an initial positive response to the week of vitamin exposure, only 4–11% showed any dramatic effect for any single nutrient, which could then be subsequently confirmed by worsening when they received the placebo.

However, although only 4–11% of children on *single* nutrients improved, the total for all groups showing verified improvement (verified by relapse on placebo) is 24%. Depending on how you look at it, these results are either impressive or discouraging. One might consider that one-quarter of the suspected vitamin responders showing confirmed dramatic improvement is a good argument for the existence of a subgroup of vitamin-responsive patients. On the other hand, about one-third of patients usually improve while on placebos in most double-blind trials. Since this trial was "open"—parents and children knew when the children were receiving the nutrients and when they got the placebo—the chance for placebo effect is even greater than usual. Moreover, there was no consistent objective measurement of change, because although the investigator used a standard checklist, this quantitative guideline could not be measured in every child.[5]

Some of those improving on vitamin B$_6$ later relapsed but then improved from adding zinc to their supplement. These children had low blood levels of zinc, suggesting that the vitamin B$_6$ treatment itself was responsible for lowering zinc levels. Some of the children who initially failed to improve with a given vitamin later did so when given higher doses. These later additions to the trial are quite instructive, for they do show some of the individuality in treatment requirements, both for dosage and interactions among the nutrients. Not all patients developed a zinc deficiency, but success in treatment apparently depended upon identifying those who did.

There are many obvious problems in interpreting this type of study: the lack of consistent measurement, variable lengths of trials, lack of double blind, and a lack of ability to pick out the responders in advance. Since there are no clear markers to identify responders, the assessment must involve a somewhat extended trial-and-error procedure, and during this time many things happen to the child and his or her family which may well influence the outcome (including the child growing older and perhaps spontaneously improving). Still, if the 25% who showed a dramatic response were responsive to one or more of the nutrients, this would be well worth knowing, and most parents would be likely to prefer this treatment over drugs, though it is far from being without risk, as we shall see.

Thus far, the evidence on hyperactivity and megavitamins appears mixed: Dr. Arnold's trial was entirely negative; but it used a fixed schedule and did not adjust for individual responsiveness to nutrient type or dose. On the other hand, Dr. Brenner's trial made these adjustments, but in doing so it lost control of the placebo response and consistent measurement of clinical effect.

Another team performed an excellent experiment with the intent of correcting these deficiencies. Dr. Robert Haslam and coworkers in Alberta, Canada, carried out the trial.[6] As with Dr. Brenner's experiment, it took place in two stages: the first to identify children responding to megavitamins; and the second to follow up those responding in a double-blind, placebo-controlled fashion.

There were many other features of this study making it a definite advance over previous ones. First, the initial trial lasted 3 months, insuring that the vitamins had plenty of time to work. Second, the next stage took place in four 6-week blocks, alternating the active nutrients and placebo (for example, active–placebo–active–placebo or placebo–active–placebo–active). If one can establish a definite on–off effect more than once, it is much more convincing than a single response.

Third, besides being completely double blind, the researchers obtained both parent and teacher ratings, and trained observers monitored the children in their classrooms, counting specific problem behaviors (such as talking out of turn, running around, disturbing other children, and so forth). It is always possible that the child will respond in one setting but not another, as is well known from drug studies, and this experiment carefully covered all the bases.

Fourth, a large group of normal children had blood samples taken to obtain normal values for vitamin B_6 and vitamin C. In this way it was possible to see whether the response in the patients related to a state of vitamin deficiency at the start of the study (it turned out not to be). Several other biochemical measurements were made in the patients as well, helping to definitively establish their nutritional status at the start of the experiment.

Finally, the nutrients recommended by Dr. Cott were *gradually* increased over the 3-month period, up to levels claimed by the orthomolecular therapists to be effective. Thus, niacinamide increased from 1 to 3 g, B_6 from 200 to 600 mg, vitamin C from 1 to 3 g, and calcium pantothenate from 400 to 1,200 mg. These dosages are 100–300 times the usual recommended daily amounts.

During stage 1 of this study, 12 patients (29% of the 41 children starting the study) showed an improvement in behavior. As defined by the authors, this meant that the children had to show a 20% decrease in symptoms for 2 weeks compared with their initial (baseline) symptom levels. Of these 12 children, 5 refused further treatment because they experienced troubling side effects, such as nausea, anorexia, gagging, and abdominal pain. So the experiment proceeded with only 7 of the original 41 patients. These 7 patients could be viewed as *possible* responders, because testing took place nonblind, and improvement might reflect placebo effects, changes in the observers' standards, and hope for improvement.

After examining the results of the double-blind crossover phase of the experiment with these 7 youngsters, however, the authors concluded that "large doses of water-soluble vitamins—niacinamide, pyridoxine, ascorbic acid, and calcium pantothenate—have no beneficial effect for children with ADD" [attention deficit disorder] (p. 110).[6] This sounds conclusive, and given the generally excellent nature of the study, we might expect the case for megavitamins in ADD to be closed for good. But before we abandon this potentially useful treatment, perhaps it is worth being the devil's advocate about this study.

First, what about the five children who initially improved but had side effects and refused to continue? Might they have made a difference in the outcome if added to the seven who carried on? It is interesting that all these children began showing their side effects only when raising supplements to their highest levels (steps 4 and 5 of the 5-step procedure). This suggests that these children were over-medicated, and they should have had the dosages lowered.

Next, the results for the teacher and parent ratings are not at all as clear cut as the authors imply in their summary: *there was a highly statistically significant improvement in teachers' ratings of inattentiveness, a result that would happen by chance less than one in a thousand times.* Curiously, the authors dismiss this finding, not even mentioning it in the abstract or the summary. Some researchers downplay some of their own findings because they feel they are flukes when most of the other tests show no results. But mothers also saw a significant improvement in psychosomatic complaints (malaise and physical complaints without a known medical basis)—a result that could occur by chance only once in a thousand times. But again, though statistically very strong, the investigators simply ignored this finding in their final conclusions. Given that there are only seven subjects, these highly significant effects must mean that *virtually every one of the children were showing some positive response to the nutrients* (or that a few are showing absolutely enormous changes). In any case, it is important to attempt to understand what is going on, and not simply to dismiss the results out of hand.

Learning-Disabled Hyperactive Children. The previous studies on hyperactivity and megavitamins were inconclusive. But there have also been claims that megavitamins are helpful in improving the learning problems which are often associated with hyperactivity. In 1979 Drs. Kershner and Hawke, at the Hospital for Sick Children in Toronto, studied this question in a group of children, all previously treated with stimulant drugs. Their parents belonged to the Association for Children with Learning Disorders (ACLD), an international organization supporting parents of children with learning disabilities.

The children studied were between 7 and 14 years of age, with a wide range of learning and behavior problems. After being withdrawn from stimulant drugs for at least 3 months, the children received a low-carbohydrate, high-protein diet, since orthomolecular practitioners often claim that this enhances the effects of megavitamins. It is worth presenting this diet because, as we shall see, it produced the only positive results of the experiment (see table on p. 202).[7]

Before randomly assigning the children (17 boys and 3 girls) to the megavitamin and placebo treatments, they were given a

High-Protein, Low-Carbohydrate Diet

Food and drink allowed

Allowable proteins: All meats, fowl, fish, shellfish, cheese, nuts, soybean products, peanut butter.

Allowable vegetables: Fresh, frozen or canned: Artichoke, asparagus, avocado, beets, black-eyed peas, broccoli, brussels sprouts, cabbage, cauliflower, carrots, celery, corn, cucumbers, eggplant, garlic, kale, lentils, lettuce, lima beans, spinach, squash, string beans, sunflower seeds, tomatoes, turnips, water cress (corn, lima beans, lentils, and peas are least desirable).

Allowable fruits: Fresh, cooked or unsweetened, frozen or canned: Apples, apricots, berries, cherries, fresh coconut, grapefruit, kumquats, lemons, limes, mango, melon, papayas, peaches, pears, pineapple, and tangerines—with or without cream but *without* sugar. Sweeten with saccharin, Sucaryl, or Sweeta.

Allowable juice: The following if unsweetened: Apple, grapefruit, orange, pineapple, tomato, vegetable, V-8; Knox gelatin may be added for protein.

Allowable beverages: Above juices; dietetic carbonated drinks except cola. Dietetic beverages must not have sugar in them; they should be 2 or less calories per serving. Herbal teas, milk, caffeine-low coffee (example: Sanka), sugar-free broth.

Absolutely none of the following

Sugar: Honey, candy, including chocolate; other sweets such as: cake, chewing gum, Jello, pastries, pie, pudding, sweet custards, sweet jelly or marmalade, and ice cream.

Caffeine: No ordinary coffee or tea (Sanka, decaf, etc., and herbal teas are okay). Beverages containing caffeine, such as Coca Cola, Pepsi Cola, other cola drinks, Ovaltine, Postum, hot chocolate are not allowed. No ordinary carbonated drinks: No grape, prune, or juices other than listed above.

Fruits: Bananas, dates, dried fruits, figs, grapes, persimmons, plums, prunes, raisins.

Starches: Macaroni, noodles, spaghetti, navy and kidney beans, potatoes, rice, ravioli.

Alcohol: Beer, cocktails, cordials, wine.

Medications containing caffeine such as: Anacin APC, 222's, A.S.A. Compound, etc., Caffergot, Coricidin, Empirin Compound, Fiorinal (plain aspirin or Bufferin permitted).

(Read the label on every can of juice, fruit, vegetable, meat, and other products. Select only those containing no syrup, honey, or sugar. These can be found at the dietetic counter in all large markets.)

battery of educational tests and ratings by parents for their aggressiveness, hyperactivity, peer relations, discipline, and attention span. The children then continued the diet and vitamin or placebo treatment.

The vitamins included ascorbic acid (vitamin C), niacinamide (vitamin B$_3$), pantothenate (vitamin B$_5$), and pyridoxine (vitamin B$_6$), given according to body weight, two to three times a day after meals. The vitamins were given in amounts many times larger than recommended daily allowances in order to approximate doses used by orthomolecular practitioners.

Vitamins produced no more changes in any measure than did placebo. Three children even appeared to experience a significant calcium loss and needed supplementation with dolomite, a form of calcium supplement. Several children in the vitamin group also had rashes or flushing of the face, a common reaction to niacin.

However, the experiment was very suggestive in another way: all the children showed significant behavioral improvement, and even some improvement in learning tests, while on the high-protein, low-carbohydrate diet. The authors are justifiably cautious about this finding because the diet was nonblind, and as we have mentioned many times, diet changes alone produce placebo-like effects. But the children did improve by everyone's estimate, a finding definitely not attributable to the megavitamins.

Thus, the diet by itself may have been important. At least the improvements are *consistent* with this presumption, though they cannot prove it. In most ways the diet is similar to the one used by Dr. Kaplan's group with poor sleepers and allergic children, which we described in Chapter 7. Since that study did have a placebo control, it is hard to avoid the implication that the diet is doing something important. Just what, of course, is unclear because of the multiple changes made at one time.

CHILDHOOD AUTISM

One of the most severe psychiatric disorders of children is the condition known as childhood autism. Fortunately, autism is rather rare, but when it strikes, it is devastating. Children with autism often appear normal until language begins to develop. Parents may notice very early that children develop words but that they are not using words as a communication to those around them. The children often act as though others were simply not there, or as if people were no different from other objects in the environment. They will usually not make eye contact and have an aversion to physical contact. It is this withdrawal, apparently into an inner world, that gives the syndrome its name of autism. There is often a form of imitative speech (sometimes with *echolalia*, in which words or phrases are simply echoed back). Sometimes the children appear retarded (IQ varies considerably in these children), but unlike retarded children, who suffer a more or less uniform loss of intellectual functions in all areas, autistic children will often have unusual areas of extreme brightness, even genius. These idiot savants often do amazing feats of calculation or memory, though they may be unable to master the simplest aspects of reading or spelling.

Autistic children are peculiar in many other ways. They often insist on a world of sameness and become highly distraught if minor changes are made in their room arrangements. They often have odd motor tics or habits, such as hand-flapping, rocking, or repetitive movements. (In this respect, they are no different from many retarded and brain-damaged children.) Emotionally, these children are very moody, labile, and sometimes severely aggressive to themselves or others, often needing restraints to prevent self-injury. While sometimes agitated and restless, at other times they may be immobile, expressionless, and withdrawn.

There are no successful treatments of autism, though behavioral and drug management will usually temper the symptoms. These children are almost always peculiar or even bizarre when they grow up, though a few cases become near normal. Early language development and IQ are important predictors of the long-term outcome. Autistic children with higher IQs and better language skills are more likely to function better in adulthood.

It is not surprising that such a severe, devastating illness should receive a good deal of attention from scientists. Most now agree that the disorder (or disorders, since there are probably several variants) is probably genetically determined in some way and that it reflects significant damage or dysfunction in the brain. But science has not been successful in defining what that damage might be or what the genetic key is that determines the occurrence of the disease.

Megavitamin Therapy of Autism

Given the general hopelessness of the condition and the failure of standard psychiatric treatments, many parents became persuaded that megavitamin therapy, as proposed by orthomolecular psychiatrists, was worth a try. Dr. Bernard Rimland, a long-time student of autism, began a study of megavitamins by collecting information from parents of 233 psychotic children, recognizing that only about 37 fit the classical autistic picture.

Parents were given a multivitamin and mineral supplement to add to the children's diets and then additional high doses of vitamin C, niacin, vitamin B_6, and pantothenic acid, one after the other. Observers used rating scales to monitor the children's behavior. Although they used no placebo nor attempts to keep parents blind, the children appeared to fall into several groups, two of which seemed to show dramatic improvement following the therapy.

In a later study, 16 of the autistic children who improved with megavitamins participated in a double-blind trial. But the results of the trial were negative (though once again, as we have seen in other diet trials, some positive results occurred, depending upon the order in which the children received placebo and vitamins). The authors admitted that the group was still quite heterogeneous, hardly representative of standard autistic diagnoses, but they still felt that the vitamins improved the overall functioning of the children.

European investigators carried out several other megavitamin studies with autistic children, again claiming significant improvements, but also employing inadequate controls and improper statistical analyses. When one reads these studies, there appears to be data *consistent* with improvements in some of the children, but the design and statistics are so questionable that the studies must be taken with a grain of salt.

Fenfluramine

One recent theory caused a wave of excitement in the medical community. Several scientists had noticed that many autistic children (usually the most impaired ones) had raised levels of the brain neurotransmitter serotonin. Dr. Edward Ritvo, a distinguished authority on autism, proposed that a drug which lowered serotonin might be beneficial to autistic children. Such a drug is fenfluramine—a drug originally developed for dieting and weight loss. In animals, fenfluramine causes a noticeably rapid decrease in brain serotonin. (We mention fenfluramine here, not because it is a vitamin, but because of its relevance to autism.)

Unfortunately, controlled studies with children once again showed the initial enthusiasm to be unwarranted, with the results disappearing after instituting proper controls. It became apparent that the drug was no better than placebo. The finding that this drug destroys the brain's serotonin neurons in animals also put somewhat of a damper on this enthusiasm.

MENTAL RETARDATION

Like autism, mental retardation produces profound deficits in intellectual ability, but in a more uniform way, and often without the peculiar emotional pattern typical of autism. Some retarded children, like those with Down's syndrome, are often extremely placid, friendly, and gentle. Scientists recognize that there are many causes of mental retardation, some being due to very early damage to the nervous system in utero, and others being due to inborn errors of metabolism (such as phenylketonuria, or PKU, a disorder in which the child does not have the ability to metabolize the amino acid phenylalanine) or genetic defects (as in Down's syndrome).

The attention of scientists was immediately captured by a report from Dr. Ruth Harrell that megavitamins were capable of raising the IQ of retarded children, especially those with Down's syndrome. Dr. Harrell's initial, preliminary study of 16 mixed types of retarded children used a supplement consisting of 8 minerals and 11 vitamins. In a rather short time—a few months—it appeared that the IQ of the children climbed an average of 5 to 10 points.

Very shortly after Dr. Harrell's report, several attempts to replicate the findings were unsuccessful. Critics of these attempts to verify Dr. Harrell's study argued that they were very different from her original studies in many ways (older subjects, lower IQs, absence of thyroid supplements, etc.). As we noted in Chapter 1, Dr. Rimland wrote a spirited defense of Harrell's study in response to its dismissal by a task force from the American Academy of Pediatrics.

Reviewing these counterstudies, I too have to agree that they are quite flawed and do not address the original findings. Thus, megavitamins for retarded children, like the treatment of attention-deficit and autistic children, has generated a lot of heat but very little light. The findings and debates with children are remarkably similar to those surrounding megavitamins for schizophrenia, leaving one with a sense of exasperation over tantalizing but inconclusive studies.

WHERE DO WE GO FROM HERE WITH MEGAVITAMINS?

The outcome of the studies of megavitamins on children are quite disappointing to the orthomolecular hypotheses. Besides worsening of some symptoms by the treatments, there is the troubling finding of abnormal liver function, calcium and zinc loss, and various side effects found in several studies of mega-vitamin supplements. This means that the high dosages of vitamins are potentially dangerous. The supposed advantage of vitamin therapy over drug therapy in being less toxic thus becomes somewhat questionable. Several investigators have substantiated the risk of megadoses of vitamins, so that at best, this is a treatment to be carried out only with close medical supervision. But putting aside these physical drawbacks of the therapy, what are we to make of the inconclusive behavioral findings?

First, we have to acknowledge that all the studies we described are enormously costly in terms of time and money. Having run similar studies, I am well aware how much effort the authors put into these trials. It is very easy to admonish Dr. Haslam and his coworkers, for example, to carry out their study with larger numbers (recall they ended up with only seven in the double-blind trial); but when you consider that the research team was tied up with each patient over a full school year (12 weeks in phase 1, and 24 weeks in phase 2), it is obvious that the experiment was very costly indeed. Dr. Brenner's study, carried out with 100 hyperactive patients (probably without research funds), is an heroic accomplishment. So one should not denigrate these efforts, despite their shortcomings. Collectively, the studies still add to our understanding.

But what is troubling to the careful reader of the studies and the counterstudies is the curious vehemence, one-sidedness, and overbearing finality of the conclusions in the face of what are often quite equivocal results *on both sides*.

I have chosen not to go into all the arguments and counterarguments about the various studies, but my own conclusion after reading them is that definitive studies on the effects of megavitamin therapy have still not been done. While we have to agree with the old Scottish maxim "Not Proven," we cannot ignore the bias which seems to permeate reporting of the issues on both sides.

In the arguments about the orthomolecular hypothesis, we see behavior which is remarkably similar to the behavior of the opponents in the sugar and food additive dialogues. *There are no clear-cut results, yet the scientific papers, in their abstracts or summaries, talk as though there were.* These portions of the papers then get cited in the research literature and nonspecialist scientists take them at face value.

This situation is particularly dangerous for the lay consumer of services. On the one hand, parents with hyperactive, autistic, or schizophrenic children are prey to unscrupulous practitioners who can cite whatever evidence supports their therapeutic program, leaving the parents open for prolonged, expensive programs. On the other hand, the possible benefits to some children (for whom these ideas might work) are lost when a parent confronts a physician who has digested only the summary with its reassuringly conclusive but negative findings. Such physicians are themselves unlikely to do careful, individualized trials with their own patients because they feel the case is already closed. Unscrupulous fringe practitioners are only too willing to step into the gap and carry out trials on individual patients, but at a very high cost and with questionable scientific safeguards.

The reason we have this predicament seems clear. Research priorities in this country simply have not been high enough to support the kinds of research needed. This is partly due to the premature and exaggerated claims of practitioners who usually insist that they are too busy curing patients to tend to mundane issues of proving their claims. These practitioners give a whole area of study a bad name, making grant review bodies justifiably concerned about supporting research in the nutrition–behavior area. There is a form of guilt by association.

Government funding for nutrition and behavior research, even for highly qualified researchers, is hopelessly inadequate. Only when parents and mental health professionals demand that such research occur in greater quantity is there any hope of change. But until such studies are done, individual parents have no choice but to take on some of the responsibility for assessing and managing their problem child's nutrition and behavior.

At present, we cannot recommend megavitamin therapy, except as a topic for sorely needed further research. Megavitamins are unlike regular multivitamin supplements, which generally do no harm and might help cognitive function, as we saw in Chapter 6; or like the Feingold diet, which is inconvenient and hard to follow but mostly safe. Megavitamin therapy can cause liver damage or interference with normal vitamin metabolism. If any of the studies contained solid evidence of benefits, then one could weigh these against the risks. But without clear benefits, the treatment has nothing to recommend it.

CHAPTER NINE

Eating Disorders and Stress in Children

In previous chapters we discussed the relationship of food to hyperactivity, aggression, intelligence, learning, and severe developmental problems in children. In this chapter we will look at eating disorders and how foods affect the ability of children to cope with stress.[1] Much of what we know about diet and stress comes from work with animals, and we must engage in some speculation when applying it to humans. But we believe this work provides fresh insights into childhood stress and suggests practical applications in dietary management.

EATING DISORDERS IN CHILDREN

The Neglected Child

Pediatricians and psychologists often see children called "psychosocial dwarfs." As babies, these children look much like those with diseases that damage the production of growth hormone. There is markedly reduced output of growth hormone, even though there is no obvious medical reason. Despite having plenty of food, these children's bodies shut down production of the hormone essential for growth. Such children are usually neglected or rejected by their parents or live in such chaotic surroundings that they are severely emotionally damaged.

Placing these children in the hospital or a caring foster home produces a remarkable change. These psychosocial dwarfs begin to gain weight and grow in height, almost exactly in lock-step with their emotional improvement. During the growth phase of a child, its brain and body are very sensitive to love and caring, and to their absence. Studies of children in orphanages show that even when babies get an adequate diet, without cuddling, talking, and appropriate stimulation they begin to look much like starving children in famine-stricken parts of the world. Catch-up growth is still possible for these children until early adolescence.

Stimulation of the child takes many forms: handling, rocking, talking, play, noise, stroking, feeding, changing diapers, and eye contact. Animals or children receiving too little stimulation become apathetic, withdrawn, and listless; or they may react in an opposite manner, displaying angry, excited, aggressive, or protesting behavior.

Tactile stimulation is important: studies of babies show that gentle stroking accelerates their growth and calms them. Movement is important: experiments with monkeys and observations of children forced to wear whole-body casts show that they need vestibular changes (the changes in the middle ear that stimulate the vestibular reflexes controlling balance and gazing). Otherwise, they become physically and mentally disturbed, often showing hyperactivity and motor and sensory deficits similar to those caused by brain damage.

Either too much or too little stimulation creates problems for the child's development. Perhaps the most important function of the mother is modulating and controlling stimulation so that it is neither too high and intense nor too low. Children under great stress or neglect are smaller, have smaller head circumferences, and usually fail to grow to their genetic potential, physically or mentally.

Babies who are over- or understimulated may refuse food or shut down their output of growth hormones and begin to look malnourished and underfed, even though they have plenty of access to food. Feeding and the body's use of food, then, are very responsive to the state of the child; and maintaining the right emotional state during feeding is essential for good nutrition.

The Battle of the Spoon

A very different type of eating disorder in children develops when mothers are *too attentive.* Some children simply stop eating after prolonged battles with their mothers, who overanxiously thrust food into the mouth at every possible occasion. These mothers are often very controlling, overprotective, and unwilling to give any leeway in how, when, and how much the child eats. They engage in a power struggle with the child over who will control the eating behavior, and this is sometimes a life-and-death struggle. One of the last resources of the child over its own destiny is the decision to stop eating. Having some control over the environment is a need so powerful that denying that control may threaten life itself. Either too much or too little caring leads the child to a sense of helplessness and to a decision to give up, even on the most basic biological needs such as eating.

Thus, both neglected and overprotected children can ultimately die of malnutrition because of severe imbalance in the care and love they need. These are extreme cases, but ones often seen in psychiatric clinics. There are many variations though, and even normal parents must learn to read the signs telling them when a child needs more or less stimulation.

The "Colicky" Child

Although not as severe as the eating disorders just discussed, the fussy, irritable, crying baby, traditionally described as having "colic," is much more common. Some of these infants are simply intolerant of the lactose in cow's milk and do well when switched to another formula. Some are unable to digest the gluten in wheat and settle down when the wheat products are removed from the baby food.

But dietary changes alone do not suffice for most children. Many people suspect that this irritable and fussy pattern is part of the child's basic temperament, but the exact causes of this age-old problem remain somewhat of a mystery. One recent experiment, however, sheds some light on the problem. Colicky children were randomly divided into two groups. One group received a new formula without cow's milk, while the other group's mothers simply checked their children for any obvious discomforts (such as wet diapers or tight clothing) and gently comforted them before returning them to the crib. Both groups showed some improvement, but the comforted group showed a much greater drop in the amount of crying and fussing.

Crying is a baby's basic signal that it is hungry, uncomfortable, or in need of stimulation. Mechanically feeding the hungry child usually will not be enough. The gentle rocking, stroking, talking, and cuddling that most mothers instinctively give when feeding a newborn turn out to be essential ingredients in the feeding process.

Finding the right level of comforting may be very difficult, however. One of the most common mistakes some parents make is comforting the child too much. Behavior therapists often find that overanxious parents respond so much to the child's cries for attention that they inadvertently reward the behavior, which then increases in frequency. Clearly, finding the right balance is a tricky problem requiring very good instincts about when to give and when to withhold attention to fussy behavior. The more devoted and loving the parents, the more likely that they will err on the side of lavishing too much attention.

Obesity

The term *malnutrition* inevitably conjures up images of starving Biafran children or dying mothers holding wasted infants with large bellies. While this form of malnutrition is truly the scourge of developing third world countries, obesity, not undernutrition, is the most common form of poor nutrition in America and the West. If fat people were indeed jolly, then we might relegate the problem to the cardiologists, because obesity is an important risk factor in cardiac disease and mortality. But fat children are anything but happy and successful, and their achievement in school is lower than their normal weight or thin classmates.

A large survey of more than 2,000 3- to 6-year-old nursery-school children in New York City found that significant obesity (defined as more than 120% of ideal body weight) affected more than 12% of the children, spanning low-, middle-, and high-income families. A study of second-grade children reported that 28.5% of boys and 33.5% of girls from middle- and upper-income families were obese or overweight for their age and height.

How do such children fare in school compared to normal weight and underweight children? A recent study of middle- and upper-income suburban grade-school children examined the achievement tests of a large sample of fifth and eighth graders, dividing the children into those who were too thin, those who were normal in size, and those who were too fat. Using the nationally standardized Metropolitan Achievement Test (MAT), the researchers found that 30% of the obese children were underachieving, contrasted with only 7.1% of the thin children. This latter figure is substantially below the percentage of underachievers in the normal group, which was 18.6%. (Clearly, the number of normal weight underachievers is not trivial but must have explanations other than nutritional status.) Obesity in children tends to persist throughout life, with as many as half of overweight schoolchildren having been excessively fat as infants. Once present, obesity becomes a lifelong problem.

The reason that obese children achieve poorly is not clear. Sometimes being an underachiever heightens anxiety and *causes* excessive eating, rather than the other way around. But in most instances, there is a vicious cycle, so that being fat promotes anxiety and social rejection, leading to poor school habits or attendance, thus leading to school failure and more anxiety. Another explanation for poor school achievement is that fat children receive less attention and help from teachers. Whatever the reason, being overweight is a risk factor for underachievement, social rejection, and poor peer relationships.

True medical causes for obesity are rare and easily dismissed as an explanation. Studies show that no more than 10–30% of obese children have medically legitimate causes for their being overweight. Most overweight children simply eat too much and exercise too little. An important element in this equation is the amount of time children spend watching television. The progressive increase in the number of obese children correlates strongly with the amount of time spent motionless in front of television.

Fat parents tend to have fat children. But obesity is like poverty: though it runs in families, it is not necessarily hereditary. That fat parents have fat children is often as much a function of lifestyle as genes, though scientists disagree on what proportion of the problem is due to heredity and environment. Obesity is an example of a nutritional condition affecting learning and behavior, but probably not through direct effects on the brain as much as through indirect effects on the social environment and self-image.

All agree, however, that once obesity occurs it is extraordinarily resistant to change over the long term. The so-called ratchet effect refers to the fact that once weight increases, it is impossible to lower it below the baseline it started from. Given these facts, *early* prevention of overfeeding, accompanied by regular exercise, seems like the soundest, perhaps the only, successful approach over the long run.

Dieting by itself may compound the problem, and it is usually not good for children. Dieting appears to disrupt the body's "set point," or homeostatic mechanism that determines hunger and satiety. But what, then, can one do with a grossly overweight preadolescent if dieting is likely to worsen the problem? One logical solution is to provide a well-balanced diet with the recommended number of calories for the age and body type and try to *maintain* a constant weight. If children maintain the same weight, they will become thinner as their natural increase in height takes place with growth spurts. This is not dieting in the sense of lowering calorie intake below normal, but limiting intake to normal levels will seem like a diet at first.

An important way of accomplishing a successful change in food intake is to monitor snack time, since often as much as 20% of the child's calories come from between-meal snacks. If the snacks are nutritionally sound and their calories counted toward the total daily intake of calories, it doesn't matter *when* they occur. In other words, it is the total quantity and quality of the diet that affects the degree of fat accumulation, not the timing during the day. Many parents keep close control over the foods provided at mealtime but fail to regulate the kind and amount of calories taken at snack times, especially in school.

Behavior therapists use a variety of techniques of self-monitoring, charting, recording, counting the number of bites, slowing the time taken to eat a meal, and so forth, in order to stem the tide of overeating. Eating more slowly results in a faster cessation of hunger urges. Counting and charting the eating rate gives feedback to help learn the proper rate. But these techniques are generally less effective in child obesity than in adult obesity because they require complete cooperation and involvement of the entire family. There is little hope of maintaining a constant weight if other family members feed at the trough in an uncontrolled fashion.

Some solutions to childhood obesity are not only silly, but dangerous. The use of adult forms of dieting with young children is an increasing national problem. Misguided parents who are rightly convinced of the health advantages of a thin lifestyle take 2-year-olds to their aerobics classes and restrict the amount of fat in the diet, often giving them skim milk in place of the recommended regular or low-fat milk. The Surgeon General's recent call for lowering the amount of fat in the adult diet gets mistakenly extrapolated to young children. Without appropriate amounts of fat in the diet, a child's nerve cells cannot develop properly. The fatty sheath that surrounds brain nerve cells, myelin, protects the nerves from "crosstalk," much like the insulation in electrical wiring. Myelin continues to grow around brain nerve cells well into late adolescence, so depriving children of fats in the diet can prevent proper growth of the brain. Children should probably not begin drinking low-fat milk until after the second or third year of life.

Anorexia Nervosa

Many suspect that the great increase in the deadly condition known as *anorexia nervosa*—a life-threatening self-induced form of malnutrition now common among adolescent girls— stems from the American obsession with being thin. Anorexics often starve themselves to death in their quest for an ideal figure. Their idea of what is "ideal" becomes so distorted that it surpasses normal boundaries. Anorexics often have actual perceptual distortion of body sizes when comparing silhouettes of human figures, grossly overestimating how fat their own figure is in relation to a standard. It is as though their basic perceptions become altered by the powerful motive to be thin.

The predisposing biochemical and hormonal factors for anorexia are not well understood, partly because so many bodily functions become deranged as a result of the intense weight reduction. Some studies implicate family factors, such as over-controlling and intrusive parenting styles. But no single psychological profile emerges, and no one knows how to catch it early or prevent it. Early preoccupation with thinness, conflicts around eating routines at meals (forcing the child to eat), and the "model child" syndrome abound in anorexics' histories. But many anorexics do not have these histories. Concordance of the disorder is higher in monozygotic than dizygotic twins; that is, identical twins are many times more likely to share the disorder than are fraternal twins. This suggests some genetic risk for the disorder.

One of the more popular current explanations of anorexia nervosa is that it is a variant of biological depressive disorders. Anorexics share a number of features with depressives, such as hyperactivity or its opposite, hypoactivity; depressed mood; lack of pleasure from ordinary activities; fatigue and loss of energy; decreased concentration and suicidal thoughts; diminished interest in sex; positive response to antidepressant drugs; and disturbed hormonal reactions such as hypersecretion of cortisol (recall that cortisol is a hormone released during emergency and stress). But many of these hormonal effects could be secondary to the starvation itself, and they cannot explain why the disorder is present mostly in young females coming from upper social classes.

Many observers have noted that anorexics can be excessively hyperactive and very intolerant of being confined. Hospitalization is often necessary for these patients, and behavioral programs usually involve getting anorexics to eat by allowing them greater freedom for activities, conditional upon eating. Applied judiciously, this same approach is appropriate as a treatment at home for less severe cases or after hospitalization teaches parent and child the right approach.

The real causes of anorexia remain a mystery. Whatever its causes, anorexia in young adolescent girls is a serious problem, with 5 to 18% of anorexics eventually dying from the effects of starvation. When an adolescent begins to show signs of serious weight loss (15% below expected weight for age), professional help should be sought and the condition treated as a medical emergency.

Bulimia Nervosa

Another increasingly common pathological form of weight loss, also found most often in adolescent girls, is *bulimia*. Bulimia is a periodic regurgitation of food, usually accomplished by mechanically causing oneself to vomit up a recent meal. The chronic use of this technique can lead to severe imbalances in body chemistry, with occasionally fatal consequences. There is usually a cycle of huge binges followed by secretively inducing vomiting.

These children can be very cunning, finding extremely imaginative ways to hide their acts. Even in specialty inpatient units for treating these children, children will outwit nurses by stowing their vomitus in some unlikely place (removing the caps from metal bedposts is one example). Or, like the alcoholic in *The Lost Weekend*, they may resort to the coverings over light fixtures to conceal their habit.

Adolescent bulimics, unlike anorexics, often maintain a normal weight and appearance, and because they are so secretive may be much more difficult to identify. Again, an excessive value placed upon thinness is usually prominent, especially among adolescents faced with physical maturation and intense comparison with their peers.

Surprisingly, both anorexics and bulimics are often high achievers and highly intelligent, only failing in schoolwork when the disorder begins to debilitate them physically. Bulimia often becomes apparent in college students away from home for the first time. Student health services usually have a heavy load of such patients (often as the result of a roommate's discovery of the secretive practices and its disgusting consequences). This pattern of high achievement supports the notion that the child suffers from the "model child" syndrome, trying to be perfect in everything, from bodily appearance to academic and social success. Needless to say, these are attitudes inculcated by the family from an early age.

THE EXPERIENCE OF STRESS

Everyone experiences stress and knows what it is at a subjective level. Scientists, however, find it difficult to define stress in a precise way. What is one person's stress may be another's thrill. Almost any event can be stressful, depending upon how it is perceived and what we are able to do about it.

The feeling of stress is a normal reaction to events perceived as threatening and requiring action. Once we feel we are *in control* of the stressful event and know what to do about it, the stress is gone. Perhaps the best way to describe stress is the sense of feeling trapped—that we must act in response to a challenge but don't know how. Once we are successful in coping with events, our stress level goes down. If we are unable to cope and to resolve the threat, our stress increases, perhaps only to a level of minor discomfort, or perhaps to a point of panic or anguish.

Ordinary events, such as taking an examination, socializing with playmates, being in a classroom, arguing with one's parents, or doing homework, are stressful events for most children. These events are not necessarily harmful or undesirable in themselves, for daily challenges allow the child to learn coping skills. But unresolved minor, cumulative stresses of everyday life can also lead to many symptoms in children. Headaches, nausea, insomnia, palpitations, temper outbursts, distractibility, and nervousness often occur when children or adults fail to recognize the stressful events impinging on them or are unable to cope with them.

The stress reaction may become intolerable or disruptive to functioning only when challenges are unmet or avoided. Chronic, *unresolved* stress immobilizes the child with anxiety, depression, or frustration, interfering with learning and normal personality development. Being in an abusive household, or being repeatedly subjected to humiliation or inescapable punishment, are extreme stressors for many children. But the fear of failure in an overachieving student can be equally stressful.

Losing a parent, a close friend, or the familiar surroundings of one's childhood may be unavoidable. These are events that invariably create chronic major stress reactions. But when a child has difficulty learning or maintaining the control required by school or parents, he or she might experience chronic stress just as severe as major life catastrophes. Crying, sadness, anger, and poor concentration are often tip-offs to a child's sense of powerlessness to control events in his or her environment. Children with undetected learning disabilities or hearing loss may be under stress for years before the condition is recognized and treated. By then, chronic stress will have permanently left its mark on their personalities.

HOW STRESS AFFECTS THE BODY AND BRAIN

The body reacts to stress as if an emergency were occurring. Heart rate and respiration increase, energy fuels mobilize for fight or flight, the body secretes hormones such as cortisol and adrenaline, and the muscles tense in readiness for action. Prolonged muscular tension often leads to headaches, as the muscles of face, head, and neck become constricted. The hormonal and gastric secretions produced by the body's emergency response system may cause nausea, stomach upset, or even ulcers.

The brain, too, increases its activity, resulting in a state of vigilance, arousal, and alertness. Insomnia may result. Along with these cognitive changes, there is usually a heightened sense of anxiety, worry, or dread. Over a long period of stress, these reactions can lead to a state of exhaustion, inertia, and the inability to experience pleasure. Worry and dread turn into apathy or depression.

Anxiety and depression go hand in hand, one often following the other. Anxiety is a state of heightened arousal and fear, but usually with lack of awareness about the source of the fear. Phobias, such as fear of open places, are severe anxiety states in which the reason for the fear is unfounded. Depression usually shows up as insomnia or early-morning awakening (psychiatrists often refer to these as DFA, or difficulty falling asleep, and EMA, early-morning awakening), sad mood, a sense of hopelessness about the future, and a sense of helplessness that anything can be done to change things. There is a general anhedonia, or inability to experience pleasure from normal events.

At times, both anxiety and depression are present simultaneously, creating a state of "agitated depression." Studies of orphans or neglected children show that they often go through a sequence of anxious, protesting distress, followed by a period of rejecting all attempts to soothe them, and ultimately, to a state of lifeless despair.

Many parents of normal children are perplexed when children taken to the hospital become angry and rejecting and even indifferent to visiting parents. In recent years, awareness of this sequence of reactions has let to greater attempts to prepare and support children during the separations attending hospitalization. The stress of separation may actually delay recovery from illness. There is evidence that stress alters the body's immune system, increasing the likelihood of infection and delaying healing of body tissues.

Some children appear to begin life very early with excessive sensitivity to stress, having unusually strong reactions to brief separations or other apparently minor stressors. These children will often complain of many bodily symptoms which no one can find a physical cause for. They may show unusually strong reactions to their first separations from home, developing nausea and vomiting, perhaps eventually becoming "school phobics." Most such apparent phobias, however, are really fears of leaving home, for children fear that something dreadful will happen to their parents when they leave. Such stress-sensitive children have headaches, nightmares, bedwetting, aches and pains, insomnia, and other classical psychosomatic symptoms, often for no apparent reason, and to an extent much greater than expected for their age. They act as if they were under intense stress, even though siblings may find the same events innocuous. Their mood is anxious, depressed, or frightened much of the time.

Stress starts in the brain, and studies of the brains of monkeys experimentally separated from their parents have shown that brain neurotransmitters change in a predictable way with their states of protest, despair, and apathy. Brain neurotransmitters involved in alertness and arousal are more abundant in the early phases of the stress response, but they become depleted during later phases. Animals subjected to unavoidable stress show characteristic impairment of exploratory activity and learning. They may freeze their bodily positions, engage in stereotyped activity, such as always turning the same way in a maze they had previously learned, or become aggressive toward litter mates previously accepted by them. They may appear frightened and "on edge" well after the stressful events have ceased.

The brain's reaction to stress is complicated and not well understood. But the excitatory neurotransmitters that we have encountered in previous chapters, norepinephrine, dopamine, and serotonin, all change under stress.* Relaxation, on the other hand, reverses most of these effects.

Dr. Herbert Benson, a Harvard cardiologist, discovered that the body has a sequence of changes just the opposite of stress, a sequence he labeled the "relaxation response." The relaxation response is a *hypo*metabolic response: a relaxation of muscles, slowing of breathing, decrease in oxygen consumption, and general slowing of metabolic activity. Relaxation allows the neurotransmitters to recuperate from the exhaustion created by stress, which is why relaxation treatments are often an effective antidote to stress.

The effects of stress on the brain are much like the effects of stimulant drugs such as Dexedrine and Ritalin. These drugs also increase the production and availability of the neurotransmitters dopamine and norepinephrine.

But if stress increases the activity of these neurotransmitters, shouldn't it actually *improve* the behavior of hyperactive children, just like stimulant drugs? To some extent it does. Many hyperactive children learn more readily and become calmer when given a moderate amount of stressful challenge. Dr. Sydney Zentall proposed the idea that hyperactive children function best with a moderate amount of stimulation in the

---

*Although we have seen that serotonin usually acts as a calming and sedating neurotransmitter, studies show that it can actually become "excitatory" in its actions under stress.

classroom, actually doing more poorly when stimulation is low (everyone knows they do poorly when stimulation is high).

These children act as if their brains need more activation than normal children. But moderate stimulation is insufficient by itself. For hyperactive children quickly tire out and readily revert to a disinhibited and frenzied pattern. After functioning rather well in the classroom for a few hours, they seem depleted and out of control. Their pattern reminds one of the normal infant who becomes cranky and irritable when tired. But tolerance for sustained attention is much less than for other children their own age, as if they become more readily depleted of some energizing ingredient available to normal children.

One such ingredient may be dietary, involving the amino acid tyrosine, found in most ordinary protein sources such as meat, fish, poultry, and eggs. Tyrosine, as we have seen before, is a precursor required in the manufacture of the neurotransmitters dopamine, norepinephrine, and epinephrine. Some scientists suggest that acute stress produces a temporary imbalance of these neurotransmitters, while chronic stress might produce a permanent imbalance. Stress creates conditions which use up neurotransmitters, and drugs can act to make more of the neurotransmitters available but usually only in a temporary way. If, for some reason, the brain did not have enough of the building blocks to manufacture more neurotransmitters, stress would improve behavior only briefly, until the supplies ran out, much as stimulants only offset poststress depression temporarily. Amphetamines used to be used to treat depression until it was found that they eventually make it worse, for the drug gradually depletes the brain's stores of excitatory transmitters.

FOOD AND STRESS

But foods can act much like these drugs. As we learned in previous chapters, the brain requires particular amino acids to be present in the diet in order to manufacture its neurotransmitters. Thus, tryptophan is needed to produce serotonin, and tyrosine and phenylalanine to produce adrenaline, noradrenaline, and dopamine. These amino acids are present in large amounts in most protein sources (meat, fish, eggs, poultry). A logical question, then, is whether these dietary amino acids might act in the same way as drugs, making more of the neurotransmitters available under conditions of stress, perhaps inoculating to some extent against the effects of stress. Perhaps the lack of energy, the poststress blues, and the irritability which often follow intense stress could be eliminated, or at least moderated, by dietary management.

Experiments with animals strongly support such a possibility. For example, in one study, rats received stress in the form of tail pinching. Their behavior following this stress showed some of the typical changes in motor behavior and alertness associated with stress, such as a decrease in exploration and grooming behavior. Examination of their brains showed a considerable depletion of norepinephrine and its by-products.

When other rats were pretreated by feeding them tyrosine—the precursor for norepinephrine—they showed fewer behavioral effects of the stress. Their brains did not show the depletion of norepinephrine which occurred without tyrosine. This protective effect of dietary tyrosine could be negated by feeding another common amino acid (valine) along with the tyrosine. Just as ordinary protein meals contain many amino acids that block each other's entry into the brain, so valine could prevent the beneficial effects of tyrosine. Valine, like other amino acids, is a common ingredient of most protein.

If tyrosine can alleviate stress, there may be other uses for amino acids. For example, studies show that the tendency of animals to self-administer amphetamine is reduced by pretreating them with tryptophan. These "rat junkies" created in the laboratory tend to establish a very stable rate of administering a fix to themselves, and this rate is substantially lowered when they are given tryptophan an hour or so beforehand. These results suggest that the dietary amino acid tryptophan can offset the need to obtain a high from the drug. Based on this type of study, some scientists have recommended that adolescent drug abusers might be treatable with antidepressants, which like tryptophan act to increase the brain's supply of serotonin.

It is just as logical to wonder whether dietary manipulation might achieve the same end; for example, by adding foods to the diet like bananas and pineapple, which are rich sources of serotonin. Though appealing, such an idea is probably too simple. It is likely that inadequate brain serotonin reflects biochemical abnormalities in the brain itself, or perhaps the ability of the serotonin nerve receptors to respond properly. Minerals like copper, magnesium, and manganese affect the brain's utilization of serotonin, as does vitamin B_6. Feeding serotonin or its precursor, tryptophan, would not correct these intrinsic limitations within the brain.

Thus far, only two studies used tyrosine to treat hyperactive children. In one study, by Dr. Eugene Arnold and colleagues at the University of Ohio, tyrosine was compared with the effects of a stimulant drug. In general, the effects were disappointing because most measures of hyperactivity showed no improvement, though there was a significant improvement in attentiveness due to the tyrosine. It was dismissed as an isolated finding, perhaps due to chance.

But a major problem with the study is that we do not know whether much of the tyrosine actually got into the brain. Since the *ratio* of tyrosine to other proteins was not measured, other amino acids may have blocked the tyrosine, much as the valine did with the rat study. Even though the blood levels of tyrosine were high, other proteins in the meal eaten at the same time as tyrosine could have blocked the latter's entry into the brain. This same criticism applies to another study, carried out with seven hyperactive children in an open, nonblind trial. In that study, tyrosine was delivered in a chocolate bar, which ought to have provided enough sugar to drive the tyrosine into the brain through the insulin response. But the authors fail to mention what other things were eaten at the same time, so competing proteins might have blocked the tyrosine action.

But there is another reason why just feeding tyrosine might not always work. The brain has a feedback system which tells it to stop manufacturing some neurotransmitters as soon as enough is produced. Only if the brain neurons are actually firing (and thus using up the neurotransmitters) will the brain allow production of these neurotransmitters from additional tyrosine. (This is unlike the situation we saw with tryptophan, where adding additional amounts to the brain usually ends up producing more of the transmitter serotonin.) Thus, only if the children fed the tyrosine were actually under some stress (thus causing the neurons to fire), would adding tyrosine to their diet have any effect. Even then, the ratio of tyrosine to other amino acids would have to be high.

In order for tyrosine to be an effective stress preventative, then, conditions would have to be just right. Obviously the child should have a protein meal containing enough tyrosine to get into the brain. But just eating the protein might not suffice to ensure that tyrosine gets to the brain, for other amino acids in the protein meal would also be elevated and compete with the tyrosine. In fact, eating a lot of protein might actually prevent the particular ones most needed at the time from gaining access to the brain.

Therefore, if competing proteins are slowing down the entry of tyrosine, some method of giving it a "push" into the brain would have to be found. One such possibility suggested by research, oddly enough, is insulin. Studies have suggested that insulin might lead to greater uptake of tyrosine by the brain, just as it does for tryptophan—first, by flushing out competing amino acids and, second, by a more direct path. In one rat study, the investigators found that oral glucose lowered tyrosine in the blood but, surprisingly, raised brain tyrosine levels, an effect they speculate might be due to a direct effect of insulin. Paradoxically then, *sugar or carbohydrate in conjunction with tyrosine could get tyrosine into the brain.*

Perhaps this is the explanation of the benefit that the protein breakfast conveyed on our hyperactive children when they received a sugar challenge. Since they were engaged in a stressful vigilance task, the brain neurons that use tyrosine would be active, and the tyrosine in the protein meal might give them a boost, with the insulin elicited by the sugar acting to get the tyrosine into the brain. This may seem contradictory, since in earlier chapters we have shown how sugar can wreak havoc with attention and possibly play a role in the low blood sugar resulting from too much insulin. But this merely emphasizes the point that sugar is neither good nor bad in itself. Its effects depend upon the condition under which it is eaten.

STIMULANT DRUGS, SUGAR, AND PROTEIN

If this line of reasoning is correct, then another benefit of a protein meal accompanied by sugar suggests itself. Why not add sugar when a hyperactive child takes his or her stimulant drug? If we are correct about insulin causing more uptake of tyrosine, and tyrosine is used to make more neurotransmitter available, just as stimulant drugs do, then adding sugar to the drug should enhance its effect. A combination of sugar, drug, and tyrosine might give an even greater effect.

Consider the following possibility. Suppose hyperactive children have a chronic deficit in one of their activating brain neurotransmitters (noradrenaline or dopamine, or perhaps both), as many scientists have suggested. The stimulant drug makes more of the neurotransmitters available but only up to a point. Especially if the hyperactive child was under stress (as is usually the case in the stressful school environment), the stimulant would eventually lose some of its effect, but increasing tyrosine in the brain at the right time should make it possible to manufacture more of the needed neurotransmitters. Thus, the drug might work better, perhaps at a lower dose, when it is taken along with sugar or other carbohydrate which stimulates enough insulin to push more tyrosine into the brain. It is safe to assume that only a modest amount of sugar, say in the form of a cookie or drink, will be necessary. Harmful effects almost always come from excessive amounts of any one food. It is only when very frequent ingestion of sugar takes place, *unaccompanied by protein*, that bodily systems are likely to become disrupted.

Our research team at Children's Hospital had suspected such a possibility, but before we could test it out, I received a phone call from a mother of a hyperactive teenager who accidentally stumbled upon this same phenomenon. Her son was taking a stimulant drug for his hyperactivity, but as in many such cases the results were not completely satisfactory. The drug worked to some extent, but the boy was far from normal at home and at school. He had many of the same problems in poor attention and getting along with classmates as he did before drug therapy.

Then one day he became nauseous, and his mother gave him an antinausea medicine along with his stimulant drug. To her complete amazement the boy had one of his best days ever. His teacher said he was completely changed; and even his father who saw him after school spontaneously said, "Who *is* that boy? He's suddenly acting terrific!" The mother noted that whenever she gave the boy the medicine along with his stimulant drug, his behavior improved compared with the stimulant alone. On the other hand, just giving the antinausea drug by itself had no effect.

When the mother called us, she gave us the name of the medicine, and to our surprise, it turned out to contain mainly sucrose and fructose: simple sugars much like table sugar or sugar found in honey. Shortly after that, we encountered another mother with a similar story. We are now testing this combination of sugar and stimulant drug in controlled trials, and the preliminary evidence is encouraging that we may have a simple dietary method of improving stimulant drug effectiveness, perhaps allowing children to take less of the drug when they have the right meal conditions. Apart from this practical advantage, if these results hold up under experimental tests, then we will have added to our understanding of the way diet affects the brain.

CONCLUSIONS

Several animal experiments show, at least in the short run, that stress acts just like amphetamine on the brain, causing release of neurotransmitters that help to mobilize for action. But chronic stress leads to an exhaustion of the neurotransmitter system, resulting in apathy and depression. We know from experience in treating depression with stimulant drugs that, over time, amphetamine also eventually leads to an exhaustion of the neurotransmitters, causing people to repeatedly increase the drug in order to get the same level of alertness and alleviation of symptoms as they did at first.

Stress, too, in the long run leads to brain depletion of these same neurotransmitters. The result is that the excitatory beneficial effects of stress are short lived. Depression, immobilization, and apathy follow. But replenishing depleted neurotransmitters by increasing the supply of the building blocks (precursors) needed for manufacturing the neurotransmitters might alleviate these effects of chronic stress. It remains to be seen whether the right meal conditions will permit a child to cope with the effects of stress better, much as stimulant drugs do in hyperactive children. This added protection from meal contents might be especially beneficial in stress-prone children who are chronically overreactive to normal events.

Theoretically, tyrosine ought to be a good prophylactic against stress, much as it is in animals. But studies with it in hyperactives are disappointing. We argued, though, that particular meal conditions may allow tyrosine to act much like stimulant drugs do, complementing their action in hyperactive children and possibly working with stress-prone children. These are experiments we are anxious to do.

CHAPTER TEN

Tracking Food, Mood, and Behavior in Children

OBSERVING AND RATING CHILDREN

Throughout this book we emphasize the tentative nature of much of our knowledge about food and behavior interactions. But science moves slowly, and parents may not want to wait until final answers are in before doing something about a suspected dietary cause of a child's problems. Until research clarifies many controversial issues we have discussed, professionals will hesitate to carry out diet–behavior programs for children outside of research studies. Moreover, there are few professionals equipped or willing to carry out systematic clinical studies for parents. But while it is generally unwise to start supplementing a child's diet (with tyrosine or megavitamins, for example) or engage in radical changes in the diet without supervision, it is still possible for parents to learn a lot about the food and mood of their children through careful observation and judicious changes in their diets.

I have encountered many observant parents who have been able to figure out important food and behavior connections on their own. Though a single observation of a child before and after a single meal can be suggestive, in most instances firm conclusions depend upon a carefully planned series of observations.

In order to find out for themselves whether a particular food, pattern of eating, or type of meal helps or hinders a child's behavior, parents must become good observers and experimenters. Whether a parent is experimenting with removing sugar, adding more protein, adding sugar to protein, removing food additives, adding sugar along with the child's Ritalin or Dexedrine, or any other dietary change, certain principles apply.

First, *be sure the overall diet is nutritionally sound.*[1] Before considering any other changes in the diet, it is important to be sure that the current diet is already meeting the basic requirements for a child of a given age. Many introductory texts on nutrition provide guidance on dietary intakes for specific nutrients, vitamins, and minerals. For parents or teachers who are computer literate, there are also computer software programs that calculate the nutrient composition of diets, specific foods, or meals.[2]

Second, *define the target behaviors.* You must define the behavior unambiguously. "Hitting the dog" is a much better target than "aggressiveness," because there is little doubt about what the target behavior is. A lot of the problems in keeping track of children's behavior stem from vague and ambiguous definitions of what constitutes the problem.

Third, *record the behavior.* Keeping records is important. One tends to forget what happened a day or two before, sometimes changing one's recollection to accord with one's wishes. By keeping records continuously over a week or two, you can begin to notice patterns of when and under what circumstances the behavior occurs. Note how often the target behavior occurs over a fixed period in a given circumstance. For example, rather than try to estimate how restless a child is generally, it is much better to record an estimate of restless behaviors for the one-hour period after dinner or during the period of afternoon home-work.

Sometimes a behavior varies more in *intensity* than in fre-quency; for example, an explosive temper outburst versus minor irritability or a mild versus a severe headache. So for these be-haviors record intensity rather than frequency of occurrence. With a subjective symptom like headache, it is often possible for older children to record their own estimate of severity.

Fourth, *record a baseline*. Count or estimate the amount, du-ration, or intensity of the behavior over several days before any changes are made in the diet, keeping a running log from which you can determine just how stable the trend is. Often one finds that as soon as one homes in on a particular behavior, it begins to decrease on its own, and it is important not to confuse these spontaneous fluctuations with the intervention. One also finds that the behavior may occur more under certain conditions than others, and finding those conditions can aid in identifying the circumstances which precede, initiate, or trigger the behaviors. Sometimes one finds that the behavior is getting worse. Without the baseline one might then attribute the worsening to the di-etary intervention. It is important, therefore, to wait until the recorded behavior stabilizes, neither getting worse nor improv-ing, before beginning a dietary change.

Fifth, having firmly established the baseline behavior, then *make a dietary change*. Again, this has to be specific (for example, adding a certain amount of a specific food suspected to improve or worsen the behavior). Make sure that you change only one thing at a time. If you were attempting to reduce sugar intake in a school-age child, it would be important to know what the child is eating when away from home. It is always easier to maintain dietary changes that are not too complicated. If you try to elimi-nate all food additives for example, you are unlikely to succeed. But starting with tartrazine or preservatives like EDTA, for ex-ample, is much easier, because you can check package labels for those specific items. You can then turn to other suspected causes of the problem, repeating the experiment as often as needed.

Sixth, continue to *record the target behaviors for several days after the change*. Then compare the rates of the target behavior with those preceding the change to see if there is improvement.

This is a mini-experiment, but by no means "scientific." Repeating it several times with the same results would give more confidence that any changes were real. Making a *different* dietary manipulation, by changing some irrelevant aspect of diet, and finding that the previous improvement failed to take place, would strengthen your case even further.

This type of experiment boils down to close observation of how the child changes under different dietary conditions. The main problem in interpreting these changes is taking account of the effects of other things that could be causing the changes. For example, if you decide to remove the sweet cola the child is drinking every night at dinner, then be aware that simply reducing liquids of any kind might account for any changes. Therefore, it would be better to substitute an alternative drink, such as milk. Of course, the child might resist such changes and become argumentative, so until the changes become a regular habit, early effects might be misleading. You could mistakenly conclude that milk makes the child argumentative!

Also *be aware of how your knowledge of dietary changes influences your judgments*. The desire for improvement often leads one to believe something positive is taking place. It is always helpful when others, not privy to a new dietary program, can verify improvement. Asking a teacher, siblings, or father to confirm the positive changes adds to the validity of an experiment.

Placebo effects are very powerful, and we have emphasized throughout this book how easy it is for any change to elicit temporary improvement. We saw examples of how effects of sugar alleged by parents were unsubstantiated by double-blind trials. Try, therefore, to document what happens by careful experiments rather than occasional impressions. Most parents coming for help at our clinic have impressions that some food affects their child's behavior, but few verify these impressions by documented experiments. Doctors are much more likely to be helpful in pursuing a suspected problem if they can see the results of an experiment backed up by careful records.

An issue that may have occurred to parents throughout this book is whether they need to worry about their children's behavior in the first place. What is normal, anyway, and how does one know what behaviors need changing? Many parents are uncertain whether some troublesome behavior is normal for a child of a given age or whether it warrants professional attention. Like medical students reading a textbook for the first time, they can begin to imagine that every problem described in a book applies to their own child.

Unfortunately, mental disorders in children are not precisely quantifiable. There is no sharp line between normal and abnormal behavior in children, and behaviors vary considerably with age and rate of development. Behavior and learning problems are quite common at all ages, and whether they deserve a label of "psychiatric disorders" is often a matter of heated debate. Very few behaviors, in and of themselves, are diagnostic of a particular abnormality. One family may decide they require professional help, whereas another family with the same problems may feel they are quite appropriate for their circumstances. What may appear to be a severe problem for one family may seem inconsequential in another.

The table on page 240 shows just how common certain problems are in children. The figures come from a sample of 482 mothers' responses about their children between 6 and 12 years of age.[3] The mothers indicated whether their children had any of these problems, and if so, how often.

It is obvious that these fears and worries are very common

Behavior Problems in Children[a]

Behavior	Percentage with problem
Fears and worries, 7% or more	43
Wetting bed within the past year	17
Nightmares	28
Temper loss	80
Biting nails	27
Fear of snakes	44
Fear of someone else's glasses, dishes, etc.	49

[a]From Lapouse & Monk, 1959.

in the general population. However, even though these problems are quite common and usually go away by themselves, if poorly handled, they can develop into major roadblocks to normal development. A child who wets the bed, for example, could be made to feel worthless and ashamed, even though the "symptom" of bedwetting occurs over a wide range of ages and usually disappears spontaneously. How one handles the problem is often much more important than any intrinsic handicap to the child. Temper tantrums and defiant or oppositional behavior are quite common in children under 5 years of age, yet if poorly managed, they can lead to major personality and behavioral impairments in later life.

There is, then, considerable uncertainty in many parents' minds about whether to ignore a particular problem, deal with it on their own, or bring it to the attention of a professional. Before investing in professional help, it is usually wise to compare the child's behavior with other children the same age. But many parents have limited experience with the behavior of other people's children, and even when they do, they may feel that the comparison is not helpful. Perhaps they feel the neighbor's child is "too good" or, conversely, that the neighbor's kid ought to be in therapy too.

One solution is to ask the opinion of a more objective and experienced person, like a teacher. While some teachers can be unusually strict or lenient, most develop a good standard based upon contacts with many children over the years. Another method is to use standards developed for normal children.

The table below lists 10 of the most common behavior problems. Thousands of parents and teachers in regular schools filled out this checklist, providing useful comparison standards. After checking each item you can sum them up, counting each item as 0, 1, 2, or 3 (for "not at all," "just a little," "pretty much," and "very much," respectively). The table shows what a total

Behavior Problem Checklist

Behavior	Score
1. Restless or overactive	
2. Excitable and impulsive	
3. Disturbs other children	
4. Fails to finish things (short attention span)	
5. Constantly fidgeting	
6. Inattentive (easily distracted)	
7. Demands must be met immediately (easily frustrated)	
8. Cries often and easily	
9. Mood changes quickly and drastically	
10. Temper outbursts: (explosive and unpredictable behavior)	
Total	

Score 0 if "not at all true"; score 1 if "just a little true"; score 2 if "pretty much" true; score 3 if "very much true."

Age	Score at which only 1% of children are higher	
	Boys	Girls
3–5	27	21
6–8	18	12
9–11	20	13
12–14	13	7
15–17	13	16

score must be in order to qualify as higher than 99% of the population. If only 1% of the population has a higher score than your child, then you can probably consider that the child has a real problem and that further attention to it is worthwhile.

To use this table, find the age of your child, and under the appropriate column (boy or girl), locate the number. If your child has a score greater than this number, then he or she has a higher score than 99% of the general population (only 1% are worse).

Notice that at all ages except 15–17, girls have lower scores than boys. A 9-year-old girl only has to get a total score of 13 before having a "severe" problem, while a boy of the same age would have to get a score of 20. This means that more problems normally occur for boys than girls of the same age, so normal boys must get higher scores to qualify as deviant. Also notice that the scores systematically decrease with age (except for 15–17-year-old girls), showing that a lot more deviant behavior is normal for younger children than older children.

Remember that in interpreting a score a single day may not be a reliable indicator of the child's usual pattern, and that filling out the scale over a week or two is more likely to reflect the *general pattern* of behavior.

It is also important to remember that these checklists are only very rough screening measures and that high scores do not necessarily show that the child suffers from a serious problem. If in doubt, always consult mental health specialists. Rather than using it as a diagnostic instrument, this brief scale is more useful for tracking the ups and downs of a child when one is trying some new tactic to cope with the problems.

But for most people there is still a lot of uncertainty when it comes to deciding just what "pretty much " or "very much" means. One guideline is that *any* problem interfering with family welfare, school functioning, or getting along with others deserves recording as "pretty much"; while "very much" applies to serious interferences with function. One must keep in mind, of course, that these are still human judgments, and that they are therefore subject to errors of many kinds, such as having too strict or too lax standards or failing to observe the child objectively.

Mental health specialists (psychologists, psychiatrists, social workers, counselors) use such information from parents and teachers, but they generally ask many other questions regarding the total pattern of the child's development, the environment, family functioning, illnesses, history of mental disorders, and specific occurrences, before deciding that the child needs treatment.

The best use of this type of checklist, therefore, is for recording behaviors before and after some intervention rather than for diagnosis. The checklist has proven very sensitive to changes in hyperactive children treated with stimulant drugs and should prove equally useful in tracking the effects of dietary manipulations in the mini-experiments suggested above.

Tracking Behavior in Older Children

Checklists and ratings are fine for younger children whose behavior is usually apparent to the naked eye. But for adolescents with some internal problems (like sadness, anger, fear, boredom, apathy), self-report rather than observation is more accurate. Older children seldom display their moods and reactions as clearly in overt behavior as they may have done as youngsters, and asking them to report their moods is usually more effective than direct observation.

Some sample items from our adolescent self-report scale are given below as examples of how one might put together a list useful for gaining information about the effects of food changes in a cooperative adolescent or older child*:

Problems with concentration:
>   I have trouble concentrating on one thing at a time.
>   My mind wanders.
>   I lose my place when I am reading.

Problems of restlessness:
>   I can't sit still for very long.
>   I have to get up and move around during homework.
>   I feel restless inside even if I am sitting still.

Problems of self-control:
>   I look before I leap.
>   I say things without thinking.
>   When I want something, I have trouble stopping myself.

Problems with anger:
>   I tend to explode easily.
>   A lot of things irritate me.

Problems with feelings:
>   I get nervous.
>   I feel sad and gloomy a lot.
>   I worry about a lot of things.

When we use such self-rating scales, we have the child rate each item on a 4-point scale, exactly like the hyperactivity checklist given above. Summing the scores for a given topic then gives an overall score (for example, for anger or restlessness) for comparison with behavior before, during, and after dietary changes.

---

*Inexpensive copies of the full scales described here, including ones for both teachers and parents, are available by writing to Multi-Health Systems, Inc., 95 Thorncliffe Park Drive, Suite 100, Toronto, Ontario, Canada M4H-1L7. Software versions for use on a home computer are also available from this source, making it easy to administer and score the scales when there are many children involved (as in school settings).

Of course, some children may not wish to cooperate in this task, especially if they feel that one is infringing upon their autonomy and privacy. But many normal children are happy to try experiments like this if they feel the results might help them to function better or understand themselves. Presented as a joint effort, and as an exercise in self-exploration and self-discovery, many adolescents will be curious enough to carry out their own experiments (for example, Does a change from coffee to juice affect my mood and homework?).

DOING EXPERIMENTS AT HOME

Many of my scientific colleagues will undoubtedly cringe at suggestions that parents do their own experiments. They are aware of how difficult it is to get even trained observers to become reliable in their recordings of behavior. They know that it is easy to kid oneself by a poor experiment lacking in controls. But scientists often work at a big disadvantage: they seldom know the children as well as parents and teachers. After listening to many parents, I believe that the failure of some experiments to validate parent observations about food and behavior is the fault of the studies, not the parents. In their own way, many parents are already carrying out experiments by making changes and seeing what happens. We are merely suggesting here that the experiments be systematic.

I have come to have great respect for the ability of some concerned parents to figure out how food operates with their children. For example, my wife and I recently entertained some friends who have a hyperactive son. Because I had been professionally consulted at one point by these parents, I already knew the son's story well. He was very hyperactive and had signs suggestive of real problems in brain function. In my clinical evaluation I had briefly discussed the role of foods, but I steered the parents into other treatments that seemed to have more immediate priority. But the child's response to foods became much plainer to me in my living room than it had in the clinic.

When it came time for dinner, the boy's mother very carefully restricted certain foods for her son. While I could only see a constantly active boy, the boy's mother knew that some of this was part of his usual pattern, while specific behaviors became more apparent after eating certain foods (she insisted on fruit rather than chocolate ice cream or cake for dessert). She had learned by experience that her son became irritable after eating chocolate in a way that was qualitatively different from his usual pattern of restless, impulsive behavior. She knew just which behaviors changed with certain foods and which were part of a general pattern that was always there. She was much better than I was at knowing what to expect of her son's behavior in a given situation. A conventional, double-blind experiment would have missed the specific changes that became apparent only after many months of familiarity with the child at home.

This mother also recounted the common experience that changes in the diet were met with tantrums and protest at first but then accepted by the child as he took part in his own behavior control program. He became quite scrupulous in monitoring his own diet. Far from embarrassment about this handicap, he was proud of his ability to manage his own behavior, and when offered chocolate cake he said, "I don't eat that, it makes me too hyper." Many attempts at changing children's diets come across as punishments, as sheer meanness, whereas skillful enlistment of cooperation through positive motivation to function better often does the trick. Keeping charts and records can be an exciting science project in which the child is both experimenter and subject.

Studies also show that food affects mood and behavior in

adults as well. Nothing gains the cooperation of children in a program of dietary change more than seeing that parents, too, take an interest in how foods affect them. Parents who blithely consume heavy loads of candy or caffeine will find their children stubbornly resistant to a unilateral disarmament program.

CHAPTER ELEVEN

Conclusions

Just as in pharmacology, where there is no "magic bullet" that strikes down a disease process in the brain, making a sick mind well, so in nutrition, there is no magic herb to calm hyperactivity, raise IQ, or soothe anxieties. Instead, there are a variety of subtle ways that food and mind interact.

FOOD CHANGES BRAIN NEUROTRANSMITTERS

The first, and most important, connection of food and behavior comes from processes of normal nutritional metabolism: foods affect neurotransmitters; indeed, foods *become* neurotransmitters. The most fundamental processes of mental activity—the transmission of nervous impulses through networks of brain neurons—involve ordinary foods we eat daily. Mental life—including remembering, planning, acting, sensing, imagining, calculating, and dreaming—requires an ever-replenished supply of these specific chemical keys, keys that fit matching receptors charged with transmitting neural messages unbroken to their many destinations.

Like alchemist's gold, the brain must take the dross of ordinary protein and turn it into neurotransmitters, the messengers assigned to carry information. The amino acids that ultimately become transmuted into these messengers appear first in food, then stomach, blood, and eventually brain. Once into the bloodstream, these precursors of mental activity must find a spot on designated transports which will ferry them across the great barrier between blood and brain. The concentration of each precursor relative to its competitors determines which will ultimately arrive within the brain cells and pass through the assembly line to become chemical messengers.

As in life, some of these competitors are more equal than others when faced with a challenge to their survival. Ever vigilant, insulin awaits the arrival of carbohydrates into the bloodstream, so it can begin the process of turning them into useful fuel or storing them as reserves. But as it begins the process of mobilizing carbohydrate into fuel, insulin sweeps through the bloodstream, purging most of the circulating amino acids. They retreat into muscle or other temporary hiding places.

But wily tryptophan has attached to a circulating molecule of albumin, and unlike its fellow amino acids, it remains unphased in the face of this challenge from insulin. Its competitors having temporarily vacated their seats on the ferry into the brain, tryptophan finds itself more likely to find a seat. Unchallenged, it crosses the great barrier into the brain itself and immediately gets synthesized into serotonin, a master neurotransmitter that carries out the brain's orders to control pain, to sleep, to modulate emotion, and to ride herd on hormones and other neurotransmitters. Thus it is that, in a sense, food becomes mind.

But if protein is eaten along with sugar or other carbohydrates, then tryptophan will find that its space on the transport ferry must be shared with other amino acids, also on their way to work in the brain's factories. For they too are essential in supplying dopamine, norepinephrine, epinephrine, acetylcholine, and other exotic messengers. So ultimately, two variables determine the outcome of this competition to get into the brain: how much protein one eats, and how much carbohydrate.

A dose of carbohydrate provokes an insulin response, and amino acids flee the scene; but eating more of them in the form of dietary protein insures that brain and body get the ones they need. This great tug-of-war between carbohydrate and protein is the cunning mechanism whereby the brain arranges for a balanced infusion of the chemicals it needs.

Some have suggested that the privileged nature of tryptophan's entry into the brain over its competitors, in the face of a carbohydrate challenge, is a way the brain uses to monitor blood sugar levels. As blood sugar rises, tryptophan responds by getting into the brain, raising the output of serotonin, and signaling the brain to stop eating and to stop sending out hormones to mobilize more fuel. Serotonin, then, might be acting as a homeostatic regulator, keeping blood sugar within bounds by signaling the organism when to stop eating carbohydrate. While some scientists doubt this serotonin-signal theory, our experiments with normal and hyperactive children are consistent with it.

Normal children given a carbohydrate breakfast respond as they are supposed to: they stop putting out hormones that mobilize more body fuel. Their brains recognize the increased blood sugar level and respond appropriately. True, they perform a little more poorly, as though the extra serotonin has a slight sedative effect. But hyperactive children perform miserably in comparison. Their vigilance deteriorates markedly as they eat a carbohydrate breakfast. However, once hyperactive children eat a protein breakfast, sugar intake actually *improves* their performance.

Whether insulin makes some exception to its scourging of amino acids by letting tyrosine from the protein meal get into the brain where it can increase excitatory transmitters, thus restoring performance to normal, or whether hyperactive children only need a little protein to offset the disturbing impact of increased brain serotonin, we cannot say. But hyperactive children react as though they are missing some essential link between the messages coming from the presence of sugar in their system and brain hormones that regulate blood sugar levels.

We believe that the missing link is one of the excitatory neurotransmitters dopamine or norepinephrine. Because tyrosine is a dietary precursor for these neurotransmitters, it might be useful in treating hyperactive children, augmenting their response to stimulant drugs. Tyrosine may also alleviate some of the effects of stress in children.

This model of competition of proteins struggling for access to the brain explains other dramatic phenomena—for instance, excessive reaction to diet drinks among some children. These processes, whereby foods gain entry into the brain and alter its functions, are well established by studies of normal nutritional metabolism. Thanks to the pioneering work of John Fernstrom and Richard Wurtman, some of the pieces of that puzzle are in place, though much more must surely follow.

FOODS PROTECT THE BRAIN

But food alters mental function in other important ways. Foods protect against damage from a polluted environment. Here, the competition is different: it is between unwanted metals competing with essential trace minerals. Which ones win affects the destiny of the brain. Some of the metals, like zinc, iron, and copper, are constructive and essential in brain function; while others, like lead and cadmium, are destructive and neurotoxic. Poor nutrition, then, makes children vulnerable to toxic environmental hazards to the brain. Even if deadly metals get to the brain, how long they remain there depends upon vitamin status. Subtle vitamin deficiencies slow the body's excretion of harmful burdens of heavy metal.

Recent evidence shows that food additives interfere with behavioral control and sleep and increase somatic complaints and allergic-like symptoms in young children. New diet studies suggest that elimination diets for removing food additives, though difficult to carry out, are useful for some young children.

FOOD AND THE DEVELOPING BRAIN

The brain continues to grow throughout childhood and adolescence, with different parts of the brain maturing at different rates. Nutritional needs of the brain are different at different ages. This varying timetable of neuronal growth is what allows vitamin and mineral supplements to elevate IQ in schoolchildren. The brain's intellectual capacities are constantly evolving. Timing nutritional supplements so that they coincide with brain growth spurts now has the potential for increasing the child's brain capacities, just as deprivation of essential nutrients can slow brain growth.

The brain's needs for energy fuel also change as the brain grows. Sudden carbohydrate craving in children may reflect rapid changes in brain needs for glucose to fuel their heightened brain activity. Parents must watch for signs that the diet itself needs changing. It cannot be rigidly restricted to fixed quantities or types of food but must be flexible, open to change, and varied. The key in management is always matching any increase in carbohydrate intake with high-quality protein.

Protein supplements for poorly nourished pregnant women and vitamin and mineral supplements for growing schoolchildren enhance mental operations and intellectual outcomes. But these findings do not simply mean that more is better. There is a real risk of toxic reactions to excessive doses of vitamins or, indeed, of any single nutrient.

IDEAS AND EMOTIONS CONTROL NUTRITION

It is easy to think of food and behavior as a one-way street. True, food alters the brain. But what the brain becomes—its beliefs, ideas, emotions, and habits—changes how and what children eat. Self-inflicted starvation—deadly anorexia—may ultimately stem from a single, powerful idea—"I am not thin enough." Obesity reflects a sedentary life-style, a lifetime of bad eating habits, and a love of food. Bulimia comes from a love of food passing through the mouth, but a hatred of it thereafter. We cannot underestimate the power of ideas and emotions in determining our nutritional status.

Stress comes from perceiving threats that we cannot control. Stress reactions lead to depression, exhaustion, anergia, anorexia, and loss of pleasure in eating. Stress uses up essential brain nutrients, much as some drugs use up brain chemicals in the process of providing a temporary cure. A child must therefore eat differently when under stress if he or she is to avoid poststress depression or exhaustion. Eating correctly can prevent some of the effects of stress, but it cannot alter the perceptions of threat which cause the stress. Treating eating disorders depends, therefore, not just on diet but on changing ideas, habits, thoughts, beliefs, and emotional reactions as well.

THE SCIENCE OF FOOD AND BEHAVIOR

Much is known from animal experiments about how food changes behavior. A little is known about food and mind in children and adult humans. But the volume of controversy far outweighs the volume of fact. Indeed, much of the scientific literature regarding food and behavior in children remains incomplete, argumentative, and biased in its presentations. This situation calls for more scientific research into the *behavioral* aspects of food and its toxicity, not just physical benefits and risks of food.

But parents and teachers must become scientists themselves to some extent—observing their children's behavior and mental functioning while systematically studying what happens when their diet changes.

For the most part, there are no "special" diets needed for children. Instead, children need a varied, well-balanced diet. High-carbohydrate, high-protein, or high-fat meals are all potentially harmful to children. Any narrow and limited food source is likely to ultimately cause more harm than good. Excesses, whether of vitamins, candy, diet drinks, meat, or vegetables are likely to interfere with optimal brain function and brain growth in children.

But even if a child is eating a reasonably well-balanced diet, there are still many questions needing answers for any specific child: Which specific foods aggravate symptoms and should be removed? Does adding vitamin and mineral supplements improve my child's brain function? Which carbohydrates does my child react to most strongly? If I remove artificial flavors and colors, will it help my child's irritability and sleep problems? And so on. For these questions, parents cannot wait while the government funds more studies and scientists continue to wrangle. Each parent must become a scientific observer—objective, systematic, and curious about their own infants and schoolchildren.

Notes

CHAPTER ONE

1. APA Task Force on Vitamin Therapy in Psychiatry: Megavitamin and orthomolecular therapy in psychiatry. *Nutrition Reviews*, Supplement, July, 1974.
2. Dr. Harrell's original report appeared in : Harrell, R. F., Capp, R. H., Davis, R. D., Peerless, J., & Ravitz, L. R. Can nutritional supplements help mentally retarded children? An exploratory study. *Medical Sciences*, 1981, *78*, 574–578.
3. Rimland, B. *Medical Tribune*, March 10, 1982.

CHAPTER TWO

1. This and other quotes on the aspartame controversy come from an article entitled: "'The most-tested additive': Lingering questions," which appeared in the *Washington Post* Outlook column, April 15, 1984, authored by Judith Randal.
2. Blundell, J. E., & Hill, A. J.: Paradoxical effects of an intense sweetener (aspartame) on appetite. *The Lancet*, 1986, 1092–1093.
3. Kreusi, M. J. P., Rapoport, J. L., Cummings, M., Berg, C. J., Ismond, D. R., Flament, M., Yarrow, M., & Zahn-Waxler, C.: Effects of sugar and aspartame on aggression and activity in children. *American Journal of Psychiatry*, 1987, 1487–1490.
4. Information on aspartame effects on seizures, blood levels, and relation to PKU and other aspects of safety appears in: *Dietary phenylalanine and brain function: Proceedings of the First International Meeting on Dietary Phenylalanine and Brain Function*, Washington, DC, May 8–10, 1987. Reprinted by the Center for Brain Sciences and Metabolism Charitable Trust, PO Box 64, Kendall Square, Cambridge, MA 02142.

CHAPTER THREE

1. Laird, D. A., Levitan, M., & Wilson, V. A.: Nervousness in school children as related to hunger and diet. *Medical Journal and Record*, 1931, 34, 494–499.
2. Lininger, F.: Relation of the use of milk to the physical and scholastic progress of undernourished school children. *American Journal of Public Health*, 1933, 23, 555.
3. Keister, M.: Relation of mid-morning feeding to behavior of nursery school children. *Journal of the American Dietetic Association*, 1950, 26, 25.
4. Matheson, N.E.: *Mid-morning nutrition and its effects on school-type tasks*. Ph.D. dissertation, University of California, 1970.
5. Dwyer, J. T., Elias, M. F., & Warren, J. H.: *Effects of an experimental breakfast program on behavior in the late morning*. Department of Nutrition, Harvard School of Public Health, 1973.
6. Tuttle, W. W., Daum, K., Larsen, R., Salzano, J., & Roloff, L.: Effects on school boys of omitting breakfast: Physiologic responses, attitudes and scholastic attainment. *Journal of the American Dietetic Association*, 1954, 30, 647.
7. Our studies of breakfast effects on attention are described in: Conners, C. K., & Blouin, A. G.: Nutritional effects on behavior of children. *Journal of Psychiatric Research*, 1983, 17, 193–201.
8. The carbohydrate–protein breakfast study was presented at the Annual Meeting of the American Psychological Association, New York City, 1987: *Hyperactives differ from normals in blood sugar and hormonal response to sucrose*.

CHAPTER FOUR

1. Seham, M., & Seham, G.: The relation between malnutrition and nervousness. *American Journal of Diseases in Children*, 1929, 37, 1.
2. Prinz, R. J., Roberts, W. A., & Hantman, E.: Sugar consumption and hyperactivity in young children. *Journal of Consulting & Clinical Psychology*, 1980, 48, 760–769.
3. Prinz, R. J., Roberts, W. A., & Hantman, E.: Dietary correlates of hyperactive behavior in children. *Journal of Consulting & Clinical Psychology*, 1980, 48, 760–769.
4. Goldman, J. A., Lerman, R. H., Contois, J. H., & Udall, J. N.: Behavioral effects of sucrose on preschool children. *Journal of Abnormal Child Psychology*, 1986, 14, 565–578.
5. Milich, R., & Pelham, W. E.: The effects of sugar ingestion on the classroom and playgroup behavior of attention deficit disordered boys. *Journal of Consulting & Clinical Psychology*, 1986, 54, 1–5.
6. Behar, D., Rapoport, J. L., Adams, A. J., Berg, C. J. & Cornblath, M.: Sugar challenge testing with children considered behaviorally "sugar reactive." *Nutrition and Behavior*, 1984, 1, 277–288.

7. Crapo, P. A., Reaven, G., & Olefsky, J.: Postprandial plasma-glucose and insulin responses to different complex carbohydrates. *Diabetes*, 1977, *26*, 1178–1183.

CHAPTER FIVE

1. The anecdotes about Dan White and the table of symptoms due to hypoglycemia are taken from an amusing and informative chapter on sugar and health by Thomas H. Jukes, *World Review of Nutrition and Dietetics*, 1986, *48*, 137–194.
2. Schauss, A. G.: *Diet, Crime and Delinquency*. Berkeley, CA: Parker House, 1980.
3. Bolton, R.: Hostility in fantasy: A further test of the hypoglycemia–aggression hypothesis. *Aggressive Behavior*, 1976, *2*, 257–274.
4. Benton, D., Kumari, N., & Brain, P. F.: Mild hypoglycaemia and questionnaire measures of aggression. *Biological Psychology*, 1982, *14*, 129–135.
5. Simeon, D., & Grantham-McGregor, S.: Cognitive function, undernutrition, and missed breakfast. *The Lancet*, 1987, 737–738.
6. Virkkunen, M.: Insulin secretion during the glucose tolerance test in antisocial personality. *British Journal of Psychiatry*, 1983, *142*, 589–604.
7. Linnoila, M., Virkkunen, M., Scheinin, M., Nuutila, A., Rimon, R., & Goodwin, F. K.: Low cerebrospinal fluid 5-hydroxyindoleacetic acid concentration differentiates impulsive from nonimpulsive violent behavior. *Life Sciences*, 1983, *33*, 2609–2614.
8. A good critical review of the diet and delinquency literature may be found in: Harper, A. E., & Gans, D. A.: Claims of antisocial behavior from consumption of sugar: An assessment. *Food technology: Symposium on behavioral reactions to foods*, January, 1986, 142–149.

CHAPTER SIX

1. Cravioto, J., & Delicardie, E. R.: Mental performance in school age children: Findings after recovery from severe malnutrition. *American Journal of Diseases of Childhood*, 1970, *120*, 404–410.
2. Rush, D., Stein, Z., & Susser, M.: A randomized controlled trial of prenatal nutritional supplementation in New York City. *Pediatrics*, 1980, *65*, 683–697.
3. Benton, D., & Roberts, G.: Effect of vitamin and mineral supplementation on intelligence of a sample of schoolchildren. *The Lancet*, 1988, 140–143.
4. Needleman, H. L., Gunnoe, C., Leviton, A., Reed, R., Peresie, H., Maher, C., & Barrett, P.: Deficits in psychologic and classroom performance of children with elevated dentine lead levels. *The New England Journal of Medicine*, 1979, *300*, 689–695.

5. Thatcher, R. W., McAlaster, R., Lester, M. L., & Cantor, D. S.: Comparisons among EEG, hair minerals and diet predictions of reading performance in children. In S. J. White & V. Teller (eds.): *Annals of the New York Academy of Sciences*. New York: New York Academy of Sciences, 1984.

CHAPTER SEVEN

1. For a nontechnical account of the testing of Feingold's hypothesis, see: Conners, C.K., *Food additives and hyperactive children*. New York: Plenum, 1980.
2. Zametkin, A.: The carrot hypothesis. *Journal of the American Academy of Child and Adolescent Psychiatry*, 1985, *24*, 240–241.
3. Rowe, K. S.: Synthetic food colourings and "hyperactivity": A double-blind crossover study. *Australian Paediatric Journal*, 1988, *24*, 143–147.
4. Beyreiss, J., Roth, N., Beyer, H., Kropf, S., Shelenzka, K., Schmidt, A., & Roscher, G.: Coincidence of immune (atopic dermatitis) and behavioral (attention deficit) disorders in children: empirical data. *Activitas Nervosa Superior*, 1988, *30*, 127–128.
5. Tryphonas, H., & Trites, R.: Food allergy in children with hyperactivity, learning disabilities, and/or minimal brain dysfunction. *Annals of Allergy*, 1979, *42*, 22–27.
6. Egger, J., Carter, C. M., Graham, P. J., & Gumley, D.: Controlled trial of oligoantigenic treatment in the hyperkinetic syndrome. *The Lancet*, 1985, 540–545.
7. Kaplan, B.J., McNicol, J., Conte, R. A., & Moghadam, H. K.: Dietary replacement in preschool-aged hyperactive boys. *Pediatrics*, 1989, *83*, 7–17.

CHAPTER EIGHT

1. Pauling, L.: Orthomolecular psychiatry. *Science*, 1968, *160*, 265–271. p.265.
2. Williams, R. J.: *Biochemical individuality: The basis for the genotropic concept*. Austin: University of Texas, 1956.
3. Lipton, M. A., Mailman, R. B., & Nemeroff, C. B.: Vitamins, megavitamin therapy, and the nervous system. In R. J. Wurtman & J. J. Wurtman (eds): *Nutrition and the Brain*. New York: Raven Press, 1979.
4. Cott, A.: Megavitamins: The orthomolecular approach to behavioral disorders and learning disabilities. *Academic Therapy*, 1972, *7*, 245–258.
5. Brenner, A: The effect of megadoses of selected B-complex vitamins on children with hyperkinesis: Controlled studies with long-term follow-up. *Journal of Learning Disabilities*, 1982, *15*, 258–264.
6. Haslam, R. H. A., Dalby, J. T., & Rademaker, A. W.: Effects of megavitamin therapy on children with attention deficit disorders. *Pediatrics*, 1984, *74*, 103–111.
7. Kershner, J., & Hawke, W.: Megavitamins and learning disorders: A controlled double-blind experiment. *Journal of Nutrition*, 1979, *109*, 819–826.

Chapter Nine

1. Good discussions of the psychiatric and metabolic aspects of eating disorders may be found in R. J. Wurtman and J. J. Wurtman (eds.): *Nutrition and the brain, volume 3: Disorders of eating and nutrients in the treatment of brain diseases.* New York: Raven Press, 1979.

Chapter Ten

1. Two standard introductory texts on nutrition, containing most information the average reader will require for creating sound diets are: Guthrie, H. A., *Introductory nutrition.* St. Louis: Times Mirror/Mosby College Publishing, 1986; and Krause, M. V., & Mahan, L. K.: *Food, nutrition, and diet therapy: A textbook of nutritional care, 7th edition.* Philadelphia: Saunders, 1984.

2. A booklet entitled "Computer software for nutrition and food education" is available from The Nutrition Information and Resource Center of the Pennsylvania State University, University Park, PA, 16802; A comprehensive and up to date nutritional software program which not only helps compose nutritionally adequate diets, but also produces a shopping list is: Nutritionist III. N-Squared Computing, 5318 Forest Ridge Rd., Silverton, Oregon 97381. Phone: (503)873-5906.

3. Lapouse, R., & Monk, M. A.: Fears and worries in a representative sample of children. *American Journal of Orthopsychiatry*, 1959, 29, 803–818.

Index

Printed in the United States
25935LVS00002B/28-33

9 780738 206202